# CANUCKS
## LEGENDS

### VANCOUVER'S HOCKEY HEROES

## JEFF RUD

FOREWORD BY **TREVOR LINDEN**

ESSAYS BY ARCHIE MCDONALD, TONY GALLAGHER, IAIN MACINTYRE, KEVIN WOODLEY

RAINCOAST BOOKS

*Vancouver*

*To all the players who have ever worn the uniform of the Vancouver Canucks*
*and to all the fans who have endured*

Title page: *Former Canucks captain
Stan "Steamer" Smyl.* (Graphic
Artists/HHOF)

Copyright © 2006 by Jeff Rud
Photograph credits, see page 256

Raincoast Books gratefully acknowledges the ongoing support of the Canada Council
for the Arts, the Province of British Columbia through the British Columbia Arts
Council and the Book Publishing Tax Credit and the Government of Canada through
the Book Publishing Industry Development Program (BPIDP).

Edited by Derek Fairbridge
Cover and interior layout by Teresa Bubela

Library and Archives Canada Cataloguing in Publication

Rud, Jeff, 1960-
Canucks legends: Vancouver hockey heroes / Jeff Rud.

ISBN 10 1-55192-809-4
ISBN 13 978-1-55192-809-8

1. Vancouver Canucks (Hockey team)—Biography. 2. Hockey players—British
Columbia—Vancouver—Biography. 3. Vancouver Canucks (Hockey team)—History.
I. Title.

GV848.V35R84 2006          796.962'092271133          C2006-901513-9

Library of Congress Control Number: 2006923688

Raincoast Books
9050 Shaughnessy Street
Vancouver, British Columbia
Canada V6P 6E5
www.raincoast.com

*In the United States:*
Publishers Group West
1700 Fourth Street
Berkeley, California
94710

Printed in China by Book Art.

10 9 8 7 6 5 4 3 2 1

# Contents

## The Third Decade: The Roaring Nineties
### *Introduction* 139

**A New York Minute** by Iain MacIntyre 200

## The New Millennium: Great Expectations
### *Introduction* 203

**Canucks Nation** by Kevin Woodley 246

# *Foreword*

## BY TREVOR LINDEN

IF SOMEBODY asked me to come up with a single mental image of my hockey career, there is absolutely no doubt I would be wearing the uniform of the Vancouver Canucks in it.

I've played for other teams, but Vancouver is where my National Hockey League career began, and where I hope it ends. And while the Canucks may not be the team I grew up watching as a young kid, they are the team I grew up with as a professional player.

I never made a secret of my fondness for the city of Vancouver and my time as a Canuck, so it might surprise some people to know how worried I was when I first found out the team I started my career with had re-acquired me from the Washington Capitals. All I could think about was that old saying you can never go home again.

Of course, the ironic thing is I'm actually from a small town in Alberta, but it didn't take long after the Canucks drafted me in 1988 for Vancouver to feel like home. Anyone who has ever spent any time in Vancouver knows it's a pretty easy place to call home and by my fourth season with the Canucks I was pretty much here full time year round.

Vancouver is a beautiful city, a place I've always felt comfortable in, and been treated extremely well by. It's been an interesting dynamic because I came here as an 18-year-old kid and in a way people probably felt like I was their son. I was wide-eyed and from a small town in Alberta and people in Vancouver seemed to connect with me as they watched me grow up. All of which made it almost as hard to come back as it was to leave.

Being traded in 1998 wasn't easy, but the hardest part was really the turmoil of that whole season; seeing something you care so much about get so messed up. After my first few seasons here I got emotionally invested in what we were trying to do — not only with the team, but with the city as well — so it was so hard to see Pat Quinn go, to see the team struggle on the ice, and having to leave it all behind didn't make it any easier.

Even after I was traded, I never stopped appreciating Vancouver. I lived here in the summers, but it wasn't easy to come back because it kind of seemed like I didn't belong. I'd listen to the radio and they'd be talking about what the Canucks were doing and it just didn't sound right because it wasn't my team any more. I'd always

felt that connection with this city and felt indebted for being allowed to be a part of its sporting landscape, which created some of my hesitation about returning in a Canucks uniform: I wondered how I could repay that debt.

After my first few shifts in Minnesota I felt it was going to be all right, and when I came back and played my first home game I had that feeling again, but it took a while to settle in and feel comfortable. My first month I still felt like a visitor — it wasn't as simple as just going home again — and I was a bit on edge because I wanted to perform well. In that way it was a lot like my first season in Vancouver.

There wasn't a lot of surprise when the Canucks chose me, and they certainly made me feel like I was a player they really wanted, but when you come to a team drafted second overall you just want to prove to everyone they didn't make a mistake.

I remember running the track at the old Empire Stadium with Stan Smyl that summer and how the way he was talking to me really made me feel accepted and put me at ease. Once the season started I got on a run where the more comfortable I felt, the better I played. You couldn't ask for a better first season, and it felt pretty good to be able to contribute.

Two years later I was part of a rotating captaincy with Doug Lidster and Dan Quinn and the following season, 1991–92, I was named captain of the Canucks. I was only 21, which made me the NHL's youngest captain, but it didn't really change much for me. I'd always been comfortable in a leadership role, and whether it was in junior or midget, I was always young for a captain, accepting the role as one of the youngest guys on the team. Sure, this time it was the NHL, but it wasn't something that was foreign to me.

I was finishing my third year as the captain when I experienced my most memorable time as a Canuck: our run to the 1994 Stanley Cup final. There's no question beating Toronto in the conference final here at home was the highlight. It was pretty much chaos in the city, not only winning the conference and going to the finals, but to beat the Maple Leafs here at home was amazing. We're playing our archrival, the game is here, and then in Game 5 we were down 3–0 and we win in overtime to clinch — it doesn't get much better than that.

There have been personal milestones as well, but when I think of my milestones, I remember winning the conference in 1994, the 100-point teams, and the teams over the last few years that have been very entertaining. When I see how much fun fans have had coming to the rink the last three years — okay not so much in 2005–06 — and I see the excitement people in British Columbia have for this team, that's what makes a special memory for me.

For me being a Vancouver Canuck is about a sense of pride, not only in how you represent the city but also in how you present yourself on the ice and the success you've had on the ice. It's also about the impact you have in the community and the legacy you leave there.

The Canucks have always believed in the importance of community, a tradition stressed to me early in my career by many of the players profiled in this book. Then, after you've been here a while, you start to make relationships and connect with people trying to do good things in the community and you try to help out. I'm grateful for the life I've been able to lead in Vancouver and always wanted to make a difference and say thanks in return.

I hope players in the future will continue in that direction. It's a path that was laid out for me and hopefully it will be a continuing legacy of my time with the Vancouver Canucks.

— Trevor Linden

The 1970s marked the long-awaited arrival of the National Hockey League in Vancouver, but the decade that also spawned disco, *Star Wars* and platform shoes by no means signalled the birth of the Vancouver Canucks. The city's beloved hockey team was conceived a full quarter century earlier, in August of 1945, at the end of World War II, when Vancouver businessman Coleman "Coley" Hall was awarded a Pacific Coast Hockey League (PCHL) franchise.

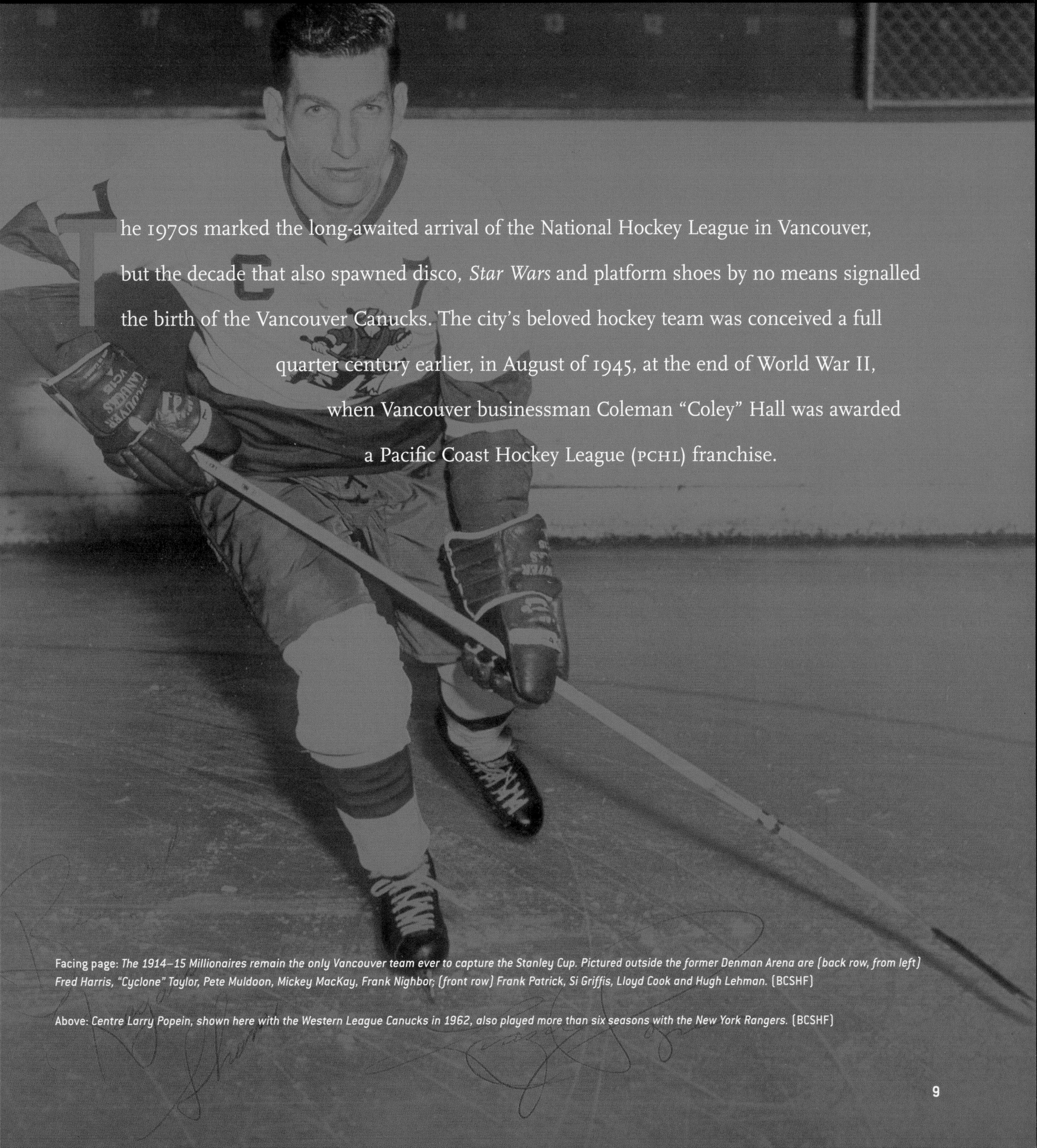

Facing page: *The 1914–15 Millionaires remain the only Vancouver team ever to capture the Stanley Cup. Pictured outside the former Denman Arena are (back row, from left) Fred Harris, "Cyclone" Taylor, Pete Muldoon, Mickey MacKay, Frank Nighbor; (front row) Frank Patrick, Si Griffis, Lloyd Cook and Hugh Lehman. (BCSHF)*

Above: *Centre Larry Popein, shown here with the Western League Canucks in 1962, also played more than six seasons with the New York Rangers. (BCSHF)*

*Coley Hall started the first edition of the Vancouver Canucks in 1945.*
(Vancouver Canucks)

Facing page: *One of the most popular combinations to have ever skated for the NHL Canucks was the line of Stan Smyl, Thomas Gradin and Darcy Rota.* (Robert Shaver/HHOF)

Hall was a streetwise high school dropout who had made his first sizable financial gain in an all-night poker game. The shrewd operator already owned the St. Regis Hotel in downtown Vancouver by the time he locked up hockey rights for the Pacific National Exhibition Forum. A hard-nosed star athlete who excelled at baseball and basketball but never played hockey himself, Hall would become one of the power players behind the sport in British Columbia by basically guaranteeing that he would be awarded the city's franchise in the fledgling PCHL.

A friend named Art Nevison advised Hall to call his new team the "Canucks." The suggestion was inspired by the cartoon character "Johnny Canuck," who symbolized the heroic war efforts of Canadian troops overseas. Hall agreed, putting a toque-wearing lumberjack on the team's first crest.

More than a half century later, that inaugural Canucks team may still rank as the most successful edition ever. Hall's first Canuck lineup won the PCHL title as well as the United States amateur crown by defeating the Boston Olympics. To this day, the 1945-46 Canucks are the only Canadian team to have captured the U.S. amateur championship.

It wasn't the city of Vancouver's most successful hockey club of all time, though. That honour goes to the Vancouver Millionaires of 1914-15. Led by Hall of Fame forward Fred "Cyclone" Taylor and steered by player-manager-owner Frank Patrick, the Millionaires captured what remains the city's lone Stanley Cup championship, beating the Ottawa Senators 3-0 in the final. The series was played at the Denman Arena, a 10,500-seat stadium built by the Patrick family at Georgia and Denman in 1911 for Can$300,000. At the time, it was the largest sporting facility in Canada.

The Millionaires won that best-of-five Stanley Cup series by scores of 6-2, 8-3 and 12-3. Their Ottawa opponents were no slouches, sporting a lineup that included legends Art Ross and goaltender Clint Benedict, but after a five-day train ride from the east the visitors reportedly were tricked by Frank Patrick. According to the late Jim Coleman, a legendary Canadian sports columnist, Patrick was smooth enough to "wine and dine" the Senators once they arrived. "Little did they realize they were being fatted for the slaughter," Coleman wrote in the Vancouver *Province*.

In those days, hockey on the West Coast was played seven-a-side, with the goalie and two defensive players keeping mainly to their end of the rink and the forwards in the offensive end. The "rover," a position played by the talented Taylor for the then princely sum of Can$1,800 a season, roamed the entire ice surface. The goaltender was not permitted to flop down on his knees to make a save.

The Millionaires are considered by many to have been the finest hockey team of that era and, fittingly for a time when many players remained on the ice for the full game, all seven of the club's starters are members of the Hockey Hall of Fame.

Although the Millionaires made other appearances in the Stanley Cup final before the trophy became the sole domain of the NHL in 1926, they never again won the fabled silverware. In fact, Vancouver isn't even the last British Columbia team to have sipped from the Cup; the Victoria Cougars of 1924-25, which were coached by Lester Patrick and included Harry "Hap"

Holmes and Frankie Fredrickson, beat the Montreal Canadiens — featuring Howie Morenz and Georges Vezina — three games to one in the best-of-five Cup final.

Vancouver teams have gone to a total of seven Stanley Cup finals since the Millionaires won the trophy in 1915, but the city has come up empty on each occasion. Despite the long drought, the name "Canucks" and hockey have been synonymous in Vancouver since Coley Hall first strung the two words together in 1945.

The founding father of the Canucks had the reputation of being extremely difficult to separate from a dollar. Star forward Eddie Dorohoy, who played for Hall's Canucks during their pre-NHL days, once said: "Coley Hall is so cheap he wouldn't give you the sleeves off his vest."

It's a good thing that Hall didn't have to worry about modern hockey economics when setting up his original Canucks squad. Each of the 15 players on that 1945-46 team reportedly was paid Can$50 a week, a far cry from the nearly US$39-million payroll that the 2005-06 Canucks boasted.

In 1948, the Pacific Coast Hockey League was swallowed up

in a merger with the Western League, a tough pro circuit that tends to be vastly underestimated by today's fans. During the 1950s and early '60s there were still only six NHL franchises, so legions of skilled and seasoned skaters patrolled Western League ice sheets. Many of these players were veterans who had been stockpiled by the "Original Six" teams, tremendous athletes who would easily have been stars or at least productive players in any sort of expanded NHL.

Among the standouts on those Vancouver Canucks teams of the old Western League were future Hockey Hall of Famers Andy Bathgate, Allan Stanley, Johnny Bower, Tony Esposito and Lorne "Gump" Worsley. A telling testament that this was a different era was the fact that Worsley was sent down to the Canucks by the New York Rangers even after winning the Calder Trophy as NHL rookie of the year in 1953.

While those early Canuck skaters and goaltenders made it to the Hall of Fame, only Cam Neely among the NHL-edition Canucks has been inducted into the shrine, although Mark Messier is a lock for a spot eventually.

Facing Page: *Robert Dirk, Sergio Momesso, Cliff Ronning, Dave Babych and Trevor Linden line up for the anthems during the Canucks' 1993–94 Stanley Cup finals season.* (Chris Relke/HHOF)

Vancouver was highly successful in the Western League, capturing four playoff titles between 1958 and 1970 and giving fans outstanding hockey each winter, highlighted by heated regional rivalries with teams from Portland, Seattle and Edmonton. Tellingly, Orland Kurtenbach, who captained the expansion Canucks into the NHL and later coached the team, says that to this day he's just as often asked by fans about his time with Vancouver in the Western League as he is about his key role in the birth of the city's NHL franchise.

Although Coley Hall subsequently sold his Canucks to the PNE and began a lucrative new Western League franchise in San Francisco in the early-1960s, he remained a key player on the Vancouver professional hockey scene until the late-1980s. He served on the NHL franchise's first board of directors and, after initial Canucks owner Tom Scallen went to jail after being convicted of misusing team funds, the savvy Hall brokered the sale of the team in 1974 to local businessman and broadcasting mogul Frank A. Griffiths, thus ensuring the Canucks would remain on the West Coast.

Hall died on August 10, 2002, at age 95. The team he named lives on, more popular than ever.

"We haven't won a lot of Stanley Cups, but we've had a lot of characters come through. There should be no shortage of interesting stories," says former Canucks goaltender and assistant coach Glen Hanlon, who still slips into using "we" though he is now head coach of the Washington Capitals.

Indeed. The NHL Canucks to 2006 have never won a Stanley Cup and they've come close only twice in 35 years; they reached the finals in 1982 and 1994. In the years between and following those two flirtations there has been plenty of misery and a big share of mediocrity, but also a decent run among the upper echelon of NHL teams. There certainly has been no shortage of interesting stories.

Through those three and a half decades, fans have witnessed the courage of Trevor Linden and Curt Fraser; the heart of Stan Smyl, Gary Lupul and Matt Cooke; the peculiar virtuosity of Gary Smith and Richard Brodeur; and the artistic petulance of Petri Skriko and Pavel Bure. Fans have revelled in the fists of fury flung by Gino Odjick and Tiger Williams; the stately elegance of Jyrki Lumme and Orland Kurtenbach; the presence and power of Greg Adams and Todd Bertuzzi; and the God-given grace of Markus Naslund and Thomas Gradin.

The team has worn a variety of uniforms, from the now-classic rink-with-a-stick original logo to the hideous gold-black-and-red V-style sweaters designed by a San Francisco marketing company in 1978, to the whale motif of today's Canucks. And they have called two different buildings home, moving from the original Pacific Coliseum, built in the late-1960s as a means to lure the NHL, to the much flashier General Motors Place, constructed in the late-1990s in part to help keep hockey's big leagues in Vancouver.

The Canucks and their doings have been faithfully recorded and reported over the years by a colourful cast of Vancouver broadcasters, columnists and reporters, a group that has managed to keep the team close to the minds and hearts of the public. Loved or laughed at, celebrated or criticized, the Canucks have always been front and centre and an easy topic of conversation from Port Coquitlam to Prince Rupert, from Nelson to Nanaimo.

Marc Crawford, the Canucks' head coach for nearly seven seasons until he was fired in April 2006 and formerly a player in the organization during the 1980s, says there is no comparison between the spotlight under which Vancouver hockey coaches and players live and play and the hockey environment in a major American city. Crawford coached the Colorado Avalanche to a Stanley Cup championship in 1996 but says the scrutiny in Vancouver is much more intense.

"In a major US city, you've got a lot of other people that you share the limelight with," he says. "And there is an ability to escape, at least for portions of the year. The pressure and attention and just the notoriety that comes from being a major sports team, that lessens on a day-to-day basis when you have other major teams to share the burden.

"In Vancouver, while there are other sports teams, I don't think anybody shares the burden with the hockey club — at least, not on a consistent basis."

The fact that the Canucks are now alone on the main stage of British Columbia professional sports means coverage of the team is a year-round project for the province's newspapers and radio and television stations. If it's not hockey season, it's time to dissect a hockey season past, or time to preview one in the future.

"The coverage is so intense," Crawford says. "The difference is a story is a story in the United States [for a reasonable period of time], where a story in Canada about the hockey club is a story until it ends. That's quite a significant change. You know, [in Vancouver], the fourth-line left-winger ... the decision you make on who's playing in that position on a nightly basis, that just falls so far below the radar in a major US city that nobody cares."

In Vancouver they do care, whether they're talking about the fourth-line left-winger or the backup goaltender. You're likely to hear fans talking about the Canucks' power-play woes on radio open-line shows or in a downtown Starbucks whether it's mid-July or mid-January.

For much of the team's 35-year history the overriding theme of those discussions has been, what's wrong with the Canucks? Let's face it: Compared with some of the more storied franchises in the NHL, there is no great lineage of success here. But positive or negative, a significant number of British Columbians are talking about the Canucks. Even during the NHL lockout of 2004-05, when fans across North America debated the future of the game or tuned out of hockey altogether, Vancouver's faithful seemed most concerned about whether captain Markus Naslund would return once the storm blew over. And after the team inexplicably collapsed down the stretch to miss the 2005-06 playoffs, the body Canuck wasn't even cold before the armchair autopsies were in full swing.

"The team really is part of the fabric of the city," says Stan Smyl, who is as big a part of that weave as any player or coach in the club's history. "I think through the '80s you could see it there, but not to the extent that it is now ... When I walk through the airport, people are so excited to talk about the team. It's such a big part of this province."

Nowhere is that more evident than in GM Place, where the Canucks have had to cap season-ticket sales at 17,000 with a waiting list thousands strong. While attendance waned considerably in the late '70s, mid-'80s and late '90s when the team floundered on the ice, fans were never far away. It seems they were always looking for an excuse to come back. Sooner or later, in every decade, they got one.

One had only to be in British Columbia during the 1982 or 1994 spring runs to appreciate just how deep love for the team goes. In 1982, after the Canucks were swept by the New York Islanders in the Stanley Cup finals, 100,000 people showed up for a parade through downtown Vancouver. In 1994, though some B.C. fans shamefully rioted in the streets after a Game 7 loss in New York to the Rangers, another 50,000 turned out at B.C. Place a couple of days later for a more fitting celebration.

"I think that this city deserves to have a winner," Naslund told reporters after his Canucks suffered a disappointing first-round defeat to the Calgary Flames in the 2004 playoffs. "This city is so excited about their hockey team, and about winning, so it would be an unreal experience."

Perhaps one day soon the Canucks will win a Stanley Cup for their enduring fans. Until then, there are plenty of stories from the team's first 35 years in hockey's big leagues.

*The once-feared West Coast Express line of Brendan Morrison, Markus Naslund and Todd Bertuzzi is now a part of Canucks history. (Vancouver Canucks/Jeff Vinnick)*

As the NHL prepared for its first expansion in February 1966, the City of Vancouver and a local group of prospective owners felt confident they would receive a franchise. After all, theirs was an attractive, vibrant and growing Canadian centre with thousands of rabid hockey fans. City council had already approved construction on the state-of-the-art Pacific Coliseum to house an anticipated NHL team and the fans felt they deserved a chance to join Toronto and Montreal on hockey's elite circuit.

But even though the NHL would add six new teams in its initial modern-era growth spurt, Vancouver wasn't on the list. Expansion franchises for the 1967 season were awarded to St. Louis, Philadelphia, Minnesota, Los Angeles, Oakland and Pittsburgh. The Canadian city's exclusion stirred anger in British Columbia and there was an economic backlash as jilted fans targeted visible *Hockey Night in Canada* sponsors.

Facing page: *Veteran George Gardner started the first-ever regular season game for the NHL Canucks, losing 3-1 to Los Angeles.* (O-Pee-Chee/HHOF)

Above: *The arrival of the National Hockey League in Vancouver drew large and enthusiastic crowds to the Pacific Coliseum.* (Vancouver Canucks)

The Pacific Coliseum was built in the late 1960s, in part to help lure the NHL to Vancouver. (Vancouver Canucks)

A tale of two draft picks. In 1970, Gilbert Perreault went number 1 to Buffalo and Dale Tallon number 2 to the Canucks. (Robert Shaver/HHOF)

"When Vancouver was turned down in '67 the people here were so upset, so angry, that they cut up all their Esso credit cards, they stopped buying Molson beer," recalls Jim Robson, at the time the play-by-play man for the old Western League Canucks. "That was the only way they could protest. They had no other weapon, but it was a pretty effective weapon."

The tactic didn't hurt. Three years later, Vancouver was awarded its coveted place in the NHL. But because the franchise fee by then had tripled from US$2 million to US$6 million — a figure that in today's NHL wouldn't buy one topline centreman for more than a single season — the previous local ownership group that had included Coley Hall and businessmen Cy McLean and Frank McMahon wasn't willing to ante up. As a result, the NHL

hand-picked its own ownership for the Canucks, bringing in American firm Medicor and its leading proponents, Thomas Scallen and Lyman Walters, as controlling partners.

Vancouver was officially awarded an expansion franchise on May 22, 1970. On June 10 of that year the Canucks and the Buffalo Sabres, the other expansion team in 1970, were permitted to pick over the cast-offs from a dozen other NHL teams during the expansion draft at Montreal's Queen Elizabeth Hotel.

The NHL's then-hefty franchise fee didn't exactly buy a load of eye-popping talent. Vancouver's first pick in the proceedings was Gary Doak, a tough, stay-at-home defenceman who had been having trouble carving out a roster spot with the Boston Bruins. All together the Canucks scavenged 18 skaters who had scored a total of 37 NHL goals the previous season, as well as goaltenders Dunc Wilson and Charlie Hodge.

After losing a coin toss to determine which team would pick first in the expansion draft, Vancouver also lost the spin of a wheel-of-chance to determine which team would select first in the 1970 amateur entry draft held June 11. That bit of bad luck proved much more costly, however, as the Sabres took Gilbert Perreault with the first pick overall and the Canucks settled for Dale Tallon with the second.

The Canucks had been assigned even numbers for that fateful spin, the Sabres odd. When NHL president Clarence Campbell spun the wheel, it ended up on what the Canucks' brain trust thought was "II" in Roman numerals, prompting general manager Bud Poile and his contingent to break into wild celebration as even Campbell exclaimed, "Number 2!"

But alas, in what was the first of many major disappointments for Canucks' fans, Buffalo general manager George "Punch" Imlach quickly pointed out that the number was actually "11" in Arabic numerals. The Sabres had won the right to take the peerless Perreault, who would don the number 11 jersey for Buffalo, win the Calder Trophy as rookie of the year and over a 17-year career stickhandle his way into the Hockey Hall of Fame. Within three seasons of acquiring Tallon, the Canucks would trade him away.

To make start-up more difficult for both the Canucks and the Sabres, the geographically challenged at NHL head office placed the new teams in the East Division, by far the most competitive of the two league segments, which included every team from the famed "Original Six" except the Chicago Black Hawks.

Although those first Canucks would become an instant hit at the box office, the team found trouble before it hit the ice. Original coach and general manager Joe Crozier was fired for "insubordination," which resulted in Poile, who was supposed to be only an adviser to Scallen, stepping in to run the Canucks and Hal Laycoe agreeing to coach. In the process, Vancouver bypassed a coaching candidate named Fred Shero, who would go on to win a pair of Stanley Cups for the Philadelphia Flyers, and Al Arbour, who would engineer four Cups for the New York Islanders.

Nevertheless, those early Canucks were by default "western Canada's team." These were the days before the upstart World Hockey Association with its eventual franchises in Calgary, Edmonton and Winnipeg. In a shrewd marketing move, the Canucks held their first training camp in Calgary, drawing more than 8,000 fans to watch simple practice scrimmages at the Corral.

When Vancouver finally entered the NHL "it was a huge thing for the city and the province," recalls Robson, who was hired by radio station CKNW to call the team's games, a job he would hold for 24 years. "We had 30 or 40 stations carrying the broadcasts. There was very little television, so when you did a radio game from Boston all of western Canada could be listening."

The Canucks' first regular-season NHL game, on October 9, 1970, was a gala affair at the Pacific Coliseum. British Columbia premier W. A. C. Bennett was there and so was Juliette, the popular singer dubbed "the People's Pet," who delivered the national anthem. Vancouver mayor Tom Campbell was booed during the pregame festivities, but Fred "Cyclone" Taylor, the hockey legend who in 1915 had led the Vancouver Millionaires to the city's only Stanley Cup, received a standing ovation.

In a dramatic foreshadowing of the team's first decade, the Canucks fell 3-1 to the Los Angeles Kings on that opening night, sending 15,062 fans home with the first of what would be a total of 414 defeats in the franchise's first 10 years.

Still, Vancouver was in the NHL. Finally.

"There was a buzz back then," recalls Doak, the original Canuck. "They had been fighting for an NHL team for years and finally they got it and we started off pretty good, and there was a buzz in the city about how well we were doing. It was a new team growing and I think it was good for the city, good for the whole area."

Despite the opening-night loss, that first Canucks team did show huge promise. It would include six 20-goal scorers and it was more than tough enough, holding its own in the NHL trenches. The infant Canucks even contended for a playoff spot early in that inaugural season, winning 17 of 39 home games in the jam-packed Pacific Coliseum. But a catastrophic knee injury to captain Orland Kurtenbach just before Christmas knocked them out of the race. The team eventually dropped to second-last in the East Division,

*Games against "Original Six" teams were a highlight in the early years. Here Andre Boudrias of the Canucks fights for the puck in front of Borje Salming of the Leafs.*
(Graphic Artists/HHOF)

finishing with a 24-46-8 record, one point ahead of the Detroit Red Wings.

All the same, "it was the NHL coming in and fans had waited a long time for it to arrive," Kurtenbach recalls of that first year. "We may not have been the most talented club, but we had a good, tough hockey club. So we weren't run out of any of the rinks and we weren't intimidated."

In their second season, the Canucks had serious trouble scoring goals. A 10-game winless streak in February and March led to a dismal campaign during which they compiled 20 wins and 48 points, totals that still stand as all-time franchise lows. That sophomore season, when the mixed blessing of expansion seemed to be sinking in for Vancouver fans, remains the only time the Canucks finished dead last in the NHL standings. Similarly dreary seasons of 22 and 24 victories followed as the team burned through head coaches Hal Laycoe, Vic Stasiuk and Bill McCreary.

The undisputed bright spot in an otherwise dismal decade came under head coach Phil Maloney during the 1974-75 and 1975-76 seasons. After floundering near the bottom of the standings for their first four years, the surprising Canucks won the

Dennis Ververgaert, whom the Canucks selected ahead of Lanny McDonald in the 1973 draft, was a key member of back-to-back playoff teams in the mid-1970s. (London Life-Portnoy/HHOF)

1974-75 regular-season championship in the newly aligned but admittedly weak Smythe Division. With 38 wins, 32 losses and 10 ties, Vancouver nipped the St. Louis Blues by two points for the Smythe championship, finishing with a total that was 27 points higher than the team's previous best.

The key to that season was the netminding of Gary "Suitcase" Smith, the loose leader of the Canucks, who had six shutouts and provided the team with a feeling of invincibility. "It's like having a great putter in golf," recalls Dennis Kearns, a defenceman on that team. "A guy can be all over the course and, all of a sudden,

he gets a par because he can get up and down. It's the same, I think, as having that great goaltender."

The Smythe Division title gave the Canucks their first playoff appearance and guaranteed them a first-round bye. In the second round, however, they would meet the Montreal Canadiens, one of the most powerful lineups in the history of the NHL, led by Guy Lafleur, Ken Dryden, Serge Savard and Guy Lapointe.

"I think it was Gerry O'Flaherty who said we got a bye in the first round and a 'bye-bye' in the second," chuckles Kearns.

The Canucks would lose that best-of-seven series 4-1, but it was a much tougher battle than the simple score lines of history indicate. The series was tied 1-1 after the Canucks won Game 2 in Montreal, a 2-1 decision in which Smith was outstanding in goal. "The teams came back to Vancouver and the place went nuts," Robson recalls.

In Game 3, winger John Gould scored for the Canucks on the very first shift and the Pacific Coliseum was buzzing. But Montreal went on to win that game 4-1, before taking Game 4 by a 4-0 score. Instead of folding in Game 5 back in Montreal, however, the Canucks forced the powerful Habs into overtime. In that extra session, forward Don Lever had two point-blank chances to win the game for Vancouver but, instead, the series ended on a fluke goal for the Canadiens: Kearns tried to knock a centring pass by Lafleur out of the air; Smith came out to intercept the pass; the puck hit Kearns' stick and floated into the Vancouver net. The Canucks' first playoff appearance was over, and the Canadiens had survived by a 5-4 margin.

"We knew it was going to be a miracle if we were going to beat them," Lever now admits. "But we gave them a pretty good series anyway. We gave them a pretty good scare so they wouldn't screw up the rest of the way."

The Canucks under Maloney would manage one more winning season, going 33-32-15 in 1975-76 to make the playoffs for the second straight year. But again they were out of the postseason in a single series, and their chemistry quickly dissolved when Smith wore out his welcome and fell into disfavour with ownership, forcing a trade.

That was pretty much the extent of the team's success in the '70s. They didn't win more than 25 games in any subsequent season and failed to make the playoffs again until 1978-79, when once more they bowed out in the first round. After a full decade in the NHL and six different head coaches, the Canucks still hadn't won a playoff series.

Vancouver *Sun* sports columnist Archie McDonald probably summed it up best when he wrote: "If an organization learns by its mistakes the Vancouver Canucks should be the smartest team in the whole darn world."

Those early Canucks did make mistakes. Their draft record was suspect — Jere Gillis (1977) and Bill Derlago (1978), each at number 4 overall, come to mind — and team management moved skaters in and out constantly, never allowing coaches or player combinations to stand long enough to establish continuity. Vancouver management didn't deal well with the very real threat of the World Hockey Association, either, during the decade allowing the rival WHA to lure away eight Canucks, including fan favourites Rosaire Paiement and Andre Boudrias.

## KEY TRADES OF THE DECADE

On May 14, 1973, the Canucks formally gave up on the first amateur draft pick in franchise history, shipping Dale Tallon to the Chicago Black Hawks. The trade turned out to be a good one for Vancouver, drawing goaltender Gary Smith and defenceman Jerry Korab in return. Smith would backstop the Canucks to the Smythe Division title in 1974-75.

The other major deal of the decade came on February 7, 1974, when the Canucks traded winger Bobby Schmautz to the Bruins for centre Chris Oddleifson, right-winger Fred O'Donnell and centre Mike "Shaky" Walton. This trade didn't work out as well. The Canucks lost the feisty scorer Schmautz, a highly questionable move. Oddleifson would later serve as captain for Vancouver for one season, but O'Donnell never reported to the Canucks and Walton joined the team only after a stint in the World Hockey Association.

## BEST OF THE DECADE

Without doubt, the 1974-75 Canucks were the highlight in a decade of growing pains. Riding an incredible goaltending season by Gary Smith, the team won the Smythe Division with a 38-32-10 record, the first time they had finished better than .500 and the first time they had earned a playoff berth.

## WORST OF THE DECADE

Thomas K. Scallen, the original owner of the Canucks, was sent to prison in 1973 after being found guilty of mismanaging team funds. He would serve eight months of a two-year sentence and be forced to sell the NHL club to Frank Griffiths.

## TOP CANUCKS OF THE DECADE

**Goal:** Gary Smith
**Defence:** Dennis Kearns, Jocelyn Guevremont
**Forwards:** Orland Kurtenbach, Andre Boudrias, Don Lever

## FOR THE RECORD

The following players skated for the first NHL edition of the Vancouver Canucks over the course of the 1970-71 season:
**Goaltenders:** Charlie Hodge, George Gardner, Dunc Wilson
**Defence:** Pat Quinn, Gary Doak, Dale Tallon, Barry Wilkins, John Schella, Poul Popiel
**Forwards:** Mike Corrigan, Dan Johnson, Wayne Maki, Andre Boudrias, Rosaire Paiement, Len Lunde, Garth Rizzuto, Orland Kurtenbach, Ray Cullen, Murray Hall, Eddie Hatoum, Bobby Schmautz, Ted Taylor, Bobby Lalonde

## CANUCK FIRSTS

**First home game:** 3-1 loss to visiting Los Angeles Kings on October 9, 1970
**First win:** 5-3 over visiting Toronto Maple Leafs, with Charlie Hodge in goal, on October 11, 1970
**First goal:** Barry Wilkins, at 2:14 of the third period, on a backhand against Los Angeles goalie Denis DeJordy
**First captain:** Orland Kurtenbach
**First head coach:** Hal Laycoe
**First general manager:** Bud Poile
**First playoff appearance:** 1974-75 against Montreal Canadiens, 4-1 series loss
**First amateur draft pick:** Dale Tallon, number 2 overall, 1970
**First player ever:** Gary Doak, number 2 overall, 1970 expansion draft

# RICK BLIGHT

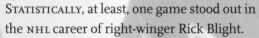

STATISTICALLY, at least, one game stood out in the NHL career of right-winger Rick Blight.

It was October 6, 1976, the opening game of his sophomore season with the Canucks. The kid from rural Manitoba scored four times for visiting Vancouver against the Pittsburgh Penguins, equalling a franchise record.

"If I'm not mistaken, I think Shaky [linemate Mike Walton] got an assist on every goal I got that night," Blight recalled years later. "He was a heckuva playmaker."

Gordie Laxton was the unfortunate Pittsburgh goalie for that game. "I think it's the last game he ever played in the NHL," Blight joked. "I think they figured if that bum can score four they might as well get rid of him."

In a characteristically Canuck twist, however, in spite of Blight's prodigious effort Vancouver managed to lose the game 9-5. "We were always behind in that one," he recalled.

Far more memorable, at least as far as Blight was concerned, was the thrill of making the NHL straight out of junior hockey, where he had been a star with the Brandon Wheat Kings on a potent line with Ron Chipperfield.

Selected 10th overall by the Canucks in the 1975 amateur draft, Blight cracked the lineup as a 19-year-old even though he was joining a team that had captured the Smythe Division title the previous season.

In his rookie campaign he played mainly on a line with Chris Oddleifson and Don Lever and at times with Ron Sedlbauer. Near the end of the season, Walton joined the team and began skating on a unit with Blight and Lever. The combination clicked.

"I was so damn happy to make the team my first year," Blight said. "I got off to a real good start, too. I got to play some power play a little earlier than I thought I would."

In his second season he shone offensively, posting the best numbers of his NHL career and leading the Canucks in goals (28) and points (68).

Blight was known as "Headley" by his teammates because he had a rather large head. He was also known for his ability to shoot the puck. But he wasn't a particularly gifted skater for a player drafted so high.

Nevertheless, he played 326 NHL games over his career, recording 96 goals and 221 points. His time in the big leagues was cut short by a late hip check from teammate Hilliard Graves during a training camp scrimmage in the fall of 1978 at Courtenay, British Columbia. It seriously injured his left knee, which was never quite the same afterward.

"That was basically the beginning of the end," Blight said. "I was a marginal skater to begin with, but that took me from being a marginal skater to a pretty poor skater."

For the next couple of seasons he was up and down between the Canucks and their Dallas farm team in the Central Hockey League before eventually being released by the Canucks in 1981.

He signed on as a free agent with the Edmonton Oilers, but he never played an NHL game with that franchise before he was traded to the Los Angeles Kings. He appeared in only two games with the Kings, then knee problems finally forced him to retire in 1983. Following his hockey career, he managed two family farm equipment dealerships in Portage La Prairie, Manitoba, where he began his junior hockey career with the Portage Terriers.

Besides his obvious knack for scoring on the ice, Blight was an outstanding golfer; he finished second in the Manitoba amateur championship in 1980. He also became a top competitive curler after his NHL days, consistently appearing in the Manitoba men's championships with skip Don Spriggs. In 2000, the rink reached the provincial final, though it lost to Jeff Stoughton.

Blight was a well-known figure in the Portage La Prairie region, which was shocked by his sudden death in April 2005. His body was found in his pickup truck in a field off the side of a Manitoba highway; his death ruled a suicide. Blight's tiny hometown of Oakville, Manitoba, honoured his memory with a public skate, an exhibition hockey game and the raising of his Canucks jersey to the rafters of the local arena in March 2006. Former teammate and Vancouver captain Chris Oddleifson spoke during the ceremony.

# ANDRE BOUDRIAS

THEY AFFECTIONATELY labelled him "Super Pest," but Andre Boudrias provided early fans of the Canucks with much more than stellar forechecking during his half-dozen years with the fledgling NHL club.

Boudrias was the first consistent offensive star for the Canucks, managing five straight seasons of 60 points or better and continually supplying his wingers with quality scoring chances.

The slick centreman was best known for his whirlwind style of play in the opponents' zone, where he moved around like a buzz saw, breaking up plays and turning them into offensive forays for Vancouver. He also managed to effectively work his way under the skin of those he played against.

"I guess I got that nickname because I was tenacious checking for the puck," Boudrias says more than 30 years later. "The forechecking part of the game was important to me. And I always wanted to give a little more on the ice to make sure the paying customers had fun."

The fans appreciated his effort in those early days at the Pacific Coliseum. A diminutive man by today's hockey standards, standing only 5'8", Boudrias was one of the most popular Canucks. "The fans were in love with me, for some reason," he says.

His linemates liked him, too. Whoever skated with Boudrias seemed to light it up. Rosaire Paiement scored a career-high 34 goals playing with Boudrias in 1970-71, Bobby Schmautz had 38 as his linemate in 1972-73 and Don Lever matched that total in 1974-75.

"Boud was a little pest. He was a little shit-disturber," Schmautz recalls, fondly. "All the guys would run after him. I don't know how many times I had to fight that [Dennis] Hextall because he'd drive Hextall crazy, and I'd jump in, and Hextall and I used to go just about every time we played.

"[Boudrias] would get [on] guys' nerves, I guess. I really don't know why, but they'd seem to go after him. When I played with him, I didn't think that was right and I'd step in."

Boudrias was sold to Vancouver by the St. Louis Blues in the summer of 1970, just months after appearing in the Stanley Cup finals against the triumphant Boston Bruins. The move proved a good opportunity for Boudrias, who finally had a chance to shine as an offensive player in the NHL.

A product of the Montreal Junior Canadiens, he had spent four years in the Habs' deep farm system where, in pre-expansion days, Montreal stockpiled scores of talented prospects. The expansion Minnesota North Stars obtained him and he also spent time with Chicago and St. Louis before ending up with the Canucks in 1970.

Although he started on the fourth line, Boudrias was eventually teamed with Paiement and Poul Popiel and he finished the year as the team's leading scorer, with an impressive 25 goals and 41 assists.

"It was exciting," Boudrias says of that first NHL season in Vancouver. "First of all, the fans got into it right away. Everything was new with the NHL coming in. But they knew about the game because the Western League had been there for years, and we got great support at home.

"We also had a great start that first year. Until [Orland] Kurtenbach got hurt, we were in the playoff picture. He was our captain and our leader."

Boudrias was durable, skilled at finding his linemates at the right time and a decent skater. He was also an outstanding penalty killer. In fact, he even scored a goal against Chicago's Tony Esposito when the Canucks were two men short, providing one of the highlights of the franchise's first season.

The pinnacle of Boudrias' career came during the 1974-75 season, when he piled up 62 assists and 78 points. That winter his linemates were Lever and Dennis Ververgaert and they both enjoyed banner seasons. Lever, in particular, had his best numbers as an NHLer, totalling 38 goals as the Canucks delighted their fans and topped the Smythe Division.

"Boudy was just a really smart little player, you know," Lever says. "He didn't have a lot of speed, but he could really pass the puck. He could see the ice, he had good vision."

*Centre Andre "Super Pest" Boudrias, who led the Canucks in scoring in each of their first two seasons, celebrates a goal against the Leafs.* (Graphic Artists/HHOF)

"Boudrias was good in the corners," adds Ververgaert, who would never find another centre with whom he worked as well. "He was just a little pest. It was hard to take the puck off him, and he allowed you time to get in position for a good scoring chance."

In 458 games with Vancouver, Boudrias accumulated 388 points. As well as his five seasons of 60 or more points for the Canucks, he went over the 70-point mark three times.

After a stint as team captain in 1975-76, he opted to leave Vancouver when the World Hockey Association's Quebec Nordiques came calling. At the time he was having a difference of opinion with Canucks management, which helped make the jump to the rival league easier.

"It was a move I had to make," he says. "The last year there, I was not used that much. I was not in the [Canucks'] plans any more. But I had six really great years in Vancouver."

The move to Quebec City was a good one. He spent two seasons with the Nordiques, winning the Avco Cup WHA championship in 1977. After his playing career ended in 1978, he had two seasons as an assistant coach with the Nordiques, then went to work for the NHL Players' Association before spending two years with the league's Central Scouting organization.

He next joined the Montreal Canadiens, serving as assistant general manager and director of scouting over a 12-year period. Working for Serge Savard, he was part of the Canadiens' Stanley Cup championships in 1986 and 1993; the Habs also made the finals in 1989. Following a 1995 management purge in Montreal, Boudrias went on to a lengthy career as an eastern-based scout with the New Jersey Devils.

"I started in major junior when I was 15 and I've never missed a day of hockey since," he says. "It's a pretty good way to live."

*Andre Boudrias was the Canucks' captain in 1975–76 but left Vancouver the following season for the WHA's Quebec Nordiques.* (London Life-Portnoy/HHOF)

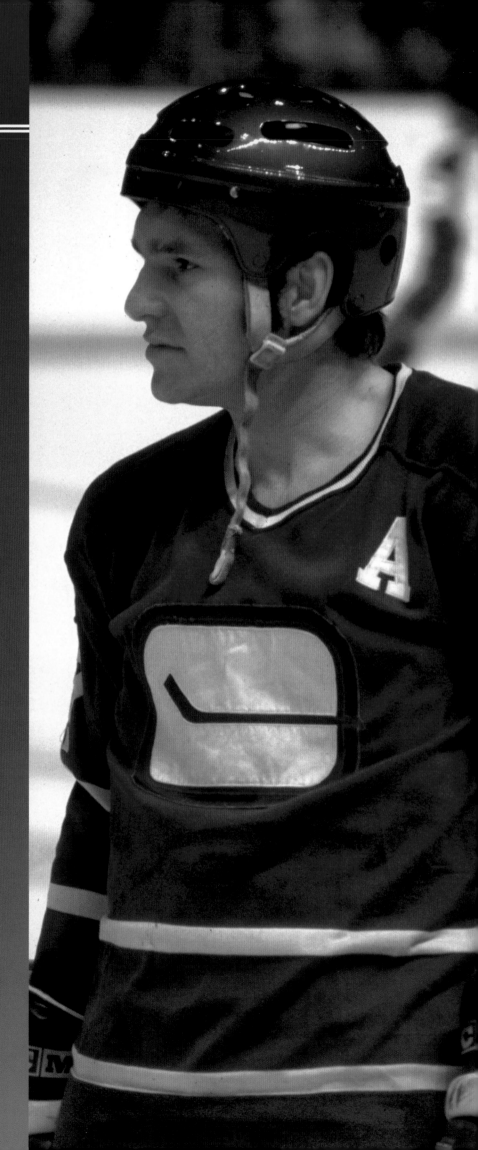

## For the record:

*Andre Boudrias made Canucks history on March 9, 1973, when he took the first penalty shot the franchise was ever awarded. The crafty centre made the most of the opportunity, scoring on Buffalo Sabres goaltender Roger Crozier.*

## Canucks Moment:

*The first Canuck sniper to score 40 or more goals in a single season was towering winger Ron Sedlbauer, who managed to hit the magic number in 1978-79, his fifth campaign with the NHL club.*

*Drafted by the Canucks in 1974 in the second round, 23rd overall, the Ontario junior product played parts of six seasons for Vancouver, but that winter was by far his best as a big-leaguer. Besides his 40 goals, the 6'3", 200-pounder also notched a career-best 56 points and contributed 15 power-play goals.*

*The 40-goal season broke the previous club scoring record of 38 goals, set by Bobby Schmautz and Don Lever. Sedlbauer's Canuck record stood until 1982-83, when Darcy Rota scored 42 times.*

**Right:** *After his retirement as a player, Andre Boudrias was part of the Montreal Canadiens' management team for two Stanley Cups.* (Robert Shaver/HHOF)

# GARY DOAK

HARD-ROCK DEFENCEMAN Gary Doak wasn't merely present for the beginning of the NHL Canucks, he was the beginning of the team. Doak's was the first name penned onto a Canucks NHL roster, when he was plucked from the Stanley Cup champion Boston Bruins on June 10, 1970, as the league held its expansion draft in Montreal.

The 24-year-old from Goderich, Ontario, had already played five seasons in the NHL, but he had yet to truly establish himself as a regular and had played in only 44 games for the Bruins the year before. So rather than being disappointed about going from the NHL penthouse — with superstar teammates Bobby Orr and Phil Esposito — to the basement suite, Doak was optimistic about the move to Vancouver.

"Boston could only protect so many players, and I was left unprotected, and Vancouver picked me first in the entry draft, which was pretty good," he recalls. "I was sort of happy, because I was a role player with the Bruins. They had a great team, and I figured this would be a chance for me to maybe get my career kicked off and get going in the right direction. I enjoyed it, and my career sort of took off forward from there."

Doak was part of a hodgepodge of players from various NHL team systems, and many of them wanted to prove themselves viable big-league regulars. That first Canucks team was an interesting mix of toughness and tenacity with surprising bits of talent thrown in. Until near Christmas, when captain Orland Kurtenbach was injured, the team was in contention for a playoff spot.

"We had players from all over the place," Doak recalls. "A lot of the guys who came to that team had kicked around the American Hockey League for a long time. Everybody was getting our first shot and we were a close-knit team. I think that's why we did so well the first year — proving that you belonged, I guess."

Although he was the original Canuck, Doak would play just one full season in Vancouver. He was paired with Pat Quinn, another defensive-minded, tough type, and the duo was far from flashy, but they laid the body on most who ventured inside the Canuck zone. The two of them were loved by the fans as hard-working, lunch-bucket players.

"Pat and I were both stay-at-home guys," Doak says, with a chuckle. "I mean, we were under heavy siege most of the time — we couldn't do anything *but* be stay-home defencemen."

Doak scored twice and had 10 assists in 77 games that inaugural season, racking up a career-high 112 penalty minutes and developing a reputation for his toughness and his temper. He played just five games the next season before being shipped off to the New York Rangers in November.

"I was a little surprised at that point [to be traded by the Canucks]. I'd had a really good season," he says. "I was an assistant captain and the team had done pretty well ... But it turned out to be a good thing for me."

He was back in the Stanley Cup finals with the Rangers in the 1972 playoffs, against his former Boston Bruin teammates. He spent the following season with the Detroit Red Wings before being traded back to Boston, where he skated for the final nine years of a solid NHL career. Doak would make a total of five trips to the Stanley Cup finals during his 16-year run.

Afterward, he served as an assistant coach to former teammate Gerry Cheevers on the Bruins bench for five years and then spent two seasons coaching college hockey in Boston before leaving the game. He now works as a recreation director for a state agency in Boston and his office isn't far from the TD Banknorth Garden, where today's Bruins play. He skates regularly for the Bruins alumni, but he still has fond memories of his brief yet key role in the history of the Canucks.

# JOCELYN GUEVREMONT

ONE OF THE EARLY knocks against the Canucks was that the organization didn't draft well. Many fans believed its scouting staff had a tendency to overlook talented juniors in western Canada in favour of prospects from the east with whom Vancouverites weren't as familiar.

The selection of Dale Tallon, from the junior Toronto Marlboros with the second pick overall in 1970, was considered by most fans to be a bust, particularly when sniper Reggie Leach was taken third that year, out of Flin Flon, Manitoba, by the Boston Bruins.

Fans in Vancouver came to view Jocelyn Guevremont in a similarly dim light. He was drafted third overall by the Canucks from a dominant Montreal Junior Canadiens team for whom he had posted 88 points and won Quebec Major Junior Hockey League defenceman-of-the-year honours, but in Vancouver he never quite lived up to his advance billing.

Guevremont was big at 6'2", and he possessed undeniable offensive skills. But he was another easterner and he wasn't particularly tough.

"It wasn't a popular decision here to draft all these guys out of the Quebec league," says Canucks play-by-play man Jim Robson, referring to Guevremont and Bobby Lalonde, another Montreal Junior Canadien taken by Vancouver in the second round that year. "Guevremont was a good shot, he had good size, but he was not physical and not particularly courageous."

Vancouver was desperate for a superstar and would have settled for one of eastern lineage, but Guevremont was neither Guy Lafleur nor Marcel Dionne, the two players taken immediately ahead of him in that 1971 amateur draft and both just tantalizingly out of reach of the Canucks.

Guevremont went on to a respectable NHL career and put up some fine offensive numbers during three seasons with Vancouver, particularly in his rookie campaign, when he had 13 goals and 51 points. At the end of that season he was even selected to the 1972 Team Canada roster that would eventually beat the Soviet Union in the historic Summit Series.

For that series, there was a stipulation that every Canadian NHL team had to be represented on the Canadian roster. So even though Vancouver probably did not have a star worthy of selection on merit alone, promising youngsters Tallon and Guevremont were chosen as the Canucks' representatives. Neither played a shift for Canada in the eight-game series, but both remain rightly proud to this day that they were members of the team.

Despite the promising start to his NHL career in Vancouver, Guevremont's offensive numbers dropped in his second and third seasons, falling to a low of 39 points in 1973-74. Ironically, that was the same year he was named Vancouver's top defenceman and represented the Canucks in the NHL All-Star Game.

Guevremont was never the physical, defensive presence the Canucks and their fans had hoped for. He was traded with Bryan McSheffrey to the Buffalo Sabres on October 14, 1974, for Gerry Meehan and Mike Robitaille. The trade paid off in a personal sense as he had a trip that season to the Stanley Cup finals, where Buffalo lost to Philadelphia.

Guevremont played five seasons in Buffalo, including a career-best 52-point effort in 1975-76 when he also led the Sabres with a plus-47 rating, making it unquestionably his finest NHL campaign. He ended his career with a 20-game stint for the New York Rangers in 1979-80.

When his playing days were over, Guevremont coached in the Quebec Major Junior Hockey League and the Ontario Hockey Association, as well as with Roller Hockey International. He also ran a fantasy hockey camp in Florida.

"Guevremont had talent but he never fulfilled the potential," Robson says, echoing the sentiments of many Canucks fans. "He never reached the level that people thought a pick that high should have."

# CHARLIE HODGE

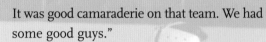

GEORGE GARDNER was the first goalie to start a regular-season NHL game for Vancouver, but Charlie Hodge will be remembered as the true starting netminder for the expansion Canucks.

Hodge played just one season in Vancouver, at the tail end of a nearly 20-year career in pro hockey. In the Canucks' inaugural year he shared goaltending duties with Gardner and Dunc Wilson, but Hodge appeared in 35 games and was easily the most successful of the trio.

While NHL expansion was a new experience for Vancouver and many of the Canucks players, it was old hat for Hodge. He had been plucked from the deep roster of the Montreal Canadiens by the California Golden Seals in the 1967 expansion draft, and in 1970 he was snatched from the Seals system by the Canucks.

Although he moved to Vancouver in the twilight of his career, the native of Lachine, Quebec, brought much-needed experience between the pipes to the Canucks. With the powerhouse Canadiens he had won two Vezina Trophies, played in three All-Star games and been a member of four Stanley Cup championship teams. He had also captured a Western League championship while with Vancouver before the team joined the NHL.

After joining the first edition of the big-league Canucks, the sturdy netminder quickly became a fan favourite. Small by today's NHL standards at 5'6" and 150 pounds, Hodge was a slightly chubby, stand-up stopper. He posted a winning record for those expansion Canucks of 15 wins, 13 losses and five ties.

He shared the first win in Canucks history, a 5-3 decision over the Toronto Maple Leafs, and he was in goal for every victory Vancouver posted against an "Original Six" NHL opponent that winter. He finished the season with a 3.42 goals-against average.

"It was exciting," Hodge says now of that first season for the NHL in Vancouver. "Actually, it was very interesting. I enjoyed my year.

It was good camaraderie on that team. We had some good guys."

But he wasn't pleased with the way his time in Vancouver — and, as it turned out, his NHL career — came to an end.

With six games left in the Canucks' expansion season, general manager Bud Poile asked Hodge to go on a scouting trip. He wanted him to check out a few of the goaltending prospects the team was considering for the upcoming amateur draft. Hodge remembers Poile telling him that the final six games of the regular season would be used to determine whether either Gardner or Wilson would be retained.

That summer, Hodge waited back home in Quebec for Poile to send him a contract for the 1971-72 season. It never arrived; Poile had sent it to Hodge's Vancouver address by mistake. By the time training camp rolled around, the goaltender still didn't have a deal. He called Poile, who told him to report to camp and said that they would work out a contract once he got there.

"I told him: 'I'm 37 years old. I'm too old to come to camp without a contract,'" Hodge recalls. He didn't report, and that was the end of his NHL career. "I would have preferred to play at least another year," he says now.

Nevertheless, he enjoyed a long career and still holds a special place in the NHL record books. He played two periods while Gary Bauman played one as the Canadiens blanked the NHL Stars 3-0 in the 1967 classic at the Montreal Forum, which will likely remain the only shutout in All-Star Game history.

Now in his seventies, Hodge lives in the Vancouver bedroom community of Langley and still works as a scout for the Pittsburgh Penguins.

# DENNIS KEARNS

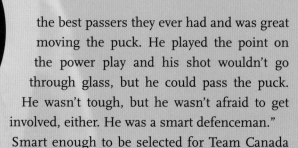

HE WASN'T DRAFTED by a NHL team. In fact, Dennis Kearns never even made it to the highest level of junior hockey. But by the time his career was over he had compiled 10 solid seasons on the Canucks' blue line and represented Canada in a pair of world championship tournaments.

Kearns was a fine passer, skilled at the difficult art of moving the puck out of his own zone. Over his career, that ability to see the ice helped him compile 321 points in 677 NHL games, including 55 assists during the 1976-77 season.

"Kearns was the kind of a player where people looked at what he couldn't do instead of what he could do," says former Canucks broadcaster Jim Robson. "They overlooked his great passing because he didn't play tough and he didn't score a lot of goals and things like that."

But Kearns did stick around, becoming a franchise cornerstone during the team's first decade. Robson remembers sharing an annual joke with the defenceman in the later years of his career. "After a few days every training camp, Kearns would come up to me and say: 'I'm going to be on this team again this year'," Robson says. And he was.

Given how Kearns arrived in Vancouver, a 10-year stay wouldn't have been easily predicted. He was brought in by Hal Laycoe, not a particularly popular coach, during the franchise's second season. Making things worse, Laycoe made room for Kearns by sitting out — and ultimately trading away — Pat Quinn, one of the team's most beloved players.

"Kearns was Laycoe's man. Quinn was a big, prominent, tough, popular guy, a great guy in the community," Robson says. "It didn't go over well."

But Kearns persevered, and he became a fixture on the West Coast and a great guy in the community in his own right. He has operated an insurance business in Vancouver since 1984 and remains extremely active with the Canucks alumni.

"Kearns was never fully appreciated as a player in Vancouver," Robson says. "He played 10 years with the Canucks, was one of

the best passers they ever had and was great moving the puck. He played the point on the power play and his shot wouldn't go through glass, but he could pass the puck. He wasn't tough, but he wasn't afraid to get involved, either. He was a smart defenceman."

Smart enough to be selected for Team Canada for the 1977 world tournament in Vienna and the 1978 tournament in Prague, experiences Kearns rates as among the best in his hockey career. "That was quite an honour for me," he says.

Although he took pride in wearing the Canucks uniform for his entire NHL career, Kearns wasn't a fan of the garish, gold, V-style jerseys the team sported in the late 1970s and early '80s. He remembers that when the team went into opposing arenas that first year — especially in cities they were visiting for the first time — the gasps were audible. He himself got into some hot water over the uniforms in 1978, the year the team adopted the unusual duds: During a visit to Toronto he told Don Cherry: "Last year we played like clowns. This year we look like clowns."

Kearns' route to the NHL would be highly unusual today. From Kingston, Ontario, he played Junior B with the Kingston Frontenacs and then made the jump to senior hockey with the hometown Aces. After four years in the minor-professional ranks he was brought up to the Canucks by coach Laycoe, who had coached Kearns with the Portland Buckaroos, with whom he played three seasons.

The time in the minors helped season Kearns, who also played a winter in Dallas, where he was a Central Hockey League first all-star.

"So much, for players like myself, depends on getting a coach who likes you and then you get your confidence," Kearns says of his gradual move up to the NHL. "And you can do a lot more once you've got your confidence."

He retired from the NHL in 1981 at age 34, after it became clear that he didn't have the confidence of then Canucks coach Harry Neale. "He and I didn't get along that well and Harry was

*In 10 seasons on the Canucks' blue line, Dennis Kearns proved to be highly skilled at moving the puck out of Vancouver's zone.* (Robert Shaver/HHOF)

the boss, so somebody had to go and it was me," Kearns recounts.

The timing meant he missed the Canucks' dramatic 1982 Stanley Cup run by a single year and had to watch the action from the stands. "Oh, I wish I would have been there, for sure," he says. "That was an exciting time in the city."

The most he earned with the Canucks for a season was Can$90,000. Although that is a pittance in today's hockey economics, he has no regrets about how his career unfolded.

"It was fantastic," he says. "I was blessed."

# ORLAND KURTENBACH

WHEN FANS TODAY are asked to identify the quintessential Canuck, they usually think of Trevor Linden, who has proudly worn Vancouver colours during two distinguished tours with the NHL team. But the rugged and stately Orland Kurtenbach, who captained Vancouver in its first four NHL seasons and later coached the team, was "Mr. Canuck" before Linden was old enough to walk, let alone lace on skates.

Kurtenbach capably carried the Canucks in that first NHL season, until he suffered a knee injury that shelved the centreman and the baby Vancouver franchise's playoff hopes. At the time, the steady veteran was enjoying the finest NHL season of his nomadic 17-year professional career, with 37 points in just 33 games.

His line, which included non-household names Wayne Maki and Murray Hall, was one of the hottest in the NHL that December. Maki had already accumulated 33 points, including 15 goals, and Hall, essentially a career minor-leaguer until that stage, was sitting with a heady 27 points. As Christmas approached, the Canucks were in an impressive fourth place overall in the East Division and possibly headed for a spot in the postseason.

But on December 23, 1970, during a 7-2 loss to the Maple Leafs, Toronto defenceman Bobby Baun levelled Kurtenbach at the blue line with a hip check that tore ligaments in the Canuck captain's left knee.

"Guys like Bobby Baun and Hilliard Graves, they all hit low," Kurtenbach recalls. "Those kinds of hits would be match penalties now. But in any case, the damage was done and I was out for, I guess, eight weeks."

He underwent surgery on Christmas Eve and didn't return to the lineup until March 3. With their captain out of commission, the Canucks sank in the standings. It had been the closest they would come to making the playoffs during Kurtenbach's tenure as captain or his subsequent 18-month stint as head coach of the team.

Orland Kurtenbach was a fan favourite in Vancouver long before the NHL finally arrived in the city. As a "can't-miss" prospect out of Cudworth, Saskatchewan, by way of the junior Prince Albert

Mintos, he made his professional debut in the New York Rangers system with the old Canucks of the Western League, and he quickly helped Vancouver to a championship during the 1957-58 season.

Kurtenbach was the Coastal Division rookie of the year that winter, collecting 54 points in 52 games. But despite his roaring offensive start as a pro, he would have a difficult time making it as a regular in the six-team NHL, spending most of his first seven years in the minors with the New York, Boston and Toronto organizations and playing in a travelogue of cities including Saskatoon, Buffalo, Springfield, Providence, San Francisco and Omaha.

When general manager Bud Poile was handed the task of assembling the first Canucks NHL team, he wanted Kurtenbach, the tough-as-nails centre who had helped him win a Western League championship in San Francisco.

Kurtenbach returned to Vancouver with a reputation as one of pro hockey's best fighters, a hard-nosed player who had spent most of his NHL nights skating on third and fourth lines.

"The game was different back then. There was a lot of competition," he recalls. "In those days there were six teams in the NHL, six teams in the American League and six teams in the Western League. There weren't very many teams."

He knew he would be going to one of the two NHL expansion teams in 1970, to either Vancouver or Buffalo. He had played for both clubs' general managers during previous stops. But he was coming back from back-fusion surgery less than two years earlier that had left him in a brace for six months, and he wasn't sure how much he would be able to contribute.

Nevertheless, he was excited about being back in Vancouver, the city where he had met his wife, Laurel. Being asked to serve as the Canucks' first NHL captain was a "big honour" and the lanky pro responded, scoring at least 20 goals for the Canucks in two straight seasons; he finally had the chance to shine as an offensive player in the NHL.

Although those early Canucks struggled in the standings,

*Orland Kurtenbach, shown here in the uniform of the Western League's Canucks, was the first captain the NHL team ever had.* [London Life-Portnoy/BCSHF]

they were never pushed around. Kurtenbach is remembered as a warrior and a proud leader; he finished his four-year stint in Vancouver with 163 points in 229 games before retiring in 1974.

"When I came to Vancouver, everything got off to a roaring start," he recalls. "Everybody was so happy to see [the NHL] and the guys played well, so it was fun."

"There is no question in my mind, we simply could not have had a better team captain," the late Hal Laycoe, the Canucks' first head coach, once said. "When you put any group together, there will always be one whose voice will carry more weight than the others, whose presence will command respect. That was Kurt with us those first two years. In all the years I have been in hockey, I have never seen one man contribute so much on his own to a team's success as Kurt did then."

"The Kraut [Kurtenbach's nickname among some of his teammates] demanded a lot of respect," says former Canuck Bobby Schmautz. "He demanded a lot of respect and got a lot of respect from everybody."

Kurtenbach wasn't the most vocal of leaders, but he was courageous in front of the net, hard-working and, as former Canucks broadcaster Jim Robson notes, "he could score, too."

"Kurtenbach was always considered a tough guy, fourth-liner, when he played in Boston and New York and Toronto," Robson says. "These guys got put in a slot and they never got a chance to show their skills. He got a chance in Vancouver to play on the power play. He got a chance to play a lot of minutes."

But he didn't get the chance to make anything close to the kind of money players in today's NHL make. When he joined the Canucks, he was paid Can$25,000 a year. At the start of his third season with the team he was offered US$150,000 a year by the Los Angeles Sharks of the World Hockey Association, over the telephone, with no negotiating. The Canucks were offering less than half that amount, but he stayed in Vancouver so that he wouldn't have to move his family back to another big American city.

"At one time, none of the [NHL] players knew what each other was making," Kurtenbach recalls. "As soon as the World Hockey Association came around, suddenly it went from $80,000 a year

to $300,000 or $400,000 and suddenly teams found the money.

"I don't begrudge the guys [today], not at all. But the game has changed a lot. Nowadays you get guys scoring eight goals or 10 goals or 12 goals and they're still making $2 million."

His fondest hockey memories are of the teams he played on or coached that won championships — none of them in the NHL. He lists as highlights being picked up from Prince Albert by the Flin Flon Bombers and winning a Memorial Cup national junior championship, as well as championship Western League stints in Vancouver, Portland and San Francisco. Winning the Centennial Cup as head coach of the B.C. Hockey League's Richmond Sockeyes in 1987 is among his best memories.

"I think it's always the championship clubs that you remember the most," he says. "I don't know how you get that, in terms of players just coming together to create the right mix."

He never enjoyed the right mix during his time as head coach of the Canucks. Vancouver general manager Phil Maloney lifted him out of the farm system in Tulsa to coach the NHL team, but the magic Kurtenbach had shown leading the Canucks as a player didn't work when he was behind the bench. He went 20-43-17 in 1977-78, his only full season as an NHL coach.

When Jake Milford took over from Maloney, Kurtenbach felt he

## For the record:

Orland Kurtenbach recorded the first hat trick in the history of the NHL Canucks on December 12, 1970, during a 5-2 victory over the California Golden Seals. The three-goal performance came against Gary Smith, who, four seasons later, would backstop the Canucks to a Smythe Division title and the team's first playoff appearance.

## Canucks Moment:

One of the finest set-up men in Canucks history was right-winger Chris Oddleifson, who posted a team-high 46 assists in 1975-76 while playing on a potent line with Gerry O'Flaherty and Garry Monahan.

A native of Brandon, Manitoba, Oddleifson played nine seasons in the NHL and was Vancouver's captain in 1976-77. But the 1975-76 season, when he added 16 goals to his 46 helpers, was his best statistical year in the NHL.

*Prior to joining the Canucks, Orland Kurtenbach underwent back fusion surgery. Action like this in front of the net obviously didn't help. [Frank Prazak/HHOF]*

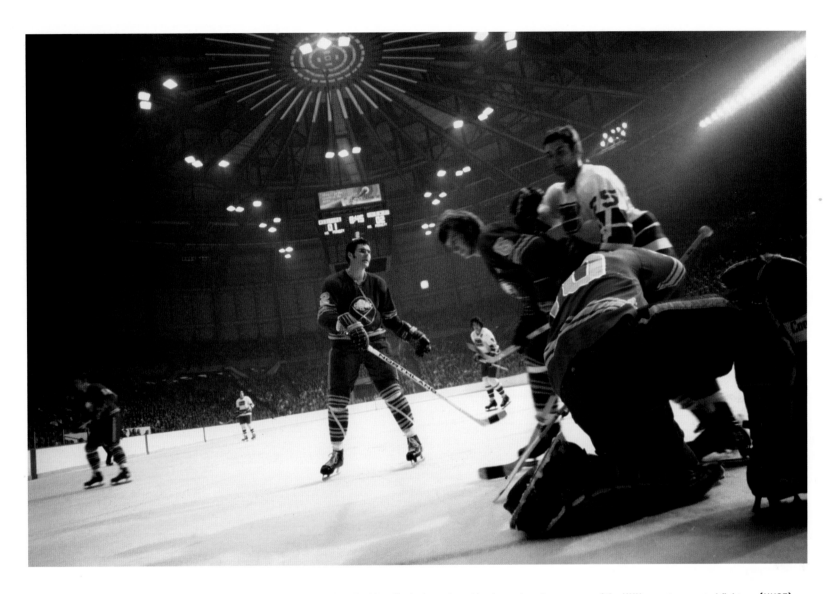

*Orland Kurtenbach was never one to shy away from the rough going. Besides displaying grit and hockey talent, he was one of the NHL's most respected fighters.* [HHOF]

didn't have the proper ingredients and he asked Milford to move some players out before the next season began: "After sitting in dressing rooms in the National Hockey League, I was not only interested in the personnel on the ice. It's the personnel off the ice, in the dressing room ... It becomes very important to me who you have in that dressing room, and I had asked Jake to move off people — and he didn't do it.

"And the first thing when Harry Neale came in [to replace Kurtenbach as coach] the next year is, those guys were gone — bang. That was part of the deal."

Kurtenbach could have returned to Tulsa to coach but that would have meant uprooting his wife and six children once again. Instead, he stayed in British Columbia, concentrated on junior hockey, opened a golf driving range in White Rock and sold insurance.

These days he works in community relations and marketing for the B.C. Hockey League. He has been active with the Canucks alumni and remains one of the franchise's true heroes.

# BOBBY LALONDE

STANDING JUST 5'5" and weighing not much more than 150 pounds, Bobby Lalonde was — and still is — the smallest player ever to have pulled on a Canucks jersey. He was certainly the most diminutive skater in the NHL when he patrolled the ice for Vancouver during six seasons in the 1970s.

The native of Montreal generated a lot of action with that frame. Canucks fans voted him the team's most exciting player for three straight seasons, from 1974-75 through 1976-77.

"He was small. That was his biggest weakness," says former play-by-play man Jim Robson. "But he got in a lot of time in the NHL, considering."

Lalonde was selected in the second round, 17th overall, by the Canucks prior to their second NHL season. He was drafted from the talent-laden roster of the Montreal Junior Canadiens, whom he had helped to back-to-back Memorial Cup national junior championships; that team included the likes of Gilbert Perreault and Rick Martin, who would go on to form Buffalo's famed French Connection Line, as well as Jocelyn Guevremont, whom the Canucks picked in the first round in 1971.

After scoring 59 goals and collecting 127 points in his final junior season, Lalonde spent most of his rookie professional year with the Canucks' farm team, the Rochester Americans of the American Hockey League. In 27 NHL contests that year, he recorded just six points.

But things went much better with one pro year under his belt. He earned 47 points, including 20 goals, for the Canucks during the 1972-73 season. He equalled that output two seasons later and then turned in his best season as a Canuck in 1975-76, when he had 14 goals and 36 assists in 71 games.

"He was a cocky little guy," Robson recalls. "I don't think he was very popular with his teammates, but he could skate. He was only five-foot-five but he had a solid build, was quick and had a good shot."

Lalonde didn't always endear himself to management. In fact, he was central in a Canucks player revolt against strict old-school coach Vic Stasiuk during a team practice in Pittsburgh in the 1972-73 season. The players were doing a drill in which they were supposed to skate down the ice, turn inside the far faceoff dot and return. Lalonde, trying to get under Stasiuk's skin, kept turning the wrong way on purpose. Stasiuk stopped practice and told Lalonde to do the drill properly, but Lalonde went back down the ice and once again turned the wrong way. Stasiuk kicked him off the ice.

Lalonde and a few other Canucks were subsequently benched by a livid Stasiuk, who brought in some young prospects to take their places. But the team was in trouble and Hal Laycoe flew in to Pittsburgh to settle matters.

"Management backed down to the players and you knew then that Stasiuk was as good as gone," Robson says.

Ankle and knee injuries hampered Lalonde during his stint in Vancouver, which ended in 1977 when the Canucks released him after a contract dispute. He was claimed by Atlanta and spent two seasons with the Flames, including a career-best 56-point output in 1978-79, before playing two seasons with the Boston Bruins.

Lalonde still shares an NHL record for most short-handed goals in a single playoff period; he scored twice for Boston while the Bruins were killing a penalty against Minnesota in April 1981, less than a year before he retired from the NHL and went on to play professionally in Switzerland.

# HAL LAYCOE

IN THE OVERALL history of the NHL, Hal Laycoe will be remembered most as the man Maurice "Rocket" Richard clubbed during a melee that led to a riot on the streets of Montreal. But when it comes to the Canucks, Laycoe is best known as the NHL franchise's first head coach, an "old-school" hockey man handed the difficult task of moulding a group of cast-offs into a competitive entity.

Laycoe didn't have much long-term luck in that regard. His team sat a surprising fourth in its division as Christmas approached in the inaugural season of the franchise. But captain Orland Kurtenbach suffered a major knee injury and the Canucks never again came as close to contention during Laycoe's remaining days behind the Vancouver bench.

Laycoe wasn't adored by Vancouver fans, many of whom remembered him as the enemy coach for the Portland Buckaroos, a powerhouse that won seven Western League titles in nine years and often listed the pre-NHL Canucks among their victims.

Following an outstanding career on the bench in the Western League, Laycoe had been hired to replace Leonard "Red" Kelly as coach of the Los Angeles Kings for the 1969-70 season. He lasted 24 games before being fired.

Less than a year later, general manager Bud Poile hired Laycoe to coach the Canucks. Poile is said to have joked about the high franchise fee Vancouver had paid to enter the NHL: "There you are, Hal, there's US$6 million worth of talent. Don't mess it up."

Laycoe was a traditional hockey man who liked his defencemen to stay at home and sometimes brought priests into the dressing room before games. He was set in his methods to the point where it rubbed some players and fans the wrong way.

He coached the Canucks for their first two seasons in the NHL, compiling an uninspiring record of 44 wins, 96 losses and 16 ties. He then served as Vancouver's general manager for one year before being replaced by Phil Maloney.

Laycoe tasted NHL success as a member of the staff of the New York Islanders for three of their four Stanley Cup seasons in the early 1980s, but he was never again offered an NHL head-coaching job.

"The game had been my life," Laycoe told Vancouver *Province* sports columnist Jim Coleman in 1991. "I spent 11 years as a player in the NHL. I spent the next 15 years as a manager or coach. After the Canucks cut me loose, with two and a half years left on an executive contract, I couldn't understand why no other team hired me ... For two and a half years, I sat waiting for the telephone to ring."

Laycoe died at age 75 on April 28, 1998, in Langley, British Columbia, following intestinal surgery. Speakers at his funeral remembered him as a "man of honesty and honour."

Former Vancouver *Sun* columnist Archie McDonald once described Laycoe as a "tireless professor of the game." Laycoe himself summed up his philosophy on coaching as this: "If a fella does his best for me, I'll do anything I can for him."

Former Canucks defenceman Dennis Kearns vouches for that. "Hal Laycoe was very, very instrumental in my career," Kearns told the *Sun* as players gathered for Laycoe's funeral. "He stuck his neck out for me and I would probably still be in Kingston working for Alcan if it wasn't for him. I guess he saw something in me perhaps I didn't see in myself."

Former Canucks sniper Bobby Schmautz remembers winning Laycoe's loyalty. After being recalled from the minors in Rochester during the 1971-72 season, Schmautz met the Canucks in Chicago.

"Laycoe comes off the bus and I'm standing there ready to greet the guys and he had no idea," Schmautz recalls. "He asked me what the hell I was doing there."

Despite the chilly reception, Laycoe became a Schmautz fan later that night when Lou Angotti of the Black Hawks took a run at the tough little winger.

"I kind of caught him with the stick and pretty much just about knocked him out and they sent Keith Magnuson after me," Schmautz says. "It just so happened I beat the hell out of Magnuson that night in Chicago and, after that, Laycoe and I, we became pretty close."

*The NHL Canucks' first coach: Hal Laycoe spent two seasons on the bench before making way for Vic Stasiuk. (Vancouver Canucks)*

Former Canucks broadcaster Jim Robson recalls that during a home game in Laycoe's second year as coach, when the team was preparing for a faceoff in the opponent's zone, Laycoe made a late change and sent out rookie defenceman Jocelyn Guevremont to play the left point. The crowd at the Pacific Coliseum booed.

"He wasn't their kind of player. They liked a tougher guy. And they didn't like Laycoe," Robson says.

The Canucks won the draw and Guevremont scored with a blistering shot from the left point. "Laycoe jumped with his hands in the air and faced the crowd on the bench, saying: 'I told you so!' The crowd still booed Laycoe."

Gary Doak says Laycoe did all right in what was a tough situation as the first head coach of the NHL Canucks. "He just tried to gel everybody together, and on the whole he did a good job."

Laycoe had played 11 seasons as a hard-hitting, stay-at-home defenceman with the New York Rangers, Montreal Canadiens and Boston Bruins. Fiery Rocket Richard broke a trio of sticks over Laycoe's back in a frightening incident late in the 1954-55 regular season and during the melee also punched out a linesman. The Rocket was suspended by then NHL president Clarence Campbell, which eventually led to the infamous "Richard Riots" in Montreal on St. Patrick's Day, 1955.

# DON LEVER

WHEN IT COMES to high-profile draft choices in the 1970s, most Vancouver fans will recall names such as Dale Tallon, Jocelyn Guevremont and Rick Blight. But Don Lever, chosen from the Niagara Falls Flyers third over-all in the 1972 entry draft, represents the Canucks' shrewdest use of a top selection during the first decade of the franchise.

Lever, a hard-working two-way winger, posted 20 goals for the Canucks in six of eight seasons, making him one of the most consistent performers in Vancouver history. Others might have been flashier, but few were as dependable.

"I played some pretty good hockey for Vancouver," says Lever, who up until the NHL lockout of 2004-05 was an assistant coach with the St. Louis Blues.

He grew up near the northern Ontario town of South Porcupine, population 2,000. That's his official hometown, but Lever was actually raised three miles away at Dome Extension, a gold-mining community where his father worked. "He didn't want me to [mine] for a living, I'll tell you that."

Hockey talent and hard work won Lever a place on the roster of the junior Flyers, for whom he stood out enough to become one of the top NHL draft picks of 1972. He was happy to be selected by Vancouver, but he remembers the high expectations that greeted the third overall pick in a city craving an NHL winner.

"I was very nervous," he admits. "I put way too much pressure on myself — I know that now — to be the saviour ... I felt that pressure, but I think I eventually eased into it."

During his first training camp with the Canucks in Calgary he hurt his ankle a couple of days in, but he kept quiet. "I didn't say anything because I wanted to make the team. You know, that kind of hurt me and set me back, but I got going again."

He doesn't remember many details of his first season, during which head coach Vic Stasiuk played him at all three forward positions with numerous linemates. But he recalls having nine goals by November before going into a slump that he couldn't shake. He finished his rookie season with 12 goals and 38 points.

"What I remember the most, I guess, about that year is Vic Stasiuk calling me 'Danny' all the time," he laughs. "It used to drive me nuts."

Lever's best year in the NHL, statistically, came in 1974-75. Playing on a line with smooth centre Andre Boudrias and physical winger Dennis Ververgaert, he compiled career-high totals of 38 goals and 68 points. The Canucks won the Smythe Division title and made the NHL playoffs for the first time that season.

"We were a pretty good line," says Lever. "We had a real good year. Boudy was a great passer. Vervy was good at going to the net. And that was the year [Canucks' goaltender] Gary Smith stood on his head."

Lever stood out, too, recording what at the time was tied for the most goals ever by a Canuck, 38, a mark not beaten until Ron Sedlbauer potted 40 during the 1978-79 season. What Lever remembers about that winter is that he could have easily had more.

"Again I got stuck [in a goal slump] at the end of the year," he says. "I got stuck for about eight or nine games. I should have easily scored 40."

Lever played nearly eight full seasons with the Canucks and served as their captain for two seasons, from 1977 to 1979. He played 593 games in a Vancouver uniform, racking up 186 goals and 407 points while skating on the power play and killing penalties. He was Vancouver's most valuable player in 1975-76.

But the 1974-75 and 1975-76 seasons were Don Lever's only appearances in the playoffs with the Canucks, who seemed to be constantly reshuffling their roster. When he was traded to the Atlanta Flames for Ivan Boldirev and Darcy Rota, he wasn't exactly heartbroken.

"They never let the team stay the same for a few years," he says. "Back then, it was always the players' fault. They would just start panicking and trade everybody."

Lever went on to play with Calgary, Colorado, New Jersey and Buffalo in an NHL career that spanned 15 years and 1,020 games. In all, he posted nine seasons of 20 or more goals and finished with 680 points. One of his career highlights came in 1981-82,

Drafted third overall in 1972, Don Lever posted six seasons of 20 or more goals for the Canucks. (Graphic Artists/HHOF)

when he represented the Colorado Rockies in the NHL All-Star Game.

Following his playing career, Lever quickly caught the coaching bug. He coached in the Buffalo organization until 2002, when he joined the St. Louis Blues. In 2005-06, he was head coach of the American Hockey League's Hamilton Bulldogs. More than 30 years after he arrived at Canucks training camp as a nervous rookie, he still clearly enjoys the camaraderie of the dressing room.

He aspires to be an NHL head coach. "It's just being in the game — it's in your blood. It's the next best thing to playing."

Although he played for a variety of NHL teams and now coaches for another organization, he still identifies with the Canucks.

"They were the first team I was with as a draft pick," he says. "And there's always a place in the bottom of your heart for where you first began."

# JACK McILHARGEY

If Jack McIlhargey wasn't the most talented defenceman to skate with the Canucks, few who came before or after him displayed as much heart.

McIlhargey played eight seasons in hockey's big leagues, including four winters during the late 1970s for the Canucks. Nicknamed "Black Jack," he competed in a pair of Stanley Cup finals with the ferocious Philadelphia Flyers and collected more than 1,100 penalty minutes while patrolling NHL blue lines.

Fans of the team today know McIlhargey as a longtime coach with the Vancouver organization and an associate coach on the Canucks' bench during the 2005-06 NHL season. For the past two decades he has been with the Canucks system either as a minor-league head coach with Milwaukee, Hamilton and Syracuse or as a bench assistant with the NHL team.

His tenure with the Canucks came to an end in June 2006 when he and other assistants were fired by incoming head coach Alain Vigneault. But long before he was guiding prospects into the NHL, McIlhargey was laying his body, and his fists, on professional opponents. The bushy-haired, hard-nosed defenceman broke in as a pro by signing a free-agent deal with the New Jersey Devils of the Eastern Hockey League in the 1972-73 season and finally earned a shot at the NHL with the roughhouse Flyers two years later.

"I wasn't a great skater or a great player," McIlhargey once told the Syracuse *New Times*. "But I worked hard. I knew, when I came to practice or a game, that I wouldn't be outworked."

His first shot at regular duty with Philadelphia came after he led the American Hockey League in penalty minutes, racking up 316 with the Richmond Robins in 1974-75.

The next season he appeared in 57 regular games for the Flyers, amassing 205 penalty minutes. More important, he recorded a plus-11 rating for the season as the Flyers went all the way to the Stanley Cup finals.

After two seasons with Philadelphia, McIlhargey was traded with Larry Goodenough to the Canucks in exchange for Bob Dailey during the 1976-77 season. He found a regular spot on the Vancouver blue line, playing his physical style for parts of four seasons before being dealt back to the Flyers in a cash deal in January 1980. He spent two seasons with the Hartford Whalers before hanging up his skates in 1982 and rejoining the Vancouver organization for which he has played an instrumental role in developing young talent.

"Jack had very limited skill as a player," says former Canucks broadcaster Jim Robson. "He wasn't that big, he wasn't a great skater, he didn't have a terrific shot, but he had a huge heart and was tough, really tough ... I remember one night in Atlanta, the Canucks lost 12-4 but McIlhargey fought everybody on the ice ... Most of the guys he fought were bigger. He was quick — he threw a lot of quick, short punches."

"Hockey has changed a lot in the last 20 years," McIlhargey told the *New Times*. "Back then, it was a more physical sport. Every team played a more physical style. There was more hitting involved. The rules have changed — for the better, I think. The game has improved. It's a faster game now. Players are bigger and stronger and better athletes."

# WAYNE MAKI

EARLY IN THE 1972-73 NHL season, while the Canucks were in the middle of an eastern road trip, left-winger Wayne Maki began experiencing severe headaches.

During two previous seasons he had been an offensive force for the fledgling Canucks, playing on the club's top line with captain Orland Kurtenbach and putting up the best numbers of his professional career. But suddenly the 28-year-old was feeling run down and suffering from horrible headaches. Prior to a game in Atlanta against the Flames, the team decided enough was enough.

"They sent him home to Vancouver from the road trip and he never played again," says former Canucks broadcaster Jim Robson.

Maki was diagnosed with brain cancer on December 14, 1972. On May 12, 1974, the native of Sault Ste. Marie, Ontario, succumbed to the deadly disease at age 29.

His death was a tragic turn for the Canucks and for his family, which included older brother and fellow NHLer Chico Maki. At the time, Vancouver general manager Hal Laycoe assured the family that the Canucks would retire number 11, the jersey that had been worn by Wayne. In 1997, however, the team allowed Mark Messier to wear number 11 when they signed him as a free agent from the New York Rangers. It was a move that upset the Maki family. Wayne's widow, Beverly, said she was heartbroken to see Messier don her husband's former number.

A product of the junior St. Catharines Black Hawks, Wayne Maki began his NHL career in Chicago in 1967, playing with Chico. He played a total of six NHL seasons, recording 136 points and 184 penalty minutes.

But he is likely best known in NHL circles for his part in a nasty stick-swinging incident that nearly killed Ted Green of the Boston Bruins. The altercation occurred during a 1969-70 preseason game in Ottawa, not long after Maki had joined the St. Louis Blues. It resulted in a fractured skull and three operations for Green and a 30-day suspension for Maki, who was eventually sent to the minors.

A year later, Maki was claimed by the Canucks in the 1970 expansion draft. He enjoyed a banner first season with Vancouver, skating on a line with Kurtenbach and Murray Hall. He collected 25 goals and 38 assists and was one of the premier players.

But he also had to suffer the wrath of Bruins fans, especially on November 10, 1970, the Canucks' first visit to the Boston Garden.

"He was a marked man," Robson recalls. "Maki got hammered every shift, mostly by Ken Hodge ... Every time Maki touched the puck he got hammered, but the kid kept coming back, coming back. Late in the game, Maki got into an exchange with Bobby Orr — in Boston. Can you imagine? In Boston? There could have been a riot. They might have killed him."

That's when Robson remembers Canucks coach Hal Laycoe doing "a wonderful thing." At the end of the game Laycoe ran off the bench, grabbed Maki by the arm and hustled him off the ice.

Maki enjoyed a solid second season with the Canucks, posting 22 goals and 25 assists. But he played in just 26 games in his third season, collecting 13 points, before being diagnosed with cancer.

"He had a good shot and was a pretty good player," Robson recalls. "And he sure had a lot of courage."

# PHIL MALONEY

His proper name is Phillip Francis Anthony Maloney. But in hockey circles he was known simply by the nickname "Fox."

Now in his eighties, the first successful coach of the Canucks still has the quick wit he used to motivate players and guide Vancouver to a surprising division title in 1974-75. When asked a couple of years ago to reflect for a few minutes upon his time with the Canucks, Maloney shot back: "I don't know if I can recall very much about it. I'm just about 78 and I have to look in my wallet every once in a while to see who I am."

That sense of humour and his easygoing style were big factors for those 1974-75 Canucks, who rode the goaltending of Gary "Suitcase" Smith and a mysterious blend of camaraderie, grit and talent to the regular-season championship in the newly created Smythe Division.

"The Fox" arrived on the scene on the heels of three "old-school" coaches who had piloted the Canucks in succession, and he seemed to be just what the players needed. He loosened the leash, allowed team members to be individuals, and it worked: Vancouver won 38 games and tied 10 in 80 starts that season.

Maloney went to Vancouver somewhat reluctantly. He had been coaching the Canucks' farm team in Seattle and had the Totems just one point out of first place. He would have preferred to remain in Seattle, biding his time until another NHL job came around, but the Canucks were struggling under rigid head coach Bill McCreary; general manager Hal Laycoe told Maloney to report to the big club.

"I went in the dressing room the first time and I just said: 'Look it, I don't care if you wear your hair down to your shoulders and you wear a dress when you come in here, but when you go on the ice, don't embarrass yourselves or your families. Do the best that you can do,'" Maloney says now. "They kind of bought it."

He had some unique ways of getting his point across. At times, he tossed lit firecrackers into the middle of the dressing room to grab the players' attention, or threw dollar bills on the floor. Sometimes he used subterfuge. During the team's first road trip under him, for example, he set an 11:30 p.m. curfew the night before a game in Detroit. He knew players would break that curfew, but instead of staying up to catch them in person he hired a hotel night worker to wait at the top of the escalator. He gave the hotel employee a hockey stick and told him to ask any player coming in after 11:30 to autograph the stick for the employee's "son."

"I gave the guy twenty bucks and he was happy as hell and I got some names on that stick and I peacefully went to sleep," Maloney says. "I didn't do anything with those names. But the players knew that I knew. I think that after that, they went to bed a little bit earlier the night before games."

The players responded positively to Maloney's approach, at least in his first full season as coach. In 1974-75 they won their division, made the playoffs for the first time in franchise history and gave the legendary Montreal Canadiens a tough test, going five competitive games in a best-of-seven playoff series.

Maloney admits, however, to running things a little "loosely" as Vancouver coach. That approach backfired during the 1975-76 season when goaltender Smith, the team's unofficial spiritual leader, insulted the wife of Canucks owner Frank Griffiths, who demanded that Smith be traded. Maloney says the fallout from that incident "really turned things around."

"I don't know if we would have been a powerhouse [without the Smith trade], but I think it would have given us some breathing room to try to improve on the team by keeping it together. I think it turned players off when I traded [Smith] for Cesare Maniago. But they must have known, I think, that it had to be done. I had no choice if I wanted to work there."

After finishing with a 33-32-15 record and once again making the playoffs in his second full season behind the Canucks bench, Maloney moved over partway through the following year to make way for former captain Orland Kurtenbach. Maloney remained general manager until the end of the 1976-77 season, when he was replaced by Jake Milford.

*Phil Maloney, known by hockey fans as "Fox," was the first coach to guide the NHL Canucks into the playoffs.* (London Life-Portnoy/Vancouver Canucks)

Rather than stay in hockey, Maloney moved on to a 12-year career selling highway tractors, dump trucks and logging trucks in Burnaby, British Columbia. He retired to an oceanfront home at Yellowpoint on Vancouver Island when he was 61.

For nearly 20 years he remained the only Canucks coach to have posted a winning record, and he had done it twice. Yet he didn't get much slack after the Smith incident. Asked if he got a fair shake, today he is blunt: "I buried myself, I think. If you don't win, you're gone. It's as simple as that."

Maloney had a long, successful career as a professional player before trying his hand at coaching and managing. The playmaking centre from Ottawa signed with the Boston Bruins in 1948 and played 158 NHL games for Boston, Toronto and Chicago over 10 years.

Although he was runner-up for the Calder Trophy in 1949-50, he spent most of his career in the Western League, where he was a standout during 14 seasons for the pre-NHL Canucks. He was the third-highest scorer of all time in the WHL, with 923 points; he once tallied eight points in a single game. He was a two-time WHL most valuable player.

# JAKE MILFORD

As THE GREGARIOUS general manager of the Canucks, Jake Milford shepherded the franchise for five years and finally reached the Stanley Cup finals in 1982. But no deal he ever made came close to being as bizarre as one he himself was subjected to as a minor-league player: He was once traded by legendary Springfield Indians general manager Eddie Shore to the Buffalo Bisons in return for a pair of used hockey nets.

As a general manager, Milford stuck to animate objects when making deals. Among those trades was a key 1980 swap in which he sent top draft picks Bill Derlago and Rick Vaive from the Canucks to the Toronto Maple Leafs in exchange for wingers Tiger Williams and Jerry Butler. That move gave the team a character and tenacity that would come in handy two years later during its run to the finals.

Milford, who had good contacts in European hockey, was also responsible for Czechoslovakian stars Jiri Bubla and Ivan Hlinka coming to Vancouver in 1981

But his best call in Vancouver came in October 1980, when he traded fifth-round picks with the New York Islanders in a seemingly trivial deal. An important throw-in that trade, however, gave the Canucks goaltender Richard Brodeur. Brodeur would go on to backstop the Canucks to the Stanley Cup finals in 1982, earning the nickname "King Richard" and certified folk-hero status in Vancouver.

Milford became Canucks general manager in 1977-78, replacing Phil Maloney, who had also served as coach. One year later,

Milford brought in head coach Harry Neale, a man who would eventually take over as general manager when Milford's health began to fail. Milford died in 1984, the same year he was inducted into the Hockey Hall of Fame as a "builder."

A product of Charlottetown, Prince Edward Island, out of junior hockey Milford turned down offers from the Detroit Red Wings and New York Rangers. He opted instead to play hockey with the Wembley Canadians and Monarchs in London, England, while also taking up competitive swimming.

He was a member of the Royal Canadian Air Force's Lion Squadron during World War II, then returned to North America to play in the American and Central professional leagues. He became a successful coach and manager in the minor-pro ranks, winning four Central Hockey League titles, and in 1973 he landed a job as general manager of the NHL's Los Angeles Kings. Under his guidance, the Kings managed a franchise-best 105 points in 1974-75.

Milford took over the Canucks in 1977-78 and the team made the playoffs in four of his five seasons as general manager — 1979, 1980, 1981 and 1982. He is now honoured by the Canucks and their alumni through the annual Jake Milford Celebrity Invitational Golf Tournament, held for charity during training camp.

"He was a helluva hockey man. He knew his business and he was very honest and polite to me," says former Canuck Dennis Ververgaert. "We hold his golf tournament every year. That tells you how respected he was in the business."

# ROSAIRE PAIEMENT

IT WAS EITHER one of the most desperate strategic moves by a general manager in the history of the NHL or one of the most brilliant public relations manoeuvres. Perhaps it was a bit of both.

In February 1972, right-winger Rosaire Paiement was struggling through a horrific slump. During the Canucks' first season he had scored an impressive 34 goals, but midway through the 1971-72 campaign "Cracklin' Rosie" found himself mired in a 37-game goalless drought.

Paiement's voice still reflects the frustration that drought caused him. "It had really been bugging me," he recalls. "There was a lot of pressure, from the club and the media."

That's when Canucks general manager Bud Poile stepped in with a decidedly unconventional approach. At a media luncheon in downtown Vancouver's stately Hotel Georgia, Poile introduced renowned hypnotist Reveen to work his magic on the slumping star. "The Man They Call Reveen," as the entertainer was billed for shows across Canada, promised to induce the winger's "superconscious state" as a group of curious hockey writers watched.

Paiement laughs now as he recalls one of the strangest moments of his career. "You know, we talked a little bit before and I told Reveen: 'I don't believe in this stuff,'" he says. "The funny thing is, just two games later, the puck bounces right out in front and I had an empty-net goal. That's how the slump ended."

Paiement's crash had been a major concern for the second-year Canucks because he had enjoyed such a superb season in the team's inaugural year. Claimed from Philadelphia in the 1970 expansion draft, the beefy winger piled up 34 goals and 62 points and became an early fan favourite in the Pacific Coliseum as the baby Canucks contended until just before Christmas, when injury grounded Orland Kurtenbach and the team. The ice time had been refreshing to Paiement, a product of the Niagara Falls Flyers who had played only 27 NHL games in any one of his four previous professional seasons.

"We were like a bunch of rejects," Paiement recalls of that first Canucks team which, aside from number 2 overall amateur draft pick Dale Tallon, was comprised of players other teams had been willing to discard. "We were from all different parts."

"We almost made the playoffs that first year. The problem was we travelled so much [because of being based in Vancouver]. I thought the travelling killed us."

Playing mainly with Andre Boudrias and Wayne Maki and sometimes with Poul Popiel, Paiement led all Canuck snipers with 34 goals that first season. His most memorable game as a Canuck came at home on February 16, 1971, against Boston, one of the NHL organizations that had previously given up on him. Paiement had three goals and two assists in that contest, figuring in every Vancouver goal as the Canucks beat the Bruins 5-4. "People still talk about that game," says former Canucks play-by-play man Jim Robson.

In one brilliant week alone Paiement counted nine goals, and he had 16 goals in a 15-game stretch for the fledgling Canucks.

But points and goals didn't come anywhere near as easily in his second season with Vancouver, when he was hit with a puck and suffered a serious eye injury. Even Reveen couldn't help Paiement's seasonal statistics and he finished with a disappointing 10 goals and 29 points in 1971-72.

He spent only two seasons with the Canucks. After his 34-goal output in 1970-71, Vancouver offered him a mere Can$3,000 raise; even salary arbitration left him making only Can$28,000 for his second season. When the rival World Hockey Association's Chicago Cougars dangled a three-year contract offer for US$300,000 the next summer, the choice was obvious.

Still, he looks back fondly on his time in Vancouver. "We did pretty good for an expansion team," he says.

Although Paiement scored 34 of his NHL career-total 48 goals in that one big season in Vancouver, he found his scoring touch again in the WHA. He put up 33 goals in his first season with the Cougars in 1972-73 and posted three straight seasons of 70-plus points with the Cougars and the New England Whalers before retiring with the Indianapolis Racers in 1978.

*"Cracklin' Rosie" Paiement had nine goals in a single week for the 1970–71 Canucks and finished with a team-high 34.* (Graphic Artists/HHOF)

He was feared in the NHL as a fighter, hence the nickname "Cracklin' Rosie." Interestingly, he rates his Canuck captain Kurtenbach as the toughest player he ever fought. The two tangled while wearing different NHL uniforms. "Kurtenbach fought like a boxer," Paiement says. "He was tough."

After retiring from pro hockey in 1978, Paiement owned and operated a popular Florida restaurant-bar-motel called The Penalty Box for many years before becoming a partner in another operation, Jester's Bar & Grill, in Fort Lauderdale.

One of 16 children from a family in Earlton, Ontario, their father a former Canadian senior arm-wrestling champion, Rosaire and his brother Wilf both made it to the NHL.

"Rosie was very popular, because he was tough and he could score," Robson says, pointing to Paiement's 152 penalty minutes in his first season with Vancouver. So tough, in fact, that he gave Bobby Orr a black eye during a fight in Boston on February 25, 1971. "Orr was supposed to do some TV commercials that week and he had a big shiner," Robson says. "Rosie might have suckered him, I don't know, but Paiement could fight."

# BUD POILE

NORMAN "BUD" POILE entered the Hockey Hall of Fame in 1990 as a "builder," a fitting description of the quintessential career hockey man. Few have done as much to build the game as Poile, who was a longtime pro coach, general manager of two NHL expansion teams — the Canucks and the Philadelphia Flyers — and a senior league executive in three different professional circuits.

But before all of that he was an outstanding hockey player, good enough to crack the lineup of the Toronto Maple Leafs as a 17-year-old kid out of Fort William, Ontario, and good enough to be a member of the Leafs' 1947 Stanley Cup team.

Poile became a Fort William folk hero in 1942 when he signed with the Leafs. The next year, playing on the Flying Forts Line with Gaye Stewart and Gus Bodnar from his hometown, he led the Leafs in playoff scoring. After serving in World War II, the hardshooting forward returned to help the Leafs capture the Cup.

His world was rocked the following year when he was involved in one of the biggest trades in hockey history. He was part of a package of five players — including the entire Flying Forts Line — the Leafs sent to Chicago in 1948 in exchange for superb centreman Max Bentley and Cyril Thomas.

Before his playing career was over, Poile skated for five of the "Original Six" teams, collecting 229 points in 311 games. But when he hung up his skates his pro hockey career was just getting started. He became a coach with the Tulsa Oilers of the United States Hockey League before moving into the Detroit organization, where he spent nine seasons as coach and general manager of the Western League's Edmonton Flyers, winning three championships.

He had hoped to succeed Jack Adams as Detroit's general manager, but the Red Wings instead hired their former superstar, Sid Abel. So Poile moved on to San Francisco of the Western League, where he won a league title with the Seals.

Poile's chance to run an NHL franchise came in 1967 when he was named general manager of the Flyers, a team he quickly turned into a success on and off the ice. In 1970 he moved on to take a similar role with the Canucks until 1973, when he became executive vice-president of the World Hockey Association.

Poile later expressed regret that the Canucks didn't fare better on the ice during his time as their boss. His initial Vancouver team was in contention for a playoff spot until captain Orland Kurtenbach was hurt just before Christmas, but that was as close as the Canucks would get under his leadership.

"From day 1 we had the support of the fans, but we couldn't get it done," Poile once told Vancouver *Sun* columnist Archie McDonald.

Though his Canucks struggled, Poile's sense as a promoter and a hockey man shone through. He tirelessly cultivated media support for the team, ensuring that the Canucks were foremost in the minds of Vancouverites, and he wasn't without his tricks.

In 1971-72, for instance, Poile brought in celebrated hypnotist Reveen to try to snap Rosaire Paiement out of a scoring slump, a move that was pure promotional genius as much as it was any kind of practical solution to Paiement's lost touch.

Bud's son, David Poile, laughs when that story is recounted to him. David followed in his father's footsteps and, after apprenticing with two other NHL teams, is now general manager of the Nashville Predators.

"He loved the game, but he loved the people, the media, all the components that came with it — the spectacle," David says of his dad. "He was always a great ambassador for the game, someone who really liked to go out there and sell the game. Whether it be out speaking or whatever, he was always selling the game ... I mean, he ran two expansion franchises in Philadelphia and Vancouver. There's a sales job that goes with each one of those jobs and I think that's where he was at his best."

David Poile says people in hockey naturally gravitated to Bud, who had a charismatic personality. Hockey was a huge topic in the Poile home and remained so as David carved out a fine career of his own.

*Bud Poile is best known for his off-ice contributions but he was also an outstanding hockey player in his younger days.* (Brian Kent/Vancouver *Sun*)

"We talked hockey three or four times a week since I've been in it."

After leaving the Canucks, Bud Poile stayed with the WHA until 1976, when he left to begin an eight-year run as commissioner of the Central Hockey League. For a period in the 1980s he ran the CHL and the International Hockey League at the same time. He continued to guide the IHL until he retired in 1989.

Bud Poile died on January 4, 2005, in Vancouver, at the age of 80. "Bud devoted his life to the service of hockey, and with his passing the game has lost a true friend and valued contributor," NHL commissioner Gary Bettman said at the time.

Besides his Hockey Hall of Fame induction, Poile's memory is honoured by an American Hockey League division championship trophy in his name. He was also awarded the Lester Patrick Trophy in 1989, for outstanding service to hockey in the United States; David won the award in 2001. David's son, Brian, also opted for a hockey career, working in the Dallas Stars organization until 2004.

"That's really the only job that either of us ever had ... the hockey business," David Poile says of his dad. "Obviously, he had a great love of the game, because he went right from playing into coaching, and then from coaching into managing, and then from managing into being the commissioner of leagues. So it came to him naturally.

"I think you'd have to say that he was rewarded for that by being inducted into the Hall of Fame."

# JIM ROBSON

IF YOU ASKED JIM ROBSON, he would tell you in his warm, "aw shucks" sort of way that he was just a boy who wanted to be a broadcaster, an eager kid who happened to be lucky enough to fall into his dream job as the voice of the Vancouver Canucks. But thousands upon thousands of fans who were raised on the rich radio tones of Robson's play-by-play would tell you the man had a gift. The Canucks could be bad at times during their early days, but one thing was certain: Their announcer was very, very good. Good enough to have earned a place in the Hockey Hall of Fame.

"I wanted to be a sports broadcaster when I was seven or eight years old," Robson says during a chat in his Kitsilano Point home in Vancouver, just steps from the beach and a short drive to General Motors Place.

Robson spent the earliest years of his life in Prince Albert, Saskatchewan, before his family moved onto a farm in British Columbia's Fraser Valley when he was eight. Like most Canadian boys of his era, he was weaned on Foster Hewitt, the legendary Maple Leafs broadcaster who was hockey's seminal play-by-play man. Winter nights at the Robsons were spent listening to hockey, not only the NHL but also minor-professional games from Vancouver and New Westminster.

"I was a Boston Bruins fan, so I hated the Leafs. But Foster Hewitt was the first one I listened to," Robson says.

It didn't take long for a young Robson to find his way into the broadcasting business. On July 1, 1952, at the age of 17 and straight out of high school, he took a job for $100 a week at radio station CJAV in Port Alberni, a small mill town on central Vancouver Island.

He was supposed to be only a copywriter, but when he arrived at the station the sports reporter had just left. Before long, Robson was calling senior men's lacrosse and basketball games. The first hockey game he broadcast was in 1953 at the Nanaimo Civic Arena, a contest between the Lake Cowichan Bruins and the Alberni Valley Flyers. But it wasn't exactly live: Robson called the morning game into a tape recorder, then drove back to Port Alberni and played it for radio listeners that afternoon.

There was plenty of such creativity in Robson's early days of radio. A few years after moving to Vancouver in 1956, he began calling games featuring the B.C. Lions of the Canadian Football League, Vancouver Mounties of minor-pro baseball, the provincial high school boys' basketball tournament and the Western League games of the pre-NHL Canucks. At times, most often with the Mounties, he wasn't able to travel with the team, so he "recreated" broadcasts using live feeds off the teletype, sound effects and his imagination.

Over 14 years he honed his broadcasting chops and incorporated his gentlemanly persona into the voice of Vancouver sports. When the Canucks were about to join the NHL in 1970, there was no other choice for radio station CKNW than to hire Jim Robson.

For Canucks fans it's difficult to imagine anyone else having been there to bring them all the action over the radio and later on television. For 24 straight seasons, Robson did every single Canucks radio broadcast. He was there like a dependable beacon through the lean years, and he related all the drama during the team's two trips to the league finals.

After Vancouver's dramatic Game 7 charge into the 1994 Stanley Cup finals, an exhausted Robson decided to back off a little, moving from radio to television to call about 30 Canucks games a season.

In 1999, after 29 years as the voice of Vancouver hockey, Robson retired fully. "It was a great job and a wonderful opportunity. But I'm a little tired of plane rides, tired of hotels," he said at the time.

He is never too far from the Canucks, however. He still attends many home games, and when asked about details of Canuck contests from years past he can quickly produce stacks of notebooks with original and amazingly accurate details of each game.

His upstairs office is like a slice of hockey heaven for anybody raised on the Canucks. Among the most prized possessions is a

*Jim Robson called every Canucks' radio broadcast for the NHL team's first 24 seasons.* (Robson Private Archives)

letter from Wayne Gretzky to Robson, congratulating him on his induction into the Hockey Hall of Fame in 1992. Another is a photo of Danny Gallivan, the legendary Montreal Canadiens broadcaster, whom Robson chose to introduce him during that induction ceremony.

An afternoon with Robson is like a guided tour of hockey in the 1970s, '80s and '90s, peppered with anecdotes about players, coaches and general managers. He claims his memory of detail is fading, but he still manages to recall at which side of the net a faceoff 20 years ago took place, and on what sort of shot a Canuck scored to clinch an important victory.

Robson will forever be associated with the Canucks, and he says the most memorable game he ever called for the team was Game 6 of the 1994 Stanley Cup finals, when the upstart Canucks beat the Rangers to send the series back to New York for Game 7.

Ask longtime Canucks fans to name the best broadcaster in hockey and they recite Robson's name with no hesitation. Robson himself deflects such talk. "Who's going to judge that?" he says. "It's all a matter of where you grew up."

Many would argue with him on that point. Over his career he called more than 2,000 NHL games on radio and TV, including five NHL All-Star Games, four Stanley Cup finals and the first NHL hockey games played in Edmonton and Calgary for the CBC's *Hockey Night in Canada.*

## "To All The Shut-Ins ..."

*Jim Robson had one of the most distinctive trademarks in sports broadcasting. During every game he called, fans heard his signature special hello "to all the shut-ins, hospital patients and people who can't make it out to the game."*

*"Well," he confides, "that was stolen."*

*A young Robson heard CKWX broadcaster Cal George use the line and decided to incorporate it into his own play-by-play.*

*It stuck. And so did Robson.*

# THOMAS K. SCALLEN

IN THE 35-YEAR NHL history of the Canucks, the name Thomas K. Scallen is often forgotten, hidden in the back of the closet like some dark family secret.

But Scallen was an integral player in the NHL's arrival in Vancouver. He was the Canucks' first majority owner and, even though he was convicted for mismanagement of funds and subsequently jailed less than four years after giving life to the franchise, Scallen still takes great pride in the role he played.

Now in his 80s, Scallen enjoys watching the Canucks when they play in Minneapolis, where he lives and has interests in the theatre and entertainment business.

"I take great pride in the fact that I was the Canucks' first owner," he says. "I've been at several of the games at the Xcel Center watching Vancouver play the [Minnesota] Wild and I'm in one of the owners' boxes and I'm always pulling for the Canucks."

Scallen says he rarely talks about his days as Vancouver owner, which ended after he was convicted on April 10, 1973, of theft, making a false statement in a prospectus and illegally manipulating US$3 million between companies. He was sentenced to two years in prison but received parole after serving eight months. Scallen says he was given a full pardon by the federal government in Ottawa nine years later.

"It was an extremely painful experience for me and totally undeserved," he says. "Listen, if I'd taken the money and run off with it and spent it, they'd have had something to complain about."

Instead, Scallen says, all he did was use money from Northwest Sports Enterprises, the company that operated the Canucks, to pay off another bank loan that was at a higher interest rate. "It was a matter of money management," he insists.

He had given all of his controlling stock in the hockey club as collateral for the loan, he adds. "So if we had not paid that loan, the [other] shareholders of Northwest Enterprises would have gotten the ownership of that team at a hugely bargain price ... There was never any opportunity for anyone to lose money on that deal.

We reported it in our audit report. It was never a secret, you know."

People behind the scenes in Vancouver who wanted control of the hockey club were instrumental in his case going to trial, he claims. "And I remember one of the lawyers saying at trial that if [Scallen] was a Canadian, he would never have been charged."

Scallen insists his conviction was "political ... The whole thing was a farce as far as I'm concerned. I think we were persecuted because a few local people wanted to try to get us to sell them the hockey club. Well, it didn't work."

He might have avoided prosecution simply by remaining in the United States, but says he wanted to return to Canada to "restore my good name."

"I could have stayed in the U.S. and there wasn't a damn thing they could have done, but I went up there because I knew I hadn't done anything wrong and I know that to this day."

He felt mistreated during the process and, more than 35 years later, the hurt lingers. But he holds nothing against the city of Vancouver or its hockey fans.

A lawyer and businessman from Minneapolis, Scallen was chief executive officer of Medicor, a company that among other things ran ice shows, when he became owner of the Canucks. Medicor owned 60 percent of the shares in the team, making Scallen controlling partner.

He made the decision to buy the franchise during a telephone conversation with NHL brass, from his hotel room in Chicago, during the late 1960s. At the time, nobody in Vancouver was willing to put up the US$6-million franchise fee, he says.

Having operated Ice Follies shows across North America, Scallen was familiar with NHL buildings and knew all the owners. So the league asked him to come on board as the Canucks' majority owner.

"I had played [Pacific Coliseum] with Ice Follies, so I knew the building," he recalls. "So I simply asked them: 'What are your expenses for the average team?' And they told me. I was in a hotel room and, just on a piece of paper, I did a rough scale of the house

*Thomas K. Scallen, shown here emerging from court in Vancouver in 1973, was the NHL team's first owner before going to prison.* (Dan Scott/Vancouver Sun)

and I knew we'd sell the thing out. I knew that we'd fill those seats, so I said: 'Yeah, I'll do it.'"

There were grumblings among Vancouver businessmen about an American owning the Canucks, but Scallen says most fans embraced him and he was excited about building from scratch an NHL franchise that all of Western Canada could support.

"I don't think they would have cared if I was a communist, they just wanted a hockey club," he recalls. "And I want to say that I have nothing but the highest regard for the people of Vancouver. I have been back there for meetings on occasion since. It's a beautiful city. And because a few bad people complicated

my life, I don't hold that against the citizenry of Vancouver. They are fine people."

He says prison was a shattering experience that nearly destroyed his life, and he has no doubt he would have remained the longtime owner of the hockey club had it not been for the criminal conviction. But the turn of events forced him to sell the Canucks to Frank Griffiths after the 1973-74 season for Can$9 million.

"I just hope those jurors who made that terrible wrong decision, I hope somehow they understand what a wrong thing they did."

# BOBBY SCHMAUTZ

MORE THAN THREE decades later, Bobby Schmautz still doesn't understand why the Canucks traded him away.

It was February 1974 and Schmautz was in the midst of a second-straight outstanding season in Vancouver. The winter before, he had led the Canucks in goals, points and penalty minutes. And 49 games into the 1973-74 season he was on pace for a similar year.

But the Canucks' brain trust traded Schmautz to the Boston Bruins for Fred O'Donnell, Chris Oddleifson and the NHL rights to Mike Walton. Neither O'Donnell nor Walton reported, opting to skate in the World Hockey Association.

"I was hurt," Schmautz says now. "It sure couldn't have been money, because in those days we weren't making money. I left practice, [was] driving home, and I heard [about the trade] on the radio."

At the time, Schmautz was making about Can$35,000 after a season in which he had scored 38 goals and had 33 assists for the Canucks. He had appeared in the NHL All-Star Game in two consecutive years. He finally felt established with an NHL team after nine seasons as a pro and now, suddenly, he was on the move again.

"As it turned out, it was probably the best thing that happened for me personally and hockey-wise," Schmautz says of the trade. "But I just never was able to figure it out. I mean, I couldn't have done much more. I don't know what they wanted me to do. You lead them in goals, scoring and penalty minutes and then the next year they get rid of you."

Schmautz would be bounced around North America by the whims of management for much of his career. He was a talented, tenacious forward with a terrific shot. He would fight anybody and beat most opponents with his fists. But he was only 5'9" and, at the most, 180 pounds, and he had a penchant for speaking his mind in an age when that was often frowned upon. His size and his feisty attitude often worked against him when it came to the men who ran hockey in the late 1960s and early '70s.

One of three tough Schmautz brothers to shine with the Saskatoon Quakers and Blades of their hometown, Bobby signed his first pro contract with the Los Angeles Blades of the Western League in 1964. He didn't get a crack at joining the NHL until the Chicago Black Hawks signed him in 1967 and didn't become an NHL regular until the following season, when he played 63 games.

But he couldn't get along with strict head coach Billy Reay in Chicago and the Black Hawks let his rights slide to the expansion St. Louis Blues in the 1969 intraleague draft.

"It was such a schmozzle there in Chicago," Schmautz recalls. "As young guys, you just didn't play. I remember one night I had to play centre because [Stan] Mikita was hurt. We're in Pittsburgh, we win 4-2, I end up with two goals, two assists. Bobby Hull ends up with the other two goals, playing on a line with [me]. The next night we go to Toronto and I didn't even dress, so ... You took what [management] said and there was nothing you could do. You could tell them to stick it, which you did, but they had control over you."

Schmautz never played a game in the NHL for St. Louis. He was traded to Montreal within three weeks of the draft and then sold to Salt Lake City of the WHL; Salt Lake in turn traded him to Seattle of the same league.

Canucks general manager Bud Poile bought Schmautz's contract outright before the NHL team's first season, giving him a solid shot at finally becoming a regular NHLer. But even at that, he began the 1970-71 season in the minors, coming to the big team in February.

By the time the 1972-73 season arrived, however, Schmautz had become an important regular for the Canucks and was clicking on a potent line with slick centreman Andre Boudrias. Schmautz collected 38 goals, 33 assists and 137 penalty minutes for Vancouver that winter, all team bests.

But just one season later, with 26 goals and 19 assists in Vancouver's first 49 games, Schmautz was traded. He went on to spend five productive seasons as a Boston Bruin, playing for coach Don Cherry, who took a liking to his style.

*Bobby Schmautz and the flying puck converge on Montreal Canadiens' netminding great Ken Dryden during the early 1970s.* (Frank Prazak/HHOF)

After brief stops in Edmonton and Colorado, Schmautz rejoined the Canucks as a free agent in 1980 but, once again, his term with the team was curiously short-lived. Though he put up 27 goals and 34 assists in 73 games during the 1980-81 season, Canucks management didn't even offer him a new contract. To this day, Schmautz blames then coach Harry Neale for his departure.

"That's the first time that I've ever heard that a guy scores almost 30 goals and can't be signed on a team and they say he's too old to play," says Schmautz, who at the time was 36. "It kind of makes you wonder: Well, what the hell did these guys want me to do?"

After mulling the idea of playing in Germany, he opted to retire. He eventually settled in Portland, Oregon, where he got into the roofing business.

Schmautz was well known as a fearless player who, though small, was willing to mix it up with anyone. "If you get scared enough, I guess you can fight," he says.

He was also known for his hard, elevating shot, which gave NHL goalies trouble. "At the end of practice, he could stand by one goal and he could put it in the top corner at the other end of the ice," recalls former Canucks broadcaster Jim Robson. "I mean, this guy could really shoot."

# GARY SMITH

His NICKNAME WAS "Suitcase," so perhaps it is understandable that Gary Smith didn't stay long in Vancouver. But while he was there, he made quite an impression. In fact, his 1974-75 season will be remembered as one of the finest ever turned in by a Canuck netminder.

Smith stood on his head that winter, backstopping the Canucks to the regular-season championship in the newly formed Smythe Division and leading the franchise to its first appearance in the NHL playoffs.

"That year, we felt like we had a chance to win all the time with him in net," says Don Lever, the left-winger who scored 38 goals to help the Canucks' cause.

The 6'4" Smith posted 32 wins and nine ties against just 24 losses between the pipes for Vancouver in 1974-75. He recorded six shutouts and a goals-against average of 3.09 and was hailed as a candidate for the Hart Trophy, the NHL's most-valuable-player award, which eventually went to Philadelphia's Bobby Clarke.

Moreover, the free-spirited netminder from Ottawa helped keep those Canucks loose, travelling on the road with a full-length lynx fur coat and rarely turning down an invitation to party. Mention Smith's name to his former Canuck teammates and the stories don't take long to percolate. Defenceman Dennis Kearns tells the tale of Smith going out on the town after a night game in New York. The team was heading to Philadelphia early the next morning.

"He got in and he called down for a 6 a.m. wake-up call," Kearns recalls, laughing, "and the hotel receptionist said, 'You just missed it.'"

During another visit to New York, Smith was brilliant en route to a shutout of the hometown Rangers. After the game, New York's Pete Stemkowski told reporters: "We could have played until four in the morning and not scored on Suitcase."

The next morning, teammates on the Canucks' bus read a hungover Smith the quote from Stemkowski. "If he'd seen me at four in the morning, he'd have scored a ton of goals," Smith laughed.

Phil Maloney, the Canucks' head coach that season, remembers Smith showing up at the airport for road trips wearing his full-length fur coat, wooden clogs on his feet and no socks.

"He would flip his foot up in the air and [a clog] would go up about 20 feet and then there'd be 25 guys yelling, 'I got it!'" Maloney recalls. "They had a helluva time together. They thought he was something, you know. The players followed Gary Smith around like he was the Pied Piper."

Smith also had his quirks come game time. Teammates recall him drinking gallons of Gatorade and wearing as many as 15 pairs of socks. Sometimes he took off all of his equipment, undressed and had a shower between periods. The extra socks were necessary, he would explain, because his skates got looser as he wore them in. And the between-periods equipment change was simply a way to relax.

Smith continually tried to stickhandle as far as he could down the ice. "He wanted to be the first goalie to score," recalls Jim Robson, the Canucks' former play-by-play man.

While fans knew him as "Suitcase" or "Smitty," Smith's teammates called him "Axe" due to his propensity for chopping at any opposing skaters who invaded his crease.

"He was in a different world. He was just a super human being," Lever says. "You know, he lived life like a lot of people would like to live it. There was a lot of party in him. But he'd do anything for you."

Smith's unconventional approach to life caught up to him while he was with the Canucks, however, and eventually led to his trade. During a Christmas reception at the tony Capilano Golf and Country Club in late 1975, the goaltender was introduced to Emily Griffiths, the wife of Canucks owner Frank Griffiths and heiress to the Ballard pet-food fortune.

"Gee. I see the resemblance on the can," Smith said as he greeted Emily, according to a Vancouver *Sun* report.

Maloney, who arrived late at the reception and missed the incident, certainly heard all about it the next morning.

"It was [the beginning of the end], because the next morning I received a call from Frank Griffiths and he told me to get rid of Gary Smith," Maloney says.

*Rangy goaltender Gary Smith had such an outstanding season in 1974–75 that many observers thought he should have won the Hart Trophy.* (Graphic Artists/HHOF)

He remembers Griffiths telling him: "I don't care what you get for him, he's got to go immediately." The Canucks' coach and general manager tried to talk Griffiths out of the move, warning that it would ruin team chemistry, but the owner wasn't relenting. So less than a year after posting a brilliant season, Smith was gone.

Maloney dealt Smith to the Minnesota North Stars for veteran goaltender Cesare Maniago. Although Maniago was team MVP in both of his seasons with the Canucks, the club never recaptured the magic it had enjoyed playing behind Smith. "I got Cesare Maniago and he was capable, but there wasn't the same mix there," Maloney says.

Smith, whose father, Des, won a Stanley Cup with the Boston Bruins in 1941, played his junior hockey in Toronto before turning pro in 1964. He was mostly a minor-leaguer until 1967, when he was taken out of the Leafs system by the expansion Oakland Seals, with whom he spent four years.

Smith was traded to Chicago in 1971 and shared a Vezina Trophy with Tony Esposito that season, when five of his 14 victories were shutouts. But he was again let go, this time back to the Canucks in 1973, moving to Vancouver along with Jerry Korab in exchange for defenceman Dale Tallon.

Over a 14-year career Smith posted an impressive 3.39 goals-against average but, true to his nickname, he played with eight different NHL teams.

He would eventually lose much of the money he had made as an NHLer, when his investment in the movie business failed. He later worked as a bailiff, sheriff, bartender and hockey scout and in various jobs around racetracks; horse-racing came as a natural love, since his father had been a horse-racing announcer.

Smith once told Vancouver *Sun* columnist Pete McMartin: "I led the league in hangovers. Fourteen years, every day." But he also told the newspaper that he wasn't the troublemaker some people made him out to be. "I was never fined a cent in my life," he said. "The only trouble I was ever in was at that one party."

# DALE TALLON

HE HAS CONSIDERED himself a Chicago Blackhawk for more than three decades now. But in the summer of 1970, Dale Tallon was both the face and the future of the Canucks.

A strapping 19-year-old out of Noranda, Quebec, Tallon was the first amateur draft pick of the fledgling franchise. Chosen second overall in 1970, he was a talented teenager who was able to step into the lineup and play both forward and defence. He was good enough to make the NHL All-Star Game and to be selected as a member of perhaps the greatest team in hockey history, the 1972 edition of Team Canada, which beat the Soviets in the Summit Series.

But in Vancouver, Dale Tallon is remembered most for who he wasn't. He wasn't Gilbert Perreault.

As they entered the NHL together, the Canucks and the Buffalo Sabres spun a wheel-of-chance at Montreal's Queen Elizabeth Hotel on June 11, 1970. The Canucks lost that spin, giving the Sabres the right to choose Perreault, the smooth-skating, ridiculously talented Montreal Junior Canadiens centre who was the consensus number 1.

The Canucks could have picked Darryl Sittler, Reggie Leach or Rick MacLeish with the number 2 selection. They picked Tallon, a forward-defenceman from the Toronto Marlboros who was good with the puck and capable of anchoring the power play.

Tallon played well for the Canucks, breaking Bobby Orr's scoring record for a rookie defenceman. But he wasn't Perreault. In spite of a solid if unspectacular NHL career, Tallon would become a symbol of the young Canucks' struggles in the NHL.

"He was either compared to Gilbert Perreault or Bobby Orr, and neither one was a very fair comparison," says former Canucks defenceman Dennis Kearns, who was sometimes paired with Tallon and witnessed the pressure the young man was under.

Tallon says he was happy to go to Vancouver and insists that the stress of being the number 2 overall pick wasn't a factor. "Not at all. I could handle it," he says. "It was the pressure of playing well, for my teammates — that was my motivation."

But there is a touch of regret in his voice when he talks about his time in Vancouver.

"When I was healthy, I had good numbers," he says. "I can only talk about things that I can control and, you know, obviously, Gilbert Perreault was a great player — I played with him all my life, against him in peewee and in junior. He was a different player. I needed good players around me and he could do more on his own, so we were different players."

They certainly were. Perreault was an offensive magician, capable of stickhandling wizardry that could lift fans out of their seats. He had two NHL seasons of more than 100 points and was the heart of the famed French Connection Line with Rene Robert and Rick Martin, once the most dangerous combination in hockey.

Tallon, meanwhile, was asked to sacrifice himself for a franchise that struggled mightily in its early years. A centreman who was switched back to defence in the last part of his final junior season in Toronto, he was moved around the Canucks' lineup like a pinball, never allowed to get comfortable in one spot. At his first NHL training camp in Calgary, he played centre and wing before finally going back to the blue line. It's a wonder they didn't slap the pads on him and put him in goal.

After breaking Orr's record as a rookie, Tallon went to his second training camp with the Canucks thinking he would again play defence. But a couple of games into his sophomore season, with the team sagging, the Canucks began to move him around.

"Then they sort of pushed the panic button and started playing me all over — played me on right wing and left wing ... I didn't complain, but I certainly wasn't happy about it."

But he enjoyed being in Vancouver and playing with veterans such as Andre Boudrias, Orland Kurtenbach, Pat Quinn and Gary Doak, who helped him adjust to the league. "They took me under their wing and they showed a lot of class toward me and they really helped me along," Tallon says. "They were terrific to me."

Canucks broadcaster Jim Robson remembers Tallon as a fine rookie, who worked hard in practice and was often on the ice both before and after team sessions. But Tallon clashed with strict head

*Bounced between forward and defence, the Canucks' first-ever amateur draft pick Dale Tallon was eventually traded to Chicago.* (Graphic Artists/HHOF)

*Dale Tallon was forever compared with two players: Bobby Orr and Gilbert Perreault. Neither comparison was fair or flattering.* (London Life-Portnoy/HHOF)

coach Hal Laycoe, suffered through injuries and sometimes let his emotions get the better of him when the fans got on his back. Tallon once gave hometown fans the one-finger salute as the boos rained down.

"He was a good player. But he was expected to be a great player and expected to be the leader and he wasn't the leader and he wasn't a great player, he was a good player," Robson says.

Tallon, who on June 21, 2005, became general manager of the Chicago Blackhawks (the name was changed prior to the 1985-86 season), says today's NHLer has so much more say about how he is played than players did in the early 1970s.

"I think maybe I was too respectful when I first came in," he says. "The line I regret ever using was when I was picked up by Hal Laycoe — the first time I came to Vancouver, for a press conference to sign my contract. He said: 'Where do you think you should play?' And I said: 'Anywhere I can help the team.'

I didn't think that he would hold me to it."

The Canucks kept Tallon playing musical positions throughout his tenure in Vancouver. Prior to his fourth year, he told the team's owners he would jump to the World Hockey Association unless he was traded and said he wanted to play in Chicago. He had met a few of their players, such as Dennis Hull and Jim Pappin, and he wanted to play in the east, closer to his family. On May 14, 1973, he was traded to the Black Hawks for goaltender Gary Smith and defenceman Jerry Korab.

Chicago imported Tallon to play centre for Bobby Hull, the NHL's most feared scoring machine, who liked to blaze down the left wing before uncorking his deadly shot. "I practised my backhand passing all summer — and then [Hull] jumped to the WHA," Tallon chuckles, ruefully.

After two seasons playing up front in Chicago, Tallon was told by coach Billy Reay to return to camp ready to play defence.

*After retiring as a player in 1980, Dale Tallon kept working in the Chicago organization. He became general manager of the Blackhawks in June 2005. (Frank Prazak/HHOF)*

He responded by scoring 62 points from the back end 1975-76, a record for Chicago defencemen. He played five seasons for Chicago and finished his career in Pittsburgh, retiring in 1980.

Vancouver remains a special place for him. "The media might have been a little tough on me, but the people were really nice to me," he says. "I still have a lot of great friends out there. It was a special place for me."

A terrific golfer, Tallon has been head pro at Highland Park Country Club in Chicago and has also played on the senior Professional Golf Association tour.

# DENNIS VERVERGAERT

IN THE WINTER of 1975-76, it seemed Dennis Ververgaert was developing into the bona fide NHL star power forward Vancouver fans had hoped for. The big right-winger notched 37 goals that season and his 71 points helped drive the Canucks into the playoffs for the second straight spring.

In the NHL All-Star Game at Philadelphia that February, Ververgaert wowed fans by scoring two goals in 10 seconds, a record at the time for the league's midseason classic, though since broken.

From Grimsby, Ontario, with shaggy hair and moustache and a blistering shot, Ververgaert seemed poised for a long and prosperous career with the Canucks. But that's not the way things worked out. Just two seasons after his 37-goal outburst, a shocked Ververgaert was traded to the Philadelphia Flyers.

Today, he says a nagging shoulder injury that never healed properly and a never-ending game of musical linemates probably did the most to keep his career as a Canuck from flourishing the way it might have.

His best year, not coincidentally, came when he played with centre Andre Boudrias and left-winger Don Lever. They formed the Canucks' top line and Ververgaert remembers finding the groove with the talented Boudrias.

"I wasn't the fastest skater, so I needed a guy who could wait until I could get my speed up and then feed me that puck just before the blue line," he recalls, describing Boudrias as just that guy.

But Boudrias was at the end of his NHL career. After the polished centreman left for the World Hockey Association, Ververgaert never found another centre with whom he clicked as well. His point output dropped from 71 in his best season to 45 in 1976-77 and 54 the next year.

"I had a different centreman every year, sometimes twice a year," he says now. "I had [Orland] Kurtenbach when I started and then Boudrias and then Lever and then Billy Derlago. So every year I'm getting a new centreman and I can't really develop with somebody."

The other thing that didn't help was a shoulder injury that occurred in Philadelphia during his second year with the Canucks. An injured knee gave out while he was skating near the boards and he ended up hurting his shoulder in the ensuing crash. The pain was excruciating, but Ververgaert wasn't diagnosed with a separated shoulder until several days later, after returning to Vancouver from a tough road trip.

"I don't think it ever got strong enough," he says. "It still hurts today — it's still weak."

Dennis Ververgaert grew up in southern Ontario and was, quite naturally, a fan of the Toronto Maple Leafs. After playing junior hockey with the London Knights, he even sat behind the Leafs' delegation at the 1973 entry draft in Montreal's Mount Royal Hotel.

"The Leafs told me I was going there" with Toronto's fourth overall pick, Ververgaert says. "For some reason, Vancouver picked me third and then Toronto took Lanny McDonald."

Jim Robson, the Canucks' longtime broadcaster, remembers announcing Vancouver's selection that year. "And everybody said: 'Dennis who?' Everybody expected them to pick Lanny McDonald."

Ververgaert made the Canucks lineup right out of junior, but he got off to a slow start. Halfway through his first season, the big winger had just seven goals. Then goaltender Gary Smith gave him a talking-to, and it worked. "It kind of woke me up," Ververgaert says. He notched 19 goals the rest of the way to finish with a team rookie-record 57 points.

In his second season in Vancouver, due to injuries he played only 57 games. But he still finished with 51 points and helped the Canucks nail first place in the Smythe Division with a strong team showing. In fact, thanks to a loss by the rival Chicago Black Hawks, the Canucks "announced it over the PA at my wedding [reception] that we just clinched first place," Ververgaert recalls. "It made for a good reception."

The following season was his finest in a statistical sense, with a 71-point output in 80 games. But after that he never put up the

*A shoulder injury during his second season with the Canucks never fully healed for forward Dennis Ververgaert.* (Robert Shaver/HHOF)

kinds of numbers hungry Vancouver fans wanted out of a third-overall pick.

Halfway through the 1978-79 season, he was traded to the Flyers for Drew Callander and Kevin McCarthy. Ververgaert joined a Stanley Cup contender in Philadelphia, a team with which he enjoyed a 35-game unbeaten streak and an appearance in the Stanley Cup finals against the New York Islanders. After one and a half seasons in Philadelphia, Ververgaert finished his NHL career with a single season in Washington.

But he hadn't planned well financially for his retirement and he struggled to make ends meet after hanging up his skates.

"It happens pretty quick," he told the Vancouver *Province* in 2003. "You're just out [of hockey] and that's it and it's kind of a shock. And back then, it took me a while to find out who my friends were. You think people are your friends when you're playing, but a lot of them were hanging out with you because of the notoriety."

With help from the Canucks alumni organization, Ververgaert found work and eventually put himself on a sound financial footing. He has owned and operated a successful general insurance business in Abbotsford for more than 15 years. He is also an active member of the Canucks alumni and says that in spite of finishing his career elsewhere, his allegiances are in British Columbia.

"Oh, I'm an avid Canuck," he says. "That's where my identity is, that's where I enjoyed it the most, and I live here."

# A GODFORSAKEN TEAM

*Seventies Canucks suffered through some serious growing pains*

## by Archie McDonald

WHEN THE PACIFIC COLISEUM opened on January 8, 1968, civic chaplain Reverend George Turpin asked God to bless the Can$6-million edifice and urged Him to guarantee that the leaders of the NHL grant a franchise to Vancouver.

Vancouver welcomed its long-awaited entry in 1970; then the dial-a-prayer line went dead. The Canucks were a godforsaken team for several years.

In no particular order: their owner went to jail for theft; illness forced general manager Bud Poile to resign; top managers were openly hostile to each other; high-scoring Wayne Maki died of a brain tumour; Orland Kurtenbach, their best player, was hobbled by injuries; their draft picks did not pan out; and they wore out three coaches in three and a half seasons.

In January 1974, following the firing of coach Bill McCreary, goalie Gary Smith noted with classic candour, "This club is unbelievably screwed up."

Problems started with ownership. The original franchise application, which had a price tag of US$2 million in 1967, was spearheaded by local interests. The NHL governors spurned them and awarded franchises to six less-qualified American cities, a move that outraged fans across Canada.

Three years later, the entry ransom had escalated to US$6 million and the original applicants balked. Medicor, a diversified service company with headquarters in Minnesota, eventually bought the team. Its flagship enterprise was Ice Follies. Its president was 44-year-old lawyer Tom Scallen.

Poile, who had put together a decent expansion franchise in Philadelphia before falling out of favour with the owners, hired Hal Laycoe as coach. Poile and Laycoe had been rivals in the Western League and there was ample evidence the rivalry continued even when they were on the same team.

A spin of a hastily assembled roulette wheel gave Buffalo, the other expansion franchise in 1970, first pick in the amateur draft. The Sabres' general manager, Punch Imlach, could scarcely contain his glee as he selected superstar-in-waiting Gilbert Perreault. The Canucks' consolation prize was defenceman Dale Tallon,

a former Canadian golf champion who had a promising rookie season before falling victim to the chaos within the organization.

The Canucks did surprisingly well in their first season, particularly before Kurtenbach was injured at Christmas. Sellout crowds — 15,570, and we thank you — turned out to see household names such as Bobby Orr, Phil Esposito, Bobby Hull, Jean Beliveau and Dave Keon, but they cheered loudest for newfound heroes Andre "Super Pest" Boudrias, tough-guy sniper Rosaire Paiement, veteran goalie Charlie Hodge and captain Kurtenbach.

The Canucks finished next to last in the East Division with 56 points, one ahead of the Detroit Red Wings. That Vancouver, the most western of cities, played in the East Division illustrates the jumbled manner in which the expansion process had been thrown together.

It was satisfying to beat out Detroit, an "Original Six" team, but the Canucks paid a price. Drafting second overall, the Wings selected Marcel Dionne, who retired 18 seasons later as the third leading scorer of all time. The Canucks opted for another defenceman, Jocelyn Guevremont, with the third choice. He rarely lived up to his advance notice and was traded after four seasons.

Year 2 spelled disaster. The Canucks finished 14th out of 14 with 48 points but were deprived of first pick in the draft, which went to the expansion New York Islanders, with Atlanta selecting second. Vancouver plucked Don Lever third and he gave them eight good seasons before being involved in a pivotal trade that brought Darcy Rota and Ivan Boldirev from Atlanta.

Laycoe was fired as coach in the off-season and replaced by Vic Stasiuk, an old friend of Poile's.

The players showed no respect for Stasiuk, an old-school guy who had played on three Stanley Cup winners. They refused to go on the ice when he called a 7:30 a.m. practice in Pittsburgh. A November 13 headline in the Vancouver *Province* shouted: CANUCK PLAYERS IN OPEN REVOLT.

Stasiuk survived the 1972-73 season but Poile didn't. He spent three weeks in hospital before Christmas suffering from exhaustion, and doctors advised him to dissociate himself from the team.

Colourful goaltender Gary Smith played an amazing 72 games for the Canucks in 1974–75 but soon wore out his welcome. (Graphic Artists/HHOF)

Laycoe, who had remained in the organization as a vice-president, became general manager and Poile was placed in charge of special projects, a fringe assignment.

The puppeteer pulling strings from the balcony was Coleman E. Hall, the original owner of the minor-league Canucks, who had been appointed club president by Medicor. With Poile on the sidelines, Hall became a persuasive force.

Laycoe said that Coley Hall left 95 percent of the operation to him. "Unfortunately," one columnist noted, "the other 5 percent were decisions."

The nadir in Canucks history occurred in 1974. A front-page picture in the Vancouver *Sun* in March showed owner Scallen escorted by two Royal Canadian Mounted Police officers, being led away to serve a two-year term in Oakalla Prison. He was found to have illegally transferred US$3 million from Northwest Sports Enterprises, parent company of the Canucks, to Medicor accounts in San Francisco and Chicago.

This team had more twists and turns than a switchback road in the high Rockies.

Earlier in the script, Poile, now assistant general manager, had declared in a radio interview that he could no longer work with "that man" — Laycoe.

Laycoe demanded Poile's resignation. They had public shouting matches. Poile resigned before he was fired.

All the while, Coley Hall was calling the shots from his vacation home in Hawaii. He fired McCreary, who had replaced Stasiuk only six months previously. He hired Phil Maloney, who had starred with the old Western League Canucks, as coach and interim general manager. Laycoe was given a leave of absence.

It was the start of a spectacular but short-lived reversal of fortunes. Under Maloney's guidance the team rallied for 34 points in its last 37 games and began 1974-75 with high hopes. The team had been sold to Western International Broadcasting, led by Frank Griffiths, and local ownership fueled the optimism ignited by the strong finish.

The league had been realigned into four divisions and the Canucks were placed in the Smythe, the weakest. Maloney laughingly referred to it as the "Sweathog Division."

Backstopped by the colourful Smith, who played an amazing 72 games, the Canucks defied the 50-to-1 odds bookmakers had given in Las Vegas and won the division with 86 points, edging St. Louis and Chicago.

Under a new playoff format, the Canucks, ninth overall in total points, faced the almighty Montreal Canadiens in a best-of-seven. The Canadiens prevailed 4-1, but the games were surprisingly close.

The change in direction, however, turned out to be a U-turn. The following season Smith, pulled from a Sunday afternoon game against Pittsburgh at the Coliseum with the Canucks trailing 5-1, stomped directly to his car. "I proved how hard it was to drive with skates on," Smith said later.

They managed to finish second but lost to the expansion Islanders in the first round.

Smith, the symbol of the team's tumultuous fortunes, was traded to Minnesota for Cesare Maniago in August 1976. Maniago would be named the Canucks' most valuable player, but they finished out of the playoffs with 63 points.

With the team struggling mightily in the 1976-77 season, Maloney was replaced as coach by Kurtenbach but remained as general manager. At the end of the season he was replaced as general manager by Jake Milford.

Milford, who had a wide and deep background in all facets of the game, brought stability to the organization. He stayed with Kurtenbach as coach for one season, then brought in Harry Neale.

Neale, who had coached the Minnesota Fighting Saints in the World Hockey Association, arrived at a propitious time. He was able to put together a line of first-year players — Thomas Gradin, Stan Smyl and Curt Fraser — who would lead the team into a better decade in the 1980s.

*Archie McDonald was a sports writer and columnist for the Vancouver* Sun *newspaper from 1957 until his retirement in 1996.*

# the **second decade**

# a moment of **near-glory**

**O**n Monday, May 17, 1982, an estimated 100,000 Lower Mainlanders jammed the sidewalks of Vancouver from the north end of Burrard Street all the way to Sunset Beach to pay an emotional tribute to their hockey heroes.

On that memorable day, the future looked bright for the Vancouver Canucks. Surely after so many lean years throughout the 1970s they had finally joined the ranks of true Stanley Cup contenders — hadn't they?

Well, in one cruel word, no.

To say that the spring of 1982 was the bright spot of the 1980s for Vancouver's NHL franchise would be like saying the Beatles were a pretty successful little combo.

*Facing page, above: Harold Snepsts and Stan Smyl hoist the Clarence Campbell Bowl after beating Chicago in 1982.* [Paul Bereswill/HHOF]

*Facing page, below: Tony Tanti and Patrik Sundstrom were a potent offensive combination for the Canucks of the mid-1980s.* [Paul Bereswill/HHOF]

*Above: When Roger Neilson took over the bench late in the 1981–82 season, some magic kicked in for the Canucks.* [Paul Bereswill/HHOF]

Within four years of that magical spring, the Canucks were struggling so badly that their lone first-round home playoff game attracted a measly 8,000 fans. And that was when the team actually made the playoffs. Three times during the 1980s, there was no postseason at all for Vancouver. And in six other years, the Canucks bowed out in the opening round.

By the midpoint of the decade, as the Canucks failed to stay within shouting distance of the punishing Calgary Flames and the dynastic Edmonton Oilers in their own Smythe Division, it seemed 1982 had been but a cruel mirage.

"We thought we had a young team that had a chance to get better," says Harry Neale, the coach-turned-general manager of those early '80s Canuck teams who was charged with making that happen.

"The problem was that in our division Edmonton was getting better, getting ready to win five Stanley Cups in seven years. And Calgary was getting a lot better, too. Everyone thought after '82 that we were just a couple of good wins away from the Stanley Cup and we were a lot further away than that, even though we never admitted it."

That 1982 run now stands out in the decade as an aberration. Not a fluke, mind you, because the team was chock full of character and work ethic and contained more talent than most people gave it credit for. And those Canucks had two things that every hockey team needs in the playoffs: momentum and great goaltending.

The momentum was sparked late in the regular season in an unusual place and manner. Members of that 1982 team will tell you that when Harry Neale went into the stands in Quebec City to try to protect Tiger Williams from an overzealous fan, his action began the ball rolling toward what would be a remarkable spring.

Until that point, with six games remaining in the regular season, the Canucks were having a mediocre year. In fact, even though they went undefeated over their final 10 games of the regular season, Vancouver finished with a sub-.500 record at 30-33-17.

But when Neale went into the stands, he set off a chain reaction that helped propel those Canucks on to greatness. For starters, the incident drew the players even closer than they had been. It also brought on Roger Neilson as a fill-in head coach for Neale, who was suspended by the NHL for the rest of the season and three games into the playoffs.

The Canucks rallied behind the tutorial Neilson, who put a system in place that every single skater, from the grinders to the gifted, bought into. Neale realized a good thing when he saw it and was wise enough to step out of the way and enjoy the ride. He was scheduled to move into the general manager's seat the next year anyway. With Neilson clearly on a roll, Neale simply vacated his coaching post a little earlier.

"I think that run was largely due to the gentleman who was coaching — Roger Neilson," Canucks defenceman Rick Lanz says now. "He basically took a group of players that really nobody expected a whole lot from, especially a playoff run like that. And you know, the players who came in to help because of the injuries we had did a fantastic job. I mean, you can look at guys like [reserve defenceman] Neil Belland and Andy Schliebener. Everybody got kind of caught up in the emotion of it all and subsequently [was] playing at the peak of their abilities. That was largely due to Roger, who kind of rallied the troops."

Lanz was reduced to observer status for those playoffs. He was one of three regular Canuck defencemen, along with captain Kevin McCarthy and Jiri Bubla, who weren't able to play in the postseason due to injuries. Another defenceman, Swede Lars Lindgren, endured the playoffs with a badly injured shoulder. The underdog Canucks managed to reach the final with a patchwork defence that included Belland, Schliebener, Doug Halward, Harold Snepsts and future NHL executive Colin Campbell. But that blue-collar crew did the job in front of the stellar netminding of Richard Brodeur, who earned his nickname "King Richard" during those 1982 playoffs with his lovable roly-poly-goalie acrobatics.

"We got on a roll and played over our heads," Neale says now. "No matter who got hurt, the guy coming in, even if he hadn't played, did a good job and we were getting excellent goaltending from Richard Brodeur. And it was just a perfect example of a team that got on a roll. When we went to the rink we *thought* we were going to win, we didn't *hope* we were going to win."

"We got good goaltending and we started believing in ourselves in a really good way," adds Lindgren. "We felt they couldn't beat us, the other teams."

Those Canucks, with their garish gold-red-and-black, flying-V jerseys, took on the Calgary Flames in the first round of the playoffs, riding the red-hot netminding of Brodeur to a three-game sweep in the best-of-five affair. The goaltender with the regal nickname allowed just five goals on 108 shots in that series and feisty Tiger Williams scored a key Game 2 overtime clincher before adding the winner in Game 3 as the Canucks captured their first playoff series in franchise history.

But just as important as what the Canucks did in that opening round was what happened elsewhere in those NHL playoffs. Vancouver benefited from the so-called "Miracle on Manchester," a reference to the location of the Los Angeles Forum, where the hometown Kings sidelined the powerful Edmonton Oilers, and the Chicago Black Hawks eliminated the other favourite from the Campbell Conference, the Minnesota North Stars.

*Richard Brodeur certainly earned his royal nickname "King" during the 1982 Stanley Cup playoffs.* (Paul Bereswill/HHOF)

Those upsets opened a lane that the Canucks could have driven a semi-trailer through. And coach Neilson, with his system that gave every skater an important role, was just the man to take the wheel.

"What a lot of people don't know is we never played a team in the first three rounds of those playoffs when we didn't have home-ice advantage," Neale says. "I don't know that you can finish where we finished in the regular season and have home-ice advantage for three straight rounds. If we'd played Edmonton, I doubt if we'd have got out of the West. And if we'd played Minnesota, they had 17 more points than we did in the regular season. When we finally played a team that was a way ahead of us, they got rid of us in a hurry."

Nevertheless, those Canucks had plenty of fun getting there and so did their fans.

"When you go on a run like that, every guy contributes, right?" says grinder Gary Lupul, a Pacific Coliseum favourite that spring for the way he never gave up on any shift.

"The way the city went nuts was really something for me," says the Powell River native. "I mean, I can remember my first year in Vancouver when I played 50 games and we played against Buffalo

in the playoffs. And I think in Game 3 there were only like 8,000 or 9,000 people there. So just to be from B.C. and to see how excited everybody got [in 1982] and to be a part of all that as a player ..."

After taking out Calgary in three straight, they faced the Kings in the second round. But Los Angeles was spent after the huge victory over the Oilers and the Canucks prevailed in five.

It wasn't easy, however and, typical of that spring, Vancouver got help from unlikely places to dethrone the Kings. Lupul scored the winner in Game 1, a 3-2 home decision. Then, after dropping Game 2 to the visitors, the Canucks had brilliant back-to-back performances from Brodeur to win two straight in Los Angeles. In Game 3, journeyman defenceman Colin Campbell, hardly an offensive threat and playing on a bad knee, scored twice, including the winner just over a minute into overtime to seal the victory and turn the series decidedly in the Canucks' favour.

That trend continued in the Campbell Conference final opener, when checker Jim Nill scored midway through the second overtime period to give the visiting Canucks a 2-1 victory in the din of Chicago Stadium.

Vancouver dropped Game 2 by a 4-1 score, but it was this game

*Slick Swedish centre Thomas Gradin was a key member of the 1982 Stanley Cup finalists.* (London Life-Portnoy/HHOF)

While fans back home in Vancouver were breaking into a frenzy, the Canucks organization was scrambling to make arrangements to play in a championship series they clearly hadn't expected to be in. By the time management made hotel reservations in New York state, the only rooms available were at a Holiday Inn on the far side of Long Island from Nassau Veterans Memorial Coliseum.

"It was kind of a schmozzle," recalls Canucks Hall of Fame broadcaster Jim Robson. "They were a couple of hours from the rink and the accommodation was isolated and not great. There was no room for the [Vancouver] media at the hotel. The team got there after a long day of travelling and they had to play Game 1 the next day."

Nevertheless, the Canucks acquitted themselves well in the opener of a best-of-seven final against the heavily favoured Islanders, who were seeking their third straight Stanley Cup.

In fact, Vancouver was unlucky not to win that game, a victory that would perhaps have created a much different series overall. But they lost 6-5 in overtime when Canuck defenceman Harold Snepsts made an ill-fated clearing pass up the middle of the ice. It was intercepted by Mike Bossy, and the Islanders' superstar sniper beat Brodeur high to the glove side with just two seconds left on the clock.

The Canucks were in Game 2 as well, leading 3-2 after two periods. But the Islanders began to assert their talent, scoring four times in the final frame to take a 2-0 lead and control of the series. The underdog Canucks had finally met their match. Even towel power couldn't stop the Isles.

"We could have won the first two games. I'm not going to say we should have, but we certainly could have," says Harry Neale. "But when the Islanders came back out to Vancouver, they made sure that our little Cinderella story was over. We couldn't compete with them, they were just too good for us. They were way better."

"The longer the series went, the cream came to the top and the Islanders started to use Bryan Trottier's line a lot more," Robson recalls. "Trottier took all the draws in Vancouver and they shut the Canucks right down."

Indeed, the Islanders were not about to let the Canucks make it a long series. They wrapped up their third of four straight Cups efficiently with 3-0 and 3-1 wins at the Pacific Coliseum.

"Every one of us had a dream to get to that level and to win the Cup but unfortunately we came up short," says Smyl, summing up the feeling in the Vancouver dressing room.

Undaunted, Canucks fans skipped work and school by the thousands to show up en masse the next day for their heroes' parade. They hadn't won the Cup, but these players had moved the Canucks from hapless also-rans into the league's elite.

that created one of the most memorable aspects of those 1982 playoffs for Vancouver. Late in the contest, Neilson chose to protest a call by referee Bob Myers by raising a white flag on the end of a hockey stick, in a form of mock surrender. A couple of players followed suit.

With Neilson's one simple gesture, "towel power" became a phenomenon that would help push Vancouver farther than it had gone before. When the Canucks returned to the Pacific Coliseum for Game 3, the stadium was transformed into a massive sea of white towels waved by roaring fans. "It sent shivers up my spine," captain Stan Smyl would later tell the Vancouver *Sun.*

Fired up by their fans and buoyed by the goaltending of Brodeur, the Canucks reeled off one- and two-goal victories to send the series back to Chicago for Game 5.

Brodeur stoned Hawks' superstar Denis Savard on a breakaway not long into that game, which was marked by numerous fights and a total of 164 minutes in penalties. The Canucks were outshot 38-28 but managed to pull away for a 6-2 win and a berth in the Stanley Cup final against the New York Islanders.

Or so they thought. Little did anybody at that parade know that the Canucks wouldn't win another playoff series for a decade.

"When you get a taste of getting to the finals, as a player especially, you always feel you can do that again," says Kevin McCarthy. "And we all felt that. We basically came back the next season to training camp and we all felt that we had the type of team that could do the same thing. But all of a sudden you're no longer that team that nobody knows about. Every game you face now, everybody's trying to show you that they could be in the finals, too. You don't have any easy games.

"We never did get to that point in that next following season where we put any kind of a string together, where we could really put ourselves in a situation of not having to worry about making the playoffs, because every game was a must-win situation from probably January on."

The rest of the 1980s were a mostly dismal time in the Canucks' history. Roger Neilson's magic touch as coach disappeared under the strain of a 78-game regular season and he was fired less than two seasons later, only to be replaced by Neale. The terrible experiment of lifting intimidating junior coach Bill LaForge onto Vancouver's NHL bench lasted just 20 games and he, too, was replaced by Neale. Tom Watt and Bob McCammon also tried their hand at coaching the Canucks, and Jack Gordon eventually took over from Neale as general manager. Nothing seemed to work.

The decade did spawn one of the best lines from any NHL coach, however: "We can't win at home, we can't win on the road," Neale once told reporters. "My failure as a coach is that I can't find anywhere else for us to play."

In spite of their run to the 1982 Stanley Cup final, the Canucks wouldn't finish a single season during the '80s with a .500 or better record. Attendance at the Pacific Coliseum dropped off severely and the team traded away some of its top young draft picks — future superstar Cam Neely and future 40-goal scorer Bill Derlago — before they had a chance to prove themselves in the NHL.

Barry Pederson, who joined the Canucks in the trade for Neely, remembers the atmosphere being "desperate" in Vancouver by the late 1980s.

"I don't think I was the only one who [felt pressure]," Pederson says. "I think if you look back at that time, not only the organization but the city and the province were very desperate to turn things around. It wasn't as if they'd had the success that they've had in the last 10 years or so ... They were pretty lean years. I think they were very, very desperate at the time for a winner, because obviously Edmonton and Calgary were in their

heyday in those years, and Winnipeg had good teams, too."

In short, the '80s were a mess in Vancouver. The only saving grace came in 1987 when owner Frank Griffiths decided to hire one of the original Canucks, Pat Quinn, to right the ship. One of Quinn's first and best moves was to draft Trevor Linden with the second overall pick from the Medicine Hat Tigers in 1988.

But even Quinn's hiring was bungled in a way of which only the 1980s Canucks were capable. Quinn was given a US$100,000 signing bonus by Vancouver while he was still coaching the Los Angeles Kings. League president John Ziegler stepped in, fined the Canucks and banished Quinn from coaching in the NHL for three seasons.

Despite all that grief, there had been that one shining springtime in 1982, when a West Coast city was captured by towel power.

"We were disappointed to lose in the final," Neale says now. "But when we looked back, we were very proud and we took the province by storm. The interest was never so high as it was during that spring."

**BEST OF THE DECADE**

In what was once referred to by the Vancouver *Sun* as the "decade of disaster," this is a no-brainer. The Canucks' unlikely dash into the 1982 Stanley Cup final remains one of the greatest happenings in British Columbia sports history.

**WORST OF THE DECADE**

Bill LaForge is hired by the Canucks as head coach to start the 1984-85 season. LaForge brings his highly successful junior coaching philosophy of PHD (pride, hustle and desire) to the pro ranks. Players don't buy into it. The experiment lasts 20 games before Harry Neale returns to the bench for a third stint. The Canucks finish dead last in the Smythe Division with 59 points.

**TOP CANUCKS OF THE DECADE**

**Goal:** Richard Brodeur
**Defence:** Harold Snepsts, Paul Reinhart
**Right wing:** Stan Smyl
**Centre:** Thomas Gradin
**Left wing:** Darcy Rota

# IVAN BOLDIREV

IVAN BOLDIREV was two years old when his family immigrated to Canada from Yugoslavia. It was in his adopted home of Sault Ste. Marie, Ontario, that he honed his hockey skills while his father forged a career in the local steel mill.

Years later, when he graduated to the NHL, Boldirev waved goodbye to Canada and began playing on a string of mostly struggling American teams. After 11 years in the league with Boston, California, Chicago and Atlanta, he was pleased to be dealt to the Vancouver Canucks in February 1980.

"That was the first Canadian city that I played in other than junior hockey," Boldirev says. "And the thing that I really liked about Vancouver and playing in a Canadian city was that the main topic was always hockey, whether it was summer, winter, fall — whatever. It was always on the news, it was always in the paper. When I grew up in Sault Ste. Marie, hockey was always number 1, but when you move to the States that's not the case. Even in Chicago, we'd be behind football, basketball, baseball and sometimes a few other sports. It wasn't the main sport. So it was kind of nice to experience that in Vancouver."

Boldirev's puck-handling and playmaking skills helped provide the kind of strength and depth at the centre position that Vancouver had never enjoyed before, and it was a factor in the Canucks advancing to the Stanley Cup final in 1982. The six-foot, 190-pound Boldirev posted 33 goals and 73 points for those 1981-82 Canucks, then added 11 points, including eight goals, during their playoff run.

"That was one of the biggest highlights of all the years I played," Boldirev says, reviewing his 16-year playing career. "It was quite a trip, really. Playing all these years in the NHL and only going once to the finals is kind of sad. But you know, at least I had a chance to experience that and it was unreal."

After two major junior seasons with the Oshawa Generals, he had been selected 11th overall by Boston in the 1969 NHL entry draft. But he couldn't crack the Bruins lineup on a regular basis and was dealt to the dismal California Golden Seals in 1971.

Less than three years later he was traded to the Chicago Black Hawks, where he had his finest statistical years, with five straight seasons of 60 or more points.

In 1979 he was surprised to be traded to Atlanta along with teammates Darcy Rota and Phil Russell in a deal that saw Tom Lysiak join the Black Hawks. Less than a year later, Boldirev and Rota were again on the move, packaged together to the Canucks in exchange for Don Lever and Brad Smith.

"We were shocked, because we had just been traded from Chicago," Boldirev recalls. "But things weren't going that well in Atlanta. I kind of had an idea that they were going to make some changes. I didn't know it was going to be us ... It was a little bit of a relief leaving Atlanta. I didn't like the area. I mean, it didn't feel like a hockey town."

In an unusual twist, he and Rota played together, sometimes on the same line, in Chicago, Atlanta and Vancouver. "You'd almost think we were a package deal, huh?" Boldirev jokes. "We were friends off the ice, so I guess that has a lot to do with [chemistry] on the ice, too."

Boldirev was one of the Canuck casualties in 1982-83 as general manager Harry Neale attempted to recapture the magic that had led Vancouver into the final the previous spring. The veteran centre was traded in January 1983 to Detroit for Mark Kirton. Boldirev believes the trade came as a result of an interview he gave to a reporter after being benched by Neale in Buffalo during the 1981 playoffs.

"I sat down with a reporter and shot my mouth off," he says. "And if I look back on that now, I would change that. I would have kept my mouth shut. You know, I would have preferred to probably finish out my career in Vancouver."

He played two more full seasons with the Red Wings and recorded a career-high 83 points in 1983-84. He slipped to 49 points the next season, after which he retired. Boldirev now lives in Val Paraiso, Indiana, where he operates a residential fire safety business.

*For Ivan Boldirev, it was exciting to be traded from Atlanta to a Canadian city that lived and breathed hockey.* (Robert Shaver/HHOF)

# RICHARD BRODEUR

DURING HIS EIGHT SEASONS with what was predominantly a weak Canucks team, goaltender Richard Brodeur produced some rather ordinary statistics. He lost more games than he won over 377 starts and posted a winning regular-season record for Vancouver just once. But for one memorable spring in a Canucks uniform, the acrobatic Brodeur was nothing short of brilliant. For one spring, he was royalty.

Perhaps more than any other player in the lineup, Brodeur was responsible for the 1982 Canucks making it to the Stanley Cup final. The diminutive goaltender from Longueuil, Quebec, enjoyed easily his finest stretch as an NHLer that spring, earning the nickname "King Richard" as he backstopped Vancouver through three straight playoff rounds.

During that run he flipped and flopped his way into the heads of opponents and teammates alike. Opposing shooters began thinking they couldn't beat the King and his lightning-quick reflexes, while teammates felt they couldn't lose with him. The result was triumph over Calgary, Los Angeles and Chicago in series that were marked by the bouncing Brodeur's flashy saves as much as anything else.

Brodeur made short work of the Calgary Flames in the opening round, allowing just five goals in a three-game sweep for a 1.55 goals-against average.

"In one of those games, we outshot them significantly," recalls Paul Reinhart, at that time an offensive defenceman for the Flames. "I seem to remember, though, it was a case of it just didn't matter. Brodeur could have turned backwards and the puck would have hit him in the back of the leg somehow. He was that good at that time."

In the Campbell Conference final against Chicago, Brodeur turned in a spectacular 46-save performance as the Canucks beat the Black Hawks and ace netminder Tony Esposito 2-1 in double overtime. Brodeur has described that game as his personal highlight of the '82 playoffs.

"It was one of those cases where a guy gets on a roll," former

Canucks broadcaster Jim Robson says of Brodeur's performance that postseason. "He flopped around. He was not a big man. He was quick for a guy who was a roly-poly goalie. He didn't seem to come out at shooters that much, he seemed to be more back in the net. But he was very effective."

The 5'7" Brodeur was a standout for the Cornwall Royals of the Quebec Major Junior Hockey League, backstopping his team to the Memorial Cup title in his final year of junior. He was drafted 97th overall by the New York Islanders in 1972, but opted instead to remain in his home province and play for the World Hockey Association's Quebec Nordiques for seven seasons. Brodeur was a star for a strong Nordiques team, posting a winning record in all but one season and winning 44 regular-season games in 1975-76 before leading the Nordiques to the Avco Cup league championship during the 1977 playoffs.

When hockey's major professional leagues essentially merged in 1979, Brodeur's NHL rights were shipped to the Islanders. But he couldn't carve out a place, because the Isles already had Billy Smith and Chico Resch in place and were on their way to becoming a Stanley Cup dynasty. Brodeur went to the minors and didn't get a chance for regular NHL action until the Canucks acquired him in a swap of fifth-round draft picks in time for the 1980-81 season.

In Vancouver he found regular duty, playing more than 50 games in six of his eight seasons there and winning the team's most-valuable-player award three times. His best NHL regular season came in 1981-82; he sported a 20-18-12 record, becoming only the second Canucks goalie after Gary Smith to win 20 games. Brodeur was even better in the playoffs that year, going 11-6 with a goals-against average of 2.70.

He remained with Vancouver until the 1987-88 season, when he was traded to the Hartford Whalers for goaltender Steve Weeks. He played briefly with Hartford that season and the next winter with the Binghamton Whalers of the American Hockey League, then retired.

*Richard Brodeur played seven seasons for his home-province Quebec Nordiques of the WHA before eventually joining the Canucks.* (BCSHF)

*Wayne Gretzky was "The Great One" but Richard Brodeur, shown here trying to disrupt Gretzky's stickhandling, was the "King" in 1982.* (Paul Bereswill/HHOF)

Brodeur was the first Canuck goalie to record 100 wins.

"He was very good for a short stretch," Robson says. "He became somewhat undependable later on. But while he was on a roll there he was very good, and in the playoffs in '82 he was sensational. You don't go far in the playoffs without goaltending and he really was great."

Current Washington Capitals head coach Glen Hanlon, who was Brodeur's backup for some of his time in Vancouver, remembers the King as a player who was able to live with his own performances even when the team wasn't playing well.

"He was the type of goaltender who could really separate the

game from just going out and enjoying his life," Hanlon says. "I could honestly feel like with Richard, you could lose 5-1 and he could feel good about his game, thinking that it should have been 8-1 or 9-1, whereas a lot of goalies would say, 'Well, I let in five goals and I cost the team the game.'

"Now, don't misunderstand me, he wasn't putting the blame on other people. But that [ability to not carry everything on one's shoulders] is an attitude that I try to instill in all the goaltenders that I come across now. Richard had a great ability to do that ... The run that he got on that year and then continued on in the playoffs was only matched, I think, by Kirk McLean in '94."

*Richard Brodeur provided the 1981-82 Canucks with one thing every playoff team needs — great, clutch goaltending.* (Robert Shaver/HHOF)

# GARTH BUTCHER

A LOOK AT GARTH BUTCHER's offensive numbers doesn't begin to convey the intangible value of the rugged defenceman to the Canucks of the 1980s. A much more revealing figure is the 1,668 penalty minutes he racked up while playing 610 games for Vancouver, second only in franchise history to Gino Odjick. Butcher wasn't overly big, at six feet and 204 pounds, and he wasn't an enforcer like Odjick, but he did play tough in every outing.

"I used to take pride in being a guy who was hard to play against, who there was no easy path around," Butcher says now. "If you do that game in and game out — versus, say, 30 out of 80 games — you're going to rack up the penalty minutes."

He certainly did that during his 14-year NHL career. A standout junior defenceman who put up impressive offensive numbers with his hometown Regina Pats of the Western Hockey League, Butcher adapted his game to the NHL and became a heart-and-soul player on the Vancouver blue line.

He showed leadership qualities early, captaining a tough Pats lineup as an 18-year-old. He was the 10th overall pick of the Canucks in 1981, but he didn't even attend the draft in Montreal. He was informed of his selection by Canucks general manager Jake Milford in an early-morning phone call, then headed out to take a biology test at Regina's Thom Collegiate.

Less than a year later, 19-year-old Butcher joined the Canucks for the tail end of their dramatic run to the Stanley Cup final, dressing for five games and playing in the last game of their championship series sweep at the hands of the New York Islanders. That winter he had been an integral part of Canada's first gold medal team at the world junior championships.

"It was really exciting to be a young guy in the Stanley Cup finals and all that," he recalls. "But for me personally, it wasn't like I was a big part of the team. I was just kind of coming up as a kid. And at that time, coming from some pretty successful teams in Regina, you thought that 'we'll be there [in the Stanley Cup finals] again, you know, it's not a big deal.'"

But he would soon find out that success at the NHL level didn't come so easily. In the next season he played 55 games with the Canucks but also spent time with the Kamloops Blazers, who by then owned his junior rights. He began the 1983-84 season with Vancouver but was sent down to the farm in Fredericton 28 games into the schedule. Back-to-back ankle injuries with the American Hockey League affiliate basically spelled the end of that campaign.

By the time 1985 rolled around, Butcher found himself still without a solid spot in the Canucks lineup. Coach Tom Watt told him he was headed to the minors again, but Butcher stood his ground. His wife was pregnant with their first child and Butcher felt he had earned a spot as a regular. In a meeting with Watt, he told the coach he should play or be traded.

"It was the old 'if you play better, you get more ice time,'" Butcher recalls of the conversation. "And, of course, the player says: 'If you give me more ice time, I'll play better.'"

Nevertheless, the meeting worked. Butcher describes it as the turning point of his career: "It really kind of took off from there." Watt began to play him in important situations and he became a key part of the Canucks defensive corps.

Though Butcher was never a flashy offensive player, he did go over the 20-point mark for the Canucks for each of the next four seasons. For five years in a row he amassed more than 200 penalty minutes, including a high of 285 in 1987-88.

Offensive defenceman Paul Reinhart says he loved being paired with Butcher after he joined the Canucks from the Calgary Flames in 1988.

"I used to joke with him. I said: 'Butch, in our end you've got both corners and the front of the net and I'll be open up top,'" Reinhart laughs. "Butchy probably in some respects exemplified what the Vancouver organization was like. They were scrappers, down and honest hard-working guys. Butchy was a small guy and he played like a really big guy."

Butcher played with the Canucks until March 5, 1991, when he

Defenceman Garth Butcher was a heart-and-soul member of the Canucks organization for 10 years. (Robert Shaver/HHOF)

was a key piece in one of the most crucial trades in Vancouver history. The franchise landed Geoff Courtnall, Cliff Ronning, Sergio Momesso and Robert Dirk from the St. Louis Blues in exchange for Butcher and Dan Quinn. The deal would be an important building block in Vancouver's 1994 charge to the Stanley Cup final.

"I kind of looked at it as a time to move on, although I considered Vancouver home and my wife is from the Vancouver area and we'd always planned on coming back to the area anyway," says Butcher.

He played three more seasons with the Blues, including a stint as team captain in 1991-92, before wrapping up his NHL career with parts of single seasons in Quebec City and Toronto.

Butcher and his family now live in Bellingham, Washington,

where he runs the city's minor-hockey programs. Although he enjoyed his time in St. Louis, he still considers himself a Canuck.

"Certainly now, being in this area and being involved with the Canucks alumni and seeing those guys, I certainly consider myself an old Canuck — well, not so old, I guess."

His competitiveness made Butcher a consistent force in the NHL for 14 seasons.

"You know, I wouldn't describe myself as a great athlete," he says. "But I think the willingness to compete, game in and game out, and sort of taking pride in showing up every night to work even when things didn't always go quite the way you wanted it to ... You could still be a special player, even if it wasn't necessarily pretty to watch — it was consistent."

# CURT FRASER

As JONI MITCHELL observes: "Don't it always seem to go that you don't know what you've got till it's gone."

That line might have been applied to left-winger Curt Fraser's departure from the Vancouver Canucks. Although they received super-sniper Tony Tanti in return from the Chicago Black Hawks in a January 1983 deal, the Canucks gave up a ton of character in what was one of the most important trades in the franchise's history.

Fraser was that rare combination, a NHLer who could score with his hands and with his fists. He was a quiet tough guy who was talented enough to play on the top line and make the most of his offensive chances.

"Curt had so much, how would I say ... hockey sense," says Thomas Gradin, a Canucks linemate of Fraser's along with Stan Smyl for several years.

"You would think Curt would be just a boomer, like a slapshotter and a hitter. But he had a lot of hockey sense. He could make those small passes. He was maybe more to my kind of play than to Stan's kind of play. And still he was the guy who could sort of take care of me because he was always on [the ice] when something heated up."

Fraser joined Gradin and Smyl to form the Canucks' rookie line in training camp of 1978. The trio clicked immediately, with Fraser and Smyl providing the grinding toughness that offset the subtler stylings of Gradin.

At six feet and 200 pounds, Fraser had proved during four standout seasons with the Victoria Cougars of the Western Hockey League that he could both score and take care of business physically. In his final year of junior the Cougar captain posted 48 goals, 92 points and a whopping 256 minutes in penalties. That winter he also helped Canada to a bronze medal at the world junior championships. His junior exploits prompted the Canucks to select him 22nd overall in the 1978 draft, ahead of Smyl, who went 40th.

Toughness was a big factor in the Canucks' decision to select him so high, but Fraser wasn't boastful or arrogant about that part

of the job. He didn't wave his arms over his head in celebration or shamelessly play to the crowd like many of today's tough guys. He fought when he had to and earned respect around the league as a premier power forward. Off the ice, "Fras" was an accomplished guitarist who made a habit of attending the theatre whenever the team was in New York.

"He was a quiet guy ... but really well-liked by his teammates," says former Canucks broadcaster Jim Robson. "He was admired because he was tough. He didn't look for it, but when he knew he had to do it, boy, he could fight. And he was a pretty good goal scorer."

One of Fraser's most memorable showdowns, at least for the effect it had on his team, came in the first round of the 1982 playoffs against Calgary. Fraser took on the much larger Willi Plett three times in the opening game of that series.

"Plett was bigger than Fraser, but Fraser had big hands," Robson recalls. "Fraser won the first fight and the other two were draws, but it sort of set the tone" for the series.

That season and the playoffs would be Fraser's finest moments as a Canuck. He compiled 28 goals and 39 assists, along with 175 penalty minutes in the regular season. During the team's run to the Stanley Cup final he collected 10 points and 98 penalty minutes in 17 games.

In spite of his performance, he was traded 36 games into the 1982-83 season as Canucks management tried to make their lineup more talented and gave away some grit and heart in the process. The hard-nosed Fraser went to Chicago and produced three straight seasons of 25 or more goals and 50-plus points as the Hawks twice reached the Campbell Conference championship. He was traded to Minnesota in 1987 and played parts of three seasons with the North Stars organization before retiring due to a shoulder injury.

The son of a minor-pro hockey player, Fraser was born in Cincinnati. That enabled him to play for the US in the 1987 Canada Cup, though he had been raised in North Vancouver.

*Forward Curt Fraser was that rare combination — a player who could score with both his stick and his fists.* (Robert Shaver/HHOF)

Fraser was diagnosed with diabetes in 1983 and became involved with the American Diabetes Association and the International Diabetes Athletic Association in the fight against the disease.

When he retired, he jumped immediately into coaching as an assistant and then a head coach of the International Hockey League's Milwaukee Admirals. He was head coach of the IHL's successful Orlando Solar Bears for four seasons and led the team to two appearances in the Turner Cup league final before becoming the first head coach of the NHL's expansion Atlanta Thrashers in 1999.

Fraser was fired by the struggling Thrashers 33 games into his fourth season with the club. He served as an assistant coach for the New York Islanders in 2003-04 before resigning after the season. During the 2005-06 season, he was an assistant coach with the St. Louis Blues.

# THOMAS GRADIN

MENTION THOMAS GRADIN to most hockey fans and the image conjured up is that of a finesse player, a smooth-skating, offensively gifted Swede who produced at nearly a point-per-game clip for the Canucks. But those who watched closely as he piled up the points for Vancouver during the 1980s saw another key ingredient: Thomas Gradin was also tough in his own way, they say.

"Toughness comes in a lot of different packages," says former Canucks coach and general manager Harry Neale. "We all know that a tough guy is one who fights or who hits, like Stan Smyl and Curt Fraser did. But Thomas Gradin's best games were against the toughest teams. He was able to do his thing in arenas and against teams where it wasn't easy. In that regard, I think Thomas was one of the toughest players I ever coached. But not 'tough' as we think of it in normal terms. He was a smart player and a hard worker and was very competitive in his own way and I remember lots of games against Philadelphia and Boston — the two most physical teams in the league at that time — Gradin was often our best player against those teams."

Gradin was hardly an imposing figure on the NHL ice surface, at 5'11" and 176 pounds. But Canucks broadcaster Jim Robson remembers that during one game in Philadelphia when the slick Swede was speared by Frank Bathe, the Flyers' hard-rock defenceman, "Gradin went down in front of the net and nobody [on the Canucks] did anything about it. But the next shift, Gradin came back up ice and ran Bathe into the Flyers' bench. That was in Philadelphia, with the Flyers well up in the game ... Gradin was a complete player and I thought he was more courageous than people gave him credit for."

Gradin chuckles when asked whether he had to prove himself physically in the NHL after joining the Canucks from Sweden as a 22-year-old in 1978. He remembers being warned by his teammates that he would be a marked man after scoring twice and adding an assist in his first-ever NHL game against the Colorado Rockies in the Pacific Coliseum. Sure enough, in a subsequent game against Chicago he was nailed by veteran Black Hawk forward John Marks.

"I still feel it in my body," Gradin says of that hit. "I knew he was coming, because everybody said: 'You watch out tonight because you have been scoring.' He was coming from the far blue line and he was just looking for me ... I didn't even know what to do. Anyway, we succeeded by not having any blood spilled."

While Gradin was tough enough to take the pounding of the rough-and-tumble NHL, he was best known for his offensive flair. Once described by the Vancouver *Province* as "elegance on ice," he collected 593 points in 677 NHL games and produced back-to-back 86-point seasons for the Canucks in 1981-82 and 1982-83.

He was practically stolen by the Canucks from Chicago, which had selected him 45th overall in the 1976 draft but had been unable to sign him. Gradin ended up in Vancouver primarily because his agent also represented Canuck defenceman Lars Lindgren, a fellow Swede. Vancouver obtained Gradin's rights for a second-round 1980 draft pick that turned out to be Steve Ludzik. Gradin chose Vancouver rather than the Swede-laden Winnipeg Jets of the rival World Hockey Association.

He was excited about playing in the NHL, of which he had heard a lot but not seen much. At that time, for young Swedish players the only glimpses of the league came at the end of hockey schools, when they would watch Super 8 movie clips of the previous year's Stanley Cup playoffs.

"That was my only thing that I knew about the National Hockey League," Gradin says. "I had heard about Phil Esposito, Bobby Orr, yes. But we hadn't really seen any games on TV."

He had even less knowledge of Vancouver. "I remember looking at the map to see where Vancouver was. We weren't really sure. 'Yeah, it's on the west coast, but where is it?' When we touched down in Vancouver, we didn't really know anything about it."

It didn't take long for him to feel right at home. He was an instant hit after Neale threw him on a line with fellow rookies Smyl and Fraser during just the second session of training camp in September 1978.

"We were put out together against Chris Oddleifson, Don Lever and Dennis Ververgaert," Gradin recalls of that first practice session.

*Swedish centre Thomas Gradin remains one of the finest players to ever wear a Canucks uniform.* (Robert Shaver/HHOF)

*Thomas Gradin led the 1981–82 Canucks with 37 goals and 86 points.*
(O-Pee-Chee/HHOF)

In the NHL it was all hockey, all the time. "Everything was perfect from the start," he says. "It was hockey from six o'clock in the morning to 12 o'clock at night."

He posted 20 goals and 31 assists in his rookie season, 1978-79, and upped those totals to 30 goals and 75 points in his sophomore season. From 1981-82 to 1983-84 he averaged more than 80 points per season, but his best campaign was in 1981-82 and the playoffs that followed.

During the 1981-82 season, Gradin scored a career-high 37 goals and finished with 86 points. He was also a career-best plus-15 on the year. In the postseason he was one of the best players in the underdog Canucks' journey to the Stanley Cup final, scoring nine goals and 19 points in 17 playoff games.

As with most of his teammates from that year, the 1982 appearance in the Cup final is the highlight of his NHL career.

"The thing I think is the most important is there was a lot of leadership on that team that year," he says. "A lot of guys from that team are still in the game. I think that's a very important thing when you want to have successful teams."

Gradin would play four more seasons for Vancouver and become one of the team's best-ever players. Robson recalls him as a "front-of-the-bus guy, who was quiet, read a lot and didn't say much." But his game spoke for itself.

"For the longest time, I said he was the best player the Canucks ever had," Robson adds. "And then Pavel [Bure] came along and I think Pavel was the best player the Canucks ever had.

"But if you had to pick a centre in the history of the Canucks, you'd probably still go to Thomas Gradin ... a wonderful, effortless skater with great hands. He didn't shoot enough, that was the knock. He'd always try and deke a goalie and slide it between his skates. For every five breakaways he'd score a goal, maybe. He didn't shoot the puck much. He tried to set somebody else up, and also he didn't seem to capitalize on as many scoring chances as he had. But he certainly had terrific skills and he was competitive, too ... He was an excellent player, one of the best the Canucks have ever had."

But after Gradin's point output dipped to 41 in 1985-86, the Canucks opted not to re-sign him as a free agent. He joined the

"We did okay. I think we scored four or five goals on them and after that day we played together for, I think, almost six and a half years."

The combination did indeed work well, with the silky-smooth Gradin using his subtle passing skills to feed off the more robust styles of Smyl and Fraser. With Fraser on the ice, Gradin usually didn't have to look far for physical backup.

"Thomas pushed me to be a better player and I pushed him to be a better player and we approached it that way every day," says Smyl. "There wasn't one day that we were not pushing each other, whether it be on or off the ice."

Gradin remembers that the biggest difference between the NHL and Swedish hockey was the level of professionalism. Before joining the Canucks, he had been studying physical education at GIH University while playing for club AIK Solna. At times, he wasn't allowed to join the Swedish national team because its games conflicted with his exams.

*Following his playing days, Thomas Gradin has served as a European scout for the Canucks.* (Robert Shaver/HHOF)

Boston Bruins, where he was able to play his final season on a line with Rick Middleton and Cam Neely.

"At the time it was disappointing," Gradin says of leaving Vancouver. "I thought for sure I was going to get the match [free-agent] offer to stay. I didn't, and that time we [he and wife Lillibeth] made the decision that we will move on and from there on move back to Sweden. We felt that the career was sort of going downhill, not going uphill. We were happy to get the chance to play in Boston."

Gradin had 43 points in 64 games with the Bruins before deciding

to return to Sweden to finish his career at home. He and Lillibeth had two of their three children by then and schooling was an issue. Gradin played three more seasons with AIK Solna, getting a chance to skate with his brother, before retiring in 1990.

Thomas Gradin eventually returned to the Canucks, becoming a scout for the organization in 1993. Today he lives in a suburb of Stockholm and scouts Europe for the Vancouver franchise.

"Every time I'm touching down in Vancouver," he says, "it feels like coming home."

# THE GRIFFITHS FAMILY

VETERAN VANCOUVER sports humorist and author Jim Taylor once relayed the following anecdote about Frank Griffiths, the quiet and well-respected owner of the Canucks from 1974 until his death nearly 20 years later.

It seems Frank was leaving a game at the Pacific Coliseum on a typically miserable, rainy Vancouver winter night. He happened to bump into a fan also heading home.

"I paid good money to watch that [expletive] team," the fan said, recognizing Griffiths and letting him have it.

"Sir," Griffiths replied, "I paid $9 million."

Frank Armathwaite Griffiths Sr. did indeed pay Can$9 million for the city's NHL team, making the decision while on a trip out of Canada in 1974.

His company, Western International Communications, bought the Canucks from American owner Medicor and its principal, Tom Scallen, who had been jailed for theft and making false statements in a prospectus. The purchase quite likely saved the Canucks from being moved elsewhere.

Griffiths was a Vancouver-born chartered accountant who had expanded into the broadcasting industry by buying his first radio station, flagship CKNW, in 1956. By 1983 his company also owned popular Burnaby television station BCTV and other TV and radio stations and satellite communications companies across the country.

Griffiths was approached about buying the Canucks by then team president Coley Hall, who brokered the deal between Scallen and the new owner. But after agreeing over the phone to buy the franchise, Griffiths returned from his trip and announced to Hall that he'd changed his mind. However, according to the Vancouver *Sun* Emily Griffiths ultimately persuaded her husband to go ahead with the deal: she had once dated a hockey player and liked the game.

Frank Griffiths, by all accounts a hard-working man of principle, stayed out of the spotlight during his two decades with the team, allowing his general managers and coaches to run the show. He was most often described by players and management as "classy,"

and the entire team was invited to his family's West Vancouver home for a Christmas party each year.

More important to Vancouver hockey fans, Griffiths had stepped in when the team desperately needed local ownership. Then, with the Canucks floundering on the ice and in the stands in the mid-1980s, he hung on to the club despite being strongly advised to sell it.

"I don't see a lot of Mr. Griffiths," Canucks general manager Harry Neale once remarked to the *Sun*. "But he's like E. F. Hutton: when he speaks, you listen."

Griffiths died at age 77 on April 7, 1994, after a lengthy illness and just as the Canucks were about to embark on only their second trip to the Stanley Cup final. The team honoured him during those playoffs by wearing a jersey patch that read "2 pts, F. G." It was a tribute to Frank's favourite hockey saying: "Let's just get the two points."

Though he remained out of the limelight, Griffiths had become a key behind-the-scenes player in the NHL. He served as league vice-chair from 1979 to 1987 and was a member of its audit and broadcasting committees; he helped a number of franchises become more financially efficient. In 1993 he was inducted into the Hockey Hall of Fame, and on the day he died he became a member of the Canadian Business Hall of Fame.

"I am sure I speak for all the members of the NHL family when I say Frank Griffiths will be sorely missed," NHL commissioner Gary Bettman said that day.

Frank and Emily Griffiths had four children, including sons Frank Jr. and Arthur. In May 1981, at age 24 and fresh out of college, Arthur had become an executive assistant to his father at Northwest Sports Enterprises, the parent company of the Canucks.

The younger Griffiths almost immediately assumed a much more public persona than his father, initially drawing scorn from the media for his habit of sometimes skating with the Canucks in practice. In those days he was generally characterized as a silver-spoon-fed kid looking to prove himself in the high-profile hockey world.

Facing Page: *Frank Griffiths (left) and son Arthur each contributed greatly to keeping the NHL in Vancouver.* (Vancouver Canucks)

Right: *Trevor Linden shares a celebratory moment with Emily and Arthur Griffiths after the Canucks win the Western final in 1994.* (Paul Bereswill/HHOF)

By the mid-1990s, however, Arthur had matured and was able to laugh at the mistakes he had made as a young executive. He was also spearheading an effort by Northwest Sports Enterprises to build a downtown arena after a satisfactory new lease arrangement for the Pacific Coliseum couldn't be reached with the Pacific National Exhibition board.

Arthur also simultaneously pursued the Grizzlies, Vancouver's one-time National Basketball Association franchise, to serve as a co-tenant in the proposed downtown General Motors Place. But the NBA franchise fee was a hefty US$125 million and the arena project eventually ballooned from Can$100 million to $163 million. Griffiths was forced to bring in cellular billionaires John and Bruce McCaw of Seattle, family friends, as partners.

Frank Griffiths "didn't want anything to do with the NBA team or the ownership of it," Arthur Griffiths told the *Sun* in a 2001 interview. "He didn't think as a family or as a company that we could afford it, which is why we restructured everything. He wasn't a fan of the game. He saw the [sense in having] the second tenant, but he didn't like the economics. He didn't come right out and say, 'You're crazy.' But in his own way, he did say it."

Initially the Griffiths family held 70 percent and the McCaws 30 percent of the Grizzlies, the Canucks and GM Place. But heavy expenses related to the NBA franchise and the 1994-95 NHL lockout resulted in John McCaw taking over in March 1995 as majority owner of Northwest Entertainment Group, the owner of the three entities. By November 1996, Arthur Griffiths had sold all of his shares in the operation to John McCaw and had become an employee.

His family having been "in the business for 22 years, this is a very difficult day for me," Arthur told reporters as the announcement was made before a Grizzlies game tipped off. "But I'm glad that I have been a part of it and been involved and didn't just stand on the sidelines."

Not long afterward he left the company, ending his family's investment in major Vancouver professional sports. But Arthur did not fade from the scene; for more than three years he worked as voluntary chair of Vancouver's effort to land the Canadian

rights to the 2010 Winter Olympics bid, helping the province of British Columbia to eventually land the Games. He was also briefly a minority owner in Vancouver's National Lacrosse League Ravens franchise and, for a time, a Lower Mainland sports radio personality.

The family may no longer own the Canucks, and the Grizzlies franchise is dead in Vancouver, but the Griffiths legacy lingers in the still sparkling General Motors Place, where the street address is 800 Griffiths Way.

"I have a great deal of respect for what the Griffiths did," former Canucks general manager and coach Pat Quinn once told the *Sun*. "There's no question that at least two times in the team's history Vancouver was in danger of losing the hockey club and both times the Griffiths were the people who stepped forward to save it."

# DOUG HALWARD

THE 1981-82 Vancouver Canucks reached the Stanley Cup final on a patchwork defence. Due to injuries, key regulars Kevin McCarthy and Rick Lanz didn't play a single playoff game, leaving others to step up on the Vancouver blue line.

Nobody stepped up more than Doug Halward, who was a tower of strength during that playoff run and scored the series-clinching goal against the Chicago Black Hawks that put Vancouver into its first Stanley Cup final.

Obtained from the Los Angeles Kings less than two years earlier, Halward was recovering from injuries during the preceding regular season and spent 22 games with the Canucks' Dallas farm team in 1981-82. But in 37 regular-season games with the big team, Halward contributed 17 points. And in those memorable playoffs he played 15 games, scoring twice and adding four assists.

"It was definitely one of the highlights of my career, that's for sure," Halward says now of that postseason. "I remember that we didn't have the most talented hockey team, but we had everybody on the same page and there weren't many teams that could outwork us. There was a real camaraderie on our team, and we stuck up for each other, and it was all-for-one."

Halward himself displayed that spirit when he went into the stands during a late-season game in Quebec City to help coach Harry Neale, who was trying to keep a fan from harming Tiger Williams. Both Neale and Halward were suspended by the NHL for their part in the melee, but most people associated with the Canucks point to that incident as a galvanizing force in Vancouver's playoff run.

Because of Neale's suspension, assistant coach Roger Neilson took over behind the bench. Halward was familiar with Neilson's educational, systematic approach to hockey because he had played for Neilson as a junior with the Peterborough Petes.

"We just all got going on the same wavelength," Halward says. "And what I remember is Roger had us really prepared, and we worked our butts off and executed his game plan, almost to perfection."

It was Neilson who had earlier helped Halward develop into a 14th-overall draft pick of the Boston Bruins in 1975. The 6'1", 200-pound defenceman posted 63 points in his final junior season with the Petes but had to bide his time in the Boston organization, spending much of his first three professional seasons with the American Hockey League's Rochester Americans.

Early in his pro career, while he was killing penalties with Wayne Cashman, the veteran Bruin grinned at Halward after a shift: "You're out there on the ice, skating around like you're a hawk, swooping in on the puck all the time." The nickname "Hawk" stuck.

The Bruins traded Halward to the Los Angeles Kings for future considerations in 1978 and he also did time with that organization's farm club, the Springfield Indians. But in the 1979-80 season he broke in as an NHL regular with Los Angeles, turning in a 56-point season. Nevertheless, the Kings dealt him to Vancouver in the 1980-81 season, setting the stage for his important role in the Canucks' push to the finals the following year.

Halward would spend six seasons with the Canucks, playing a lot with defensive mate Garth Butcher. "Dougie was the rushing defenceman type of guy," Butcher says, "so I kind of took on the role as the guy who was supposed to stay back."

Halward's stint with the Canucks ended 10 games into the 1986-87 season when he was traded to the Detroit Red Wings. The deal followed closely on the heels of what the team contended was a case of "intentionally missed curfew" by Halward on a road trip. Halward says that wasn't the case.

At the time, he was hurt and travelling with the team. "They blew that [incident] way out of proportion," he says. "I didn't intentionally miss curfew. I was hurt. I couldn't play." Still, the trade was welcome, he says now. "You know, we had some tough years here and it was time for me to get a fresh start with somebody else."

He played parts of three seasons with the Red Wings before finishing his NHL career with a 24-game stint for the Edmonton Oilers in 1988-89. He settled in the Vancouver area and heads a successful recycling company with branches in Vancouver, Winnipeg and Florida.

# GLEN HANLON

IT WAS WELL AFTER midnight in a nearly abandoned Pittsburgh airport and the weary members of the Vancouver Canucks were waiting for their luggage. The team was in the midst of one of its typically stupefying late 1970s road trips. Coming off a loss that night, players were half asleep and grumpy as they scanned the baggage carousel.

"All of a sudden, this little rubber screen sort of opens up and out comes Glen Hanlon, lying, pretending he's asleep, on the track for the baggage," laughs former Canucks broadcaster Jim Robson. "That really broke the ice. Everybody just broke up."

Hanlon, the red-haired goaltender known as "Carrot" by fellow players, was like that. He was a team guy, well-liked by his peers and absolutely devoted to the Vancouver franchise.

All of which made it extremely difficult for him when he was traded by the Canucks at the deadline in 1982, heading to St. Louis in the very spring the Canucks were headed for some playoff magic.

Struggling at the time to live up to the tag as Vancouver's "franchise" goalie, Hanlon went to the Blues in exchange for Jim Nill, Tony Currie and Rick Heinz in what turned out to be a poor trade for the Canucks. Currie was released less than a year later and Heinz would serve as backup to Richard Brodeur in the Canucks' playoff run before being shipped back to the Blues in what was basically a prearranged short-term lease.

"I always say that I'm directly responsible for the team going to the finals. They traded me," Hanlon says now. "It was unfortunate and it was one of the most difficult things — juggling [my] happiness for the players going to the finals but coming home and watching it and not being part of it. Selfishly, I was just sort of wishing that I was part of it."

Simply being traded by the Canucks was the most difficult thing for Hanlon, who had played for the team since being drafted 40th overall from the Western Hockey League's Brandon Wheat Kings in his hometown in 1977. His father and brother had worked for the same companies all their lives and he shared that sort of loyalty. Being dealt away by the only NHL team he had known took him by surprise and he became choked up and cried as he tried to address reporters following the news.

"Boy, the first of anything in your life is something that you don't forget," he says today. "I was devastated. You know, at the time, there was no talk about me moving … When you're young and you've never had it happen to you, you don't really ever think about those things, you know. It was a tough day."

Hanlon would go on to nine more NHL seasons with the Blues, New York Rangers and Detroit Red Wings. But after ending his playing career he returned to the Canucks, hired by Pat Quinn as a goaltending coach in 1991, and he moved up to regular assistant duties four years later.

"It was a natural fit and I think they knew my love for the organization," Hanlon says. "As it's turned out, it was the best move of my career to get started in coaching there."

After four seasons as a Canucks assistant, he left Vancouver for Maine to become head coach of the Portland Pirates of the American Hockey League. Three seasons later, he became an assistant coach with the NHL's Washington Capitals. On December 10, 2003, he was named head coach of the Capitals.

An acrobatic goalie who liked to challenge shooters, Hanlon says that as a player he never aspired to become a coach.

"No, my very first goal [upon retiring] was to not have to work in the summer, so I wanted to stay in the game," he laughs. "And then, within about a week or two, I realized that coaching was where, perhaps, likely more of my calling was than playing goal. Then we [he and his wife] said our goal is going to [be to] become a head coach.

"I knew that hockey is my love and, outside of personal relationships, it's about the only thing I really do love in this world. It's something I could do every day, all day."

Robson remembers Hanlon as a player who had that excitement for the game from Day 1. He was certainly excited as a

*Glen Hanlon says he never aspired to be a coach while playing goal in the NHL. But in 2003 he became the head coach of the Washington Capitals.* (Robert Shaver/HHOF)

youngster being drafted by Vancouver, although he didn't attend the draft in person. Instead, he waited in the offices of the Brandon *Sun* newspaper for the teletype results to come in.

Going to Vancouver was perfect for him. He had spent some time in New Westminster as an 18-year-old after being picked up to play for the New West Bruins in the Memorial Cup championship and he loved the beauty of the west coast.

"I was so excited about getting drafted, period, I guess I could have gone anywhere," he says. "But I really wanted to play for a Canadian city that I knew a lot about. Another priority was to stay in the western part of the country because of family and friends. Being drafted by the Canucks was a wonderful thing. It was a natural, and consequently I made my home there. You know, I've never moved; we still spend our summers on the west coast in Point Roberts, Washington."

He cherishes the memories of being part of a young, up-and-coming Canucks team in the late 1970s and early '80s along with Stan Smyl, Curt Fraser and Thomas Gradin. The four youngsters all arrived at roughly the same time as the team gradually improved. "We sort of grew up there," Hanlon says.

One of his biggest moments as a Canuck came when he recorded the first Pacific Coliseum victory over the Montreal Canadiens in franchise history, a 5-2 decision. "As silly as it sounds, just beating Montreal [was a big thing]," he says. "Most times, organizations are talking about winning Stanley Cups, but you have to go through some growing pains. The majority of the people in the rink that night were Montreal fans. When we finally beat them, for the Canuck fans who were there it was sensational."

Hanlon fondly recalls veterans such as Jack McIlhargey, Don Lever and Cesare Maniago unselfishly helping him adjust to the NHL.

"They were just terrific people," he says. "My career wasn't laced with Stanley Cups — mine was laced with relationships. I wish I had one Cup and maybe one less relationship."

He played 137 games for the Canucks over five seasons, with four shutouts. He remains one of the most popular players the franchise has had, a feeling that is mutual.

"I just loved the Canucks and I still do love the Canucks," he says. "Sometimes I have to wrestle with myself [over whether] I'm supposed to be saying that when I'm coaching in the same league."

# IVAN HLINKA

HE WAS A PIONEER for Czech hockey, first as a player for the Vancouver Canucks of the early 1980s and later during a brief stint as head coach of the Pittsburgh Penguins.

Ivan Hlinka began the Czech invasion of the NHL when he and countryman Jiri Bubla joined the Canucks in the fall of 1981. The pair were among the first Czechs to jump to the NHL, paving the way for future stars such as Jaromir Jagr, Robert Lang and Tomas Vokoun. In 2000, Hlinka reached another milestone when he became the first Czech head coach in NHL history, taking over from the legendary coach of the 1980 gold-medal-winning US Olympic team, Herb Brooks, and leading the Pittsburgh Penguins into the Eastern Conference final.

Hlinka was killed at age 54 in an automobile accident near Prague in August 2004.

"It was not that he was just a coach, but he was sort of like Herb Brooks was for America," Vokoun said upon Hlinka's death.

Hlinka was an outstanding centre for the Czechoslovakian national team, helping his country capture world titles in 1972, 1976 and 1977 as well as Olympic bronze in 1972 and silver in 1976. The big centre with the booming wrist shot was named his country's top hockey player of all time and was selected best forward during the star-studded 1976 Canada Cup tournament, when Czechoslovakia fell in the final to Canada.

By the time he arrived in Vancouver, Hlinka was in his early 30s and the twilight of his career. Nevertheless, he scored 42 goals and 123 points over 137 games for the Canucks and was well respected by his teammates.

"We saw him near the end of his career, as was the case with Bubla, and in their prime those two were two of the best players in the world," says former Canucks play-by-play man Jim Robson, who remembers Hlinka chain-smoking off the ice.

"He was the same calibre in Czech hockey like Wayne Gretzky and Bobby Orr to Canada," Bubla told the Vancouver *Sun* when his longtime friend died.

Canucks fans might have not fully recognized Hlinka's stature in the sport, says Robson. The star scored an impressive 132 goals in 256 games for his national team and had played for the Czech club Litvinov for 19 years before he arrived in Vancouver.

"We have a tendency — at that time, especially — to not fully recognize the Europeans," Robson says. "Hlinka was sort of nearing the end of his career, but he still could be a dominant player and he was very good on the draw."

"I can just imagine what he was like as a 20-year-old," adds Rick Lanz, a Czech-born teammate who translated for Hlinka after he arrived in Vancouver. "He was a big guy who had a tremendous wrist shot. He provided a presence, a size, and more importantly, you never saw him panic with the puck. I mean, he was so cool with it and he was always able to set up a play. And his tremendous experience in international hockey was a great asset to that team."

Hlinka's presence gave a gritty Vancouver lineup unusual depth, talent and experience at centre and he was a big reason the Canucks were able to advance to the Stanley Cup final. He contributed two goals and six assists in 12 playoff games after setting a team "rookie" record with 60 points in the regular season.

"He was an integral part of our 1982 playoff team and it's too bad we only got a chance to see him play in the NHL during the latter part of his career," Former Canucks head coach Marc Crawford, a teammate of Hlinka's in that 1982-83 season, said after his death. "He was a good man and he will be greatly missed."

After finishing his playing days in Europe, Hlinka became an extremely successful coach, guiding the Czech Republic to the gold medal in the 1998 Olympics in Nagano, Japan, when NHL players made their debut at the Games.

He was killed just a few days before he was scheduled to open training camp as coach of the Czech Republic's 2004 World Cup entry. On his way to a golf course, his car was hit by a large truck.

Vladimir Ruzicka, who stepped in to coach that World Cup

*Czechoslovakian star Ivan Hlinka came to Vancouver in the twilight of his career but he was nevertheless effective at centre.* (Robert Shaver/HHOF)

team after Hlinka's death, told the Prague *Post* that replacing Hlinka would be impossible: "I know that I can say this about every single human being, but Ivan is irreplaceable ... no one can fill the gap after him."

"He was a charismatic leader and a hero for our generation," Jaromir Jagr said in the same *Post* article.

"We feel horrible ... It was actually Hlinka who taught us to play hockey," added team captain Robert Reichel.

## Sneaky, Sneaky

*One of the most memorable plays of Ivan Hlinka's brief NHL career came Feb. 11, 1982, during a 4-4 tie in Detroit when Vancouver was awarded not one but two penalty shots in the third period.*

*Early in that period, Thomas Gradin scored on the first penalty shot for the Canucks. Then, with Vancouver trailing 4-3 and in the last minute of the game, the Canucks were awarded a second penalty shot when Stan Smyl was hauled down as he was breaking in on the right wing.*

*Coach Harry Neale sent out a teammate to instruct Smyl to stay down, so that somebody else could take the shot. Neale then had*

*Gradin skate in circles in front of the Vancouver bench, as if he was going to take it. But suddenly Hlinka skated out, picked up the puck, rushed in and scored a highlight-reel goal, surprising goaltender Gilles Gilbert.*

*"The guys were laughing at the bench because he just put on so many moves, he was like standing still at the edge of the crease when he snapped it up underneath the crossbar," recalls Jim Robson. "Some guys couldn't even do that without a goalie in there."*

# RICK LANZ

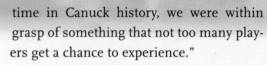

HIS FAMILY WAS vacationing in Bulgaria when Soviet tanks rolled into Prague in 1968. His parents decided on the spot not to go home at all, but to emigrate to Canada with their two young sons.

A dozen years later, Rick Lanz was living the all-Canadian dream as a first-round NHL draft pick of the Vancouver Canucks.

In between, there was a steep learning curve, not the least of which was mastering the basics of hockey. Lanz didn't begin playing the game until he was 10, late for anybody with hopes of making it to the NHL. And he had to learn English on the fly at school in London, Ontario, where the family settled in a small apartment after flying into Montreal and then travelling to Ontario by train.

"My parents made a very, very difficult decision at the time," Lanz says now. "They left everything behind and we just came to Canada ... That was a real experience for our family and probably more difficult for my parents than my brother and I, who respectively were seven and 10 years old. It was kind of like an adventure for us."

The adventure took on a magical twist for Lanz when the 6'2", 195-pound defenceman was drafted by the Canucks after a strong junior hockey career with the Oshawa Generals. Lanz was the Canucks' first pick — seventh overall — in the 1980 draft.

He responded with a solid rookie season, collecting 29 points as a 19-year-old in 1980-81. He went on to post three seasons of 48 points or better on the Vancouver blue line during his seven years with the Canucks.

Lanz's biggest disappointment was being injured when the Canucks made their dramatic run to the 1982 Stanley Cup final. That season, he tore the anterior cruciate ligament in his left knee in January and was out the rest of the way.

"There was a group of us who had the misfortune of being injured at that time and were forced to basically watch from the sidelines," he says. "Despite that, I think we were all very privileged to be part of a group that made it that far and, for the first time in Canuck history, we were within grasp of something that not too many players get a chance to experience."

Lanz was healthy when he returned to the Canuck lineup the following season, and he began to use his offensive flair and much-feared shot from the point to post some impressive numbers while also continuing to learn the defensive intricacies of the NHL. He had 48 points in 1982-83, 57 the next season and 53 in 1985-86, mainly paired with defence-minded partner Jiri Bubla.

"I enjoyed that part of the game," Lanz says of the offensive end. "I enjoyed jumping up in the play and creating something."

But during the 1986-87 season he broke his jaw and then tried to come back from the injury too soon. "I really kind of struggled because my mouth was wired shut, so during the games it was difficult to try to get oxygen and the team was struggling, too."

General manager Jack Gordon responded by trading Lanz, then an assistant captain, to the Toronto Maple Leafs for Dan Hodgson and Jim Benning on December 2, 1986. Although Lanz had enjoyed his stay in Vancouver, the change came at a good time.

"I was kind of at a point where I really wasn't enjoying playing hockey, period," he recalls. "I had thoughts of retirement running through my mind, and I think I took some time away from the game to kind of rethink everything and was able to get back on track with the trade and playing the game in a different town."

He played parts of three seasons for the Leafs before joining the Chicago Blackhawks organization. But injuries to his spine that had occurred during his junior career began to exact a toll and he underwent spinal fusion during the 1989-90 season.

After 25 games with the International Hockey League's Atlanta Knights in 1992-93, Lanz retired as a player and began a coaching career, most recently with the Burnaby Express, 2005-06 B.C. Hockey League champions.

*Defenceman Rick Lanz was the seventh overall pick of the Canucks in 1980 NHL draft. (Robert Shaver/HHOF)*

# IGOR LARIONOV

ONE OF THE BIGGEST mistakes ever made by the Vancouver Canucks was failing to hang on to Igor Larionov.

They had been smart enough to bring him over from the Soviet Union with Vladimir Krutov, another member of Russia's famed KLM Line, in time for the 1989-90 season. The pair, along with defenceman Slava Fetisov, who went to New Jersey, were among the first established Soviet stars to break into the NHL.

Larionov moved to the NHL after eight seasons with the power-house Soviet Red Army squad. The year before arriving in Vancouver, he was named the Soviet player of the year and he was a four-time Soviet League all star. He also gained notoriety and respect for bravely speaking up for the rights of Russian players prior to the fall of the Communist regime, being especially critical of how players were kept in barracks and away from their families.

Whereas Krutov was a complete bust in Vancouver, showing up overweight and appearing unenthused about learning the NHL ropes, Larionov was the opposite. He fit in well with his teammates, displayed his world-famous passing and stick-handling skills in an understated way and became the consummate NHL pro.

"It was such a contrast, those two men," recalls Canucks broadcaster Jim Robson. "Krutov was so much of a loner, didn't talk to anybody, couldn't speak the language, couldn't adjust to the travel, the life. He just sat on the bus like a stone. You know, he never showed any emotion. Every once in a while, he'd show a flash on the ice of his past greatness but he appeared to be overweight and out of shape and uncaring. When he got here, he just was lost, whereas Igor was very personable and talked to all the other players. They liked Iggy."

Larionov would eventually develop into the NHL's elder statesman and one of the league's most respected personalities, playing 14 seasons and skating well into his forties. Unfortunately, in only three of those NHL seasons did he wear a Vancouver uniform.

Despite a 65-point effort, including 44 assists, during the 1991-92 season when he helped a young Pavel Bure emerge as a star NHL sniper, Larionov was not retained by the Canucks past the terms of his original deal.

Vancouver owner Frank Griffiths was by then fed up with the Soviet hockey federation, having been forced to pay them for the disappointing Krutov. Griffiths refused to shell out more money to the federation to keep Larionov, even though the Russian star had performed well in the NHL.

Larionov instead went to play with the Swiss club Lugano for one season. He returned to the NHL in 1993-94 and would have rejoined the Canucks had he cleared waivers. He didn't, and instead he was astutely picked up by the San Jose Sharks. After two seasons in San Jose Larionov joined the Detroit Red Wings, where his keen hockey skills, leadership and sense for the game were a natural fit in a powerhouse organization.

Larionov once told the Detroit *Free Press* that being with the Red Wings was "where I finally found my harmony. In my years with the Red Army and national teams I had success, but not much fun. But in Detroit, I found what I was looking for when I came over in 1989 — good teammates and freedom for what I wanted to do on the ice and off the ice."

He played a total of eight seasons in Detroit, winning three Stanley Cups, and spent a single season in both Florida and New Jersey before retiring from pro hockey.

During the summer of 1997, Larionov and Fetisov became the first Russian players to take the Stanley Cup home. Included in that trip was a stop in Voskresensk, a city of about 90,000 just outside Moscow where Igor Larionov and many other NHLers to follow first learned the game.

# LARS LINDGREN

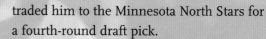

HE PLAYED for five seasons with the Canucks, skated in 394 NHL games, helped Vancouver reach the 1982 Stanley Cup final and appeared in an NHL All-Star Game. But Lars Lindgren, the defenceman from Pitea, Sweden, is most often remembered for one single, bizarre play.

Unfair as it might seem, Lindgren goes down in history as the Canuck player who tied up a close game in Edmonton during the 1982-83 season with a shot that caught the top corner of the net. Unfortunately for Lindgren, the net in question belonged to the Canucks. His ill-fated clearing attempt with 10 seconds left tied the game for the Oilers, depriving Vancouver of what would have been a rare victory in Edmonton.

"I remember that incident very clearly," says former Canucks play-by-play man Jim Robson, who called that game.

Edmonton was pressing for the equalizer with a faceoff in the Canucks' zone. Vancouver's Thomas Gradin won the draw cleanly and the puck went to Lindgren, who wheeled around and fired it. The Swedish defenceman was trying to put the puck behind the net and around the other side to the opposite wing so the Canucks could clear the zone.

"But he puts it just inside the post, perfect," Robson says. "That tied the score 3-3. In those days, there was no overtime. That's the way it ended.

"After the game, they asked Lindgren about it and he said: 'Oh, it's the stick boy's fault, he gave me the shooting stick.'"

Lindgren, who now works for the Swedish hockey federation trying to build that country's youth programs, retains a good sense of humour about the goal.

"I heard a lot about it," he laughs over the telephone from Sweden. "Even [coach] Roger Neilson was laughing when I came in the dressing room after that game. It was different, but every goal counts. It happens."

It's too bad that one incident overshadows the fact that Lars Lindgren was a fine passer with good mobility. He was a big contributor for the Canucks from 1978 until 1983, when the team traded him to the Minnesota North Stars for a fourth-round draft pick.

After reaching Vancouver, Lindgren also developed into a solid defensive player and was a key member of the patched-up blue-line corps that helped an unlikely Canucks squad into the 1982 Stanley Cup final against the New York Islanders. The Swede describes that series as the highlight of his hockey career.

"I've been in some other big things, too, with the Swedish national team, but that was a really good feeling," he says. "I mean, it's the best league in the world and going to the finals ... I wouldn't have minded going a little bit further and if we'd won the finals, but the Islanders had a really good team at that time and we just couldn't score the goals that we needed against them."

Lindgren's skills won him a spot in the 1980 NHL All-Star Game, where he represented Vancouver, and a place on Team Sweden for the 1981 Canada Cup tournament.

He says his adjustment to North America wasn't difficult, given that fellow Canucks Thomas Gradin, Lars Zetterstrom and Roland Eriksson all came from Sweden at the same time, followed closely by Czechoslovakians Jiri Bubla and Ivan Hlinka.

Besides, he was there to experience something different. "I was going there to see another country and to see another style of hockey, so it wasn't important to me to have Swedes around, not at all."

Nicknamed "Lurch," Lindgren scored 138 points and collected 325 penalty minutes in 394 NHL games. All but 59 of those games came in a Vancouver uniform.

"He had little tricks," Robson says. "He would grab his opponent's stick in traffic and put his other glove in the guy's face. He did little things like that and they'd get mad at him and he didn't fight. But he'd do things and they'd get furious with Lindgren in front of the net. He was a smart player."

Lindgren moved to the Canucks as a free agent after three seasons in the Swedish Elite League with Modo. After playing 59 games for Minnesota in 1983-84, he retired from the NHL and returned to Sweden.

*Defenceman Lars Lindgren (left) shares an on-ice laugh with Ivan Boldirev during the early 1980s.* (Paul Bereswill/HHOF)

The trade from Vancouver in 1983 wasn't a disappointment, he says. In fact, the Canucks had wanted to sign him to a long-term deal but Lindgren and his family knew they wanted to return soon to Sweden. So Vancouver allowed him to choose a list of clubs to whom he wanted to be traded. Minnesota was on that list.

"I had a great time in Vancouver. But at that time they were talking a new contract and I didn't want to sign a new contract because we were thinking about moving back home,"

Lindgren says. "They were really good to me."

Back in Sweden he played five more seasons, three for Lulea and two for Pitea in the Swedish second division, before retiring as a player in 1988 to coach.

He still has friends, fond memories and even a boy in British Columbia. His son Michael, in his early twenties, works in the construction business in Vancouver.

# GARY LUPUL

FOR A SCRAPPY, undersized kid from the coastal British Columbia mill town of Powell River who had played all his junior hockey on Vancouver Island, there was no better feeling than skating in the Stanley Cup final for the Vancouver Canucks.

Gary Lupul soaked up every last drop of that atmosphere in the spring of 1982, the undisputed highlight of a seven-year career in the NHL, all with the Canucks.

Fans in the Pacific Coliseum loved Lupul, the little guy with the huge heart who pestered opponents, scored a few goals and never, ever backed down from a challenge. Whenever he stepped onto the ice, the chants of "Loop! Loop! Loop!" would rain down from the stands.

"To be a part of that," Lupul says now, "is something that you never forget. Growing up in Powell River and then watching the first game [of the Canucks franchise in 1970] and then getting an opportunity to play for them. And then in '82, you know, to be a part of that — that's what everybody dreams about, right?"

He certainly dreamed of that as he grew up a talented, multisport athlete in the blue-collar town of Powell River, where his father worked in the mill. At age 16 he joined the Nanaimo Clippers on Vancouver Island, helping the team to a B.C. Hockey League championship. After one winter there, he moved down to Victoria to play three seasons of major junior with the Cougars, skating with teammates such as Barry Pederson, Brad Palmer and Torrie Robertson, each of whom would later be NHL draft picks.

Although he put up some big offensive numbers, including a 53-goal, 54-assist season in his final year with the Cougars, Lupul was not drafted by an NHL team. His 5'8", 175-pound frame did not seem to impress the scouts.

Undaunted, he signed as a free agent with the Canucks and was sent to play with the Dallas Black Hawks of the Central Hockey League. After just 26 games — and 24 points — with Vancouver's top farm team, he was called up and played 51 NHL games as a rookie for the Canucks, scoring 20 points.

For the next few years he split his play between Dallas and Vancouver. Each time he was called up he produced decent offensive numbers, including 28 points in 40 games in 1982-83, but he didn't become a full-time NHLer until the 1983-84 and 1984-85 seasons.

"During my whole time I was up and down, and it's all about confidence, right?" Lupul says. "You look back and you go: 'Well, if I just did ...' But at the end of the day, you just realize how lucky you were to play in the NHL."

Never did he feel more lucky than in those 1982 playoffs, when the Canucks captured the hearts of a province.

"He loved the idea of playing for the Canucks," Vancouver play-by-play man Jim Robson says of Lupul. "And the crowd loved him, because he buzzed around and hit people and threw the gloves off. Oh, he was a real favourite, a little guy who just put all out."

Lupul remembers that coach Roger Neilson, who took over for the suspended Harry Neale late in the year, gave him a clearly defined role and regular playing time. Lupul responded by contributing two goals, five points and plenty of hits in 10 playoff games as the Canucks reached the Cup final before losing to the New York Islanders.

"Roger made me feel a part of the team," Lupul says. "Before that I wasn't getting much ice, and then I got to play with Ron Delorme and Tiger Williams and he gave me a role to play, right? Roger was just a real calming influence. Before that I was basically going to games and, even sitting on the bench, I didn't know if I was going to get on the ice. Whereas Roger just told you: 'This is what you're going to do.' Nobody was bigger than the team. He made everybody feel a part of it."

By the 1985-86 season, however, Neilson was gone and Lupul wasn't feeling part of the Canucks' plans any more. He spent most of that season in the minors in Fredericton before deciding it was time to try Europe; he joined the Berlin Prussians of Germany's top professional league.

Lupul left the NHL after playing 293 games and scoring 145 points. "I was only 27 and basically, back then, [NHL teams] only

*Powell River native Gary Lupul, breaking in here on Brian Hayward of the Winnipeg Jets, became a fan favourite in the Pacific Coliseum.* (Paul Bereswill/HHOF)

had 20-man rosters and when you got up to 29 or 30 they considered you old," he says. "And I liked to party a bit. Maybe that was against me a bit, but whatever ..."

He spent two seasons in Europe before retiring, getting married and having a baby girl. But retirement was a rough adjustment; Lupul had never known much besides hockey. He tried a series of jobs, including roofing, and in the latter an accidental spill of hot tar left him with third-degree burns on his hands.

"I went through some personal things, [including] a divorce. You know, when you get out of hockey it's like you're [no longer] up there on a pedestal kind of thing. And you can't live through other people's eyes. Like, if you were a ditchdigger, who cares, right? I got into real estate, I got into a lot of different things that just didn't pan out. Plus my lifestyle was a little haywire. But at the end of the day, I mean, I don't look back. I've had a lot of good experiences, so I'm just happy to be where I'm at now. You live and learn, right?"

With some help and advice from the Canucks alumni along the way and a job offer from former teammate Ron Delorme to scout for the Canucks, Lupul seems to have found his calling. He is based in Kitchener, Ontario, for the winters, scouting college and junior hockey for Vancouver, the organization he has always loved.

"I had a tough time adjusting career-wise when I got out of hockey," he says. "So now I found something that I'm good at. And being loyal to the organization and [their] having faith in me, it's worked out really well."

# KEVIN McCARTHY

KEVIN McCARTHY couldn't believe what was happening. The captain of the Canucks sat dejected on a table in the Vancouver dressing room, listening to the bad news from team trainer Larry Ashley.

McCarthy's left ankle was broken. He would not play in the 1982 NHL postseason. After four seasons of building with a young Vancouver team toward what would prove to be its shining moment, the talented defenceman would be sitting in the press box for the playoffs.

"It was a tough time," he says.

The injury occurred just one day after the end of the 1981-82 regular season at an optional practice for the Canucks, who were preparing to play the Calgary Flames in the first round of the playoffs. McCarthy decided to skate. It turned out to be an unlucky decision: during a relaxed scrimmage, he and Curt Fraser became entangled along the boards and, in a freak occurrence, McCarthy's ankle snapped.

"The biggest thing [during his time with the Canucks] was going to the finals, obviously," McCarthy says. "But it was kind of a bittersweet thing for myself. All the injured players, we got to travel with the team for every game. Management made you feel like you were part of the team. But at the same time, when you're not on the ice contributing and you're not on the ice sweating and taking the hits and making the hits and being part of the game, there's still that feeling that you're just not part of the group. That's just a natural reaction.

"As they kept on going further and further into the playoffs, you just felt even more and more distant from the team because you weren't out there helping the guys get to where they were. It was great to see the team doing so well, but at the same time it was really tough not to be part of it."

A fine offensive-style defenceman and a strong skater, McCarthy returned to the lineup healthy the next season, but by then things had changed. Head coach Roger Neilson decided that the Canucks would stick with Stan Smyl as captain; Smyl had taken over for the injured McCarthy in the playoff run.

Today, with more than 15 seasons of professional coaching under his belt, McCarthy says he can understand Neilson's logic as a coach. "But at the time, I wasn't ready to accept that as a player. You always want to be the captain of your team; you feel that you didn't do anything not to be the captain other than getting hurt. But at the same time, now looking back, I probably should have handled that a lot differently than I did. I didn't really accept it and I went on with the team not wearing the 'C' but I never really came to grips with the reality of it. And looking back ... I wish I would have just accepted it and [gone] on and, you know, maybe things might have changed."

Instead, he wound up being traded midway through the 1983-84 season to the Pittsburgh Penguins despite having posted four straight seasons of more than 40 points on the Vancouver blue line. He believes his lack of enthusiasm over losing the captaincy was a factor in that trade.

"I think that sort of went into their thinking [in making the deal], as the season went on and we weren't having much success as a team and I definitely wasn't playing up to my capabilities. You know, probably if I would have handled that differently from the outset it might not have come to that point."

Although the Penguins were a poor team, McCarthy says leaving Vancouver was almost a relief after the trade rumours that had constantly swirled around him. Still, it was difficult to leave behind his wife, Rhonda, who was seven months pregnant and unable to fly. McCarthy took a brief leave from the Penguins and flew back to Vancouver later that season to be present for the birth of his second child. He didn't see his new daughter again for another six weeks.

He began his NHL career in Philadelphia, which plucked him from the Winnipeg Monarchs with the 17th overall draft pick in 1977. He was only partway through his second season with the Flyers when they traded him and Drew Calendar to the Canucks in exchange for Dennis Ververgaert on December 29, 1978.

McCarthy played just one game for the Canucks that season,

*Rushing defenceman Kevin McCarthy was the Canucks' captain in 1981–82 but broke his left ankle and missed the playoffs.* (Robert Shaver/HHOF)

however, due to bone chips in his hip joint that caused Vancouver to lodge a complaint to the NHL about the trade. Surgery scuttled the remainder of the 1978-79 season for the Winnipeg native, but he rebounded the following season to become one of Vancouver's best players.

Initially shocked to be traded by Philadelphia, McCarthy quickly warmed to the idea of playing in Vancouver and took over as captain before the 1979-80 season. His best numbers as an NHLer came the following season, when he had 16 goals and 53 points, paired mostly with Lars Lindgren, and represented Vancouver in the NHL All-Star Game.

"That's kind of where I got my career untracked as far as getting to the level of play that I was hoping to get to when I first got drafted," McCarthy says of Vancouver. "It was a great place to play, a great city and a good team and I really enjoyed playing for Harry Neale."

As the leader of the Canucks after practice during a road trip to Winnipeg, the outgoing McCarthy once directed the team bus to his parents' house instead of back to the hotel. "The whole team got out and Mrs. McCarthy had prepared lunch for them," recalls Canucks broadcaster Jim Robson. "There were 22 hockey players gathered in this little house in Winnipeg. It was a memorable get-together."

The trade to Pittsburgh marked the beginning of the end of McCarthy's NHL career. He spent less than two seasons with the Penguins before signing with Philadelphia, becoming an emergency defensive replacement and eventually a playing assistant coach with the Flyers organization.

That led to a fine coaching career for McCarthy, who has spent 15 seasons in the Hartford/Raleigh NHL organization, including two trips to the Stanley Cup finals as a bench assistant with the Carolina Hurricanes, who won the Cup in 2006.

# HARRY NEALE

HARRY NEALE had no idea of the chain reaction he was about to ignite when he left the Canucks bench during a game in Quebec City on March 20, 1982. All the head coach knew was that one of his players, talented tough guy Tiger Williams, was being physically attacked by a fan who had made his way down to the glass from his seat a few rows up. Williams, who had initiated the melee by roughing up Nordiques' star Peter Stastny, was at the time being pinned to the boards near the Vancouver bench by Quebec's Wilf Paiement.

Neale charged into the stands after the fan. Three of his Canuck players followed to back him up. By the time the smoke cleared, Neale had been suspended by the NHL for 10 games and a strange momentum had begun that would carry the Canucks all the way into the Stanley Cup final.

Neale remembers there had been plenty of pregame tension after Williams made some objectionable comments toward the French Canadians in an interview shortly before that game. "We knew it was going to be a lively crowd and it was, like it often was in Quebec."

Making the situation more volatile was the fact that the stands in Le Colisée were not separated from one end of the bench and the protective glass extended only two feet above the boards, giving players access to fans and vice versa.

The offending fan "had been a mouthy fan," Neale says. "I'd known him from the WHA days when I coached Hartford. I ran off to try and get him. I never quite got to him, and I think Marc Crawford and Doug Halward and I forget who else ... three guys came with me, so I was going to be all right if a fight started."

Perhaps it was Neale's show of support for Williams, perhaps it was a feeling that NHL suspensions handed to the team were unfair — whatever the reason, many around the 1982 Canucks point to the Quebec City fracas as the galvanizing force behind that team's magical spring.

The Canucks, who had experienced a mediocre season to that point, had already embarked on a mini hot streak when the incident occurred. But from that point on they went on a tear, winning their final five of their last six games of the regular season and the first four of the playoffs.

Since it had already been long decided that Neale would move over the following season and replace Jake Milford as general manager, and that assistant Roger Neilson would become head coach, it was determined that Neilson should remain behind the bench for the rest of the 1982 playoffs. That decision would lead to "towel power," when fans emulated Neilson and waved white towels as the Canucks eventually skated all the way to the Cup finals.

"When Roger had won the last two games of the season and the first three of the playoffs, I didn't have to be [Montreal Canadiens general manager] Sam Pollock to figure out 'this guy's got something going with this team'," Neale says now. "And we were going to make the change anyway, so we made it then."

As planned, Neale became general manager the next season. He served in that capacity for three years before being fired after a 25-win 1984-85 season in which Vancouver missed the playoffs.

"When you get fired, you're upset," he says. "I worked harder the two or three years when I was the Canucks' manager than I did when I coached, trying to get the team better with trades and drafts and so on. You know, firing is something you wish hadn't happened, but there aren't many guys in this business ... who don't get fired when they don't get the job done."

Neale was subsequently hired to coach the Detroit Red Wings, a once proud franchise that was coming off its 12th straight losing season. But he was fired less than halfway through the 1985-86 season and never coached again.

"I coached in Detroit for 35 games and then I was harder to find than Jimmy Hoffa," he says. That kind of wit helped him quickly land a job with CBC Television as a colour analyst.

More than 20 years later he is still behind the microphone. Teamed with play-by-play man Bob Cole, the pair have formed the number 1 broadcasting team at *Hockey Night in Canada*. Neale is well-known by hockey fans across Canada for his witticisms and

*By going into the stands to battle an unruly fan, Canucks' coach Harry Neale kick-started Vancouver's 1981–82 momentum. (Vancouver Canucks)*

often dry humour when assessing Saturday night games.

"When I first got the job, it was a job and I needed one," Neale says of broadcasting. "After two or three years, I got some inquiries about getting back into the coaching or assistant coaching business, but I got to like the TV — and it didn't take me very long to realize that I was still in the game, but that I never lost, and I got to the finals every year."

Still, he looks back on his coaching career with pride. After plenty of seasoning in the rival World Hockey Association, he became the Canucks' head coach in 1978, taking over a team that had finished 23 games under .500 and totalled just 57 points the previous season under Orland Kurtenbach.

Over the next four seasons, the Canucks improved to 63-, 70-, 76- and 77-point totals under Neale's guidance. That development came on a new base of players that GM Jake Milford had drafted.

"I was lucky in this regard, in that my first year was the rookie year of Thomas Gradin, Curt Fraser and Stan Smyl," Neale says. "They all came in as draft picks and made the team and became vital parts of any success we had in Vancouver.

"Those three guys were certainly ... I don't know whether you'd call them favourites, but they were coach's delights. They were competitive, they were sensible, they worked hard, they had some talent and they played real well together."

It wasn't all rosy for the coach, however. Play-by-play man Jim Robson remembers one home game against Montreal in the late 1970s in which Larry Robinson rushed through the entire Canuck team and scored just after Neale had told his crew between periods to watch out for that very thing.

"And the crowd goes nuts, because in those days the place [Pacific Coliseum] was full of Montreal Canadiens' fans," Robson says. "The cheer was so loud you'd think the game was in Montreal."

Robson remembers Neale being livid, first with his players and then with the fans. In a live postgame interview with Al Davidson of CKNW, Neale said: "Al, these assholes don't deserve a winner."

Davidson cautioned: "You're live on the radio right now, Harry."

"You're right, Al," Neale replied. "I shouldn't call these assholes assholes."

By the spring of 1982 Neale's and the team's fortunes had improved dramatically, but after the Canucks reached the Stanley Cup finals expectations went through the roof. Neale found it impossible to live up to those hopes when the Canucks' skill level couldn't match that of their two Western Canadian rivals in the Smythe Division.

In trying to find the right combination he traded Fraser and Williams, two of the players who had given those '82 Canucks so much grit and toughness. Neale eventually fired Neilson and the disastrous coaching experiment that was Bill LaForge, climbing

*Harry Neale and sportscaster Bernie Pascall appear on CTV's* Wednesday Night Hockey. *Neale, of course,
has gone on to a lengthy TV career with* Hockey Night in Canada. *(Vancouver Canucks)*

back behind the bench himself in both cases. Nothing seemed to work.

"We had two teams in our division, Calgary and Edmonton, whose skill level was way beyond ours," Neale says. "We thought, to get up to them and to be able to play with them, that we had to improve the skill level of our team. And what happened was we took away from what got us to the '82 finals — heart and grit and work and toughness and good defensive play — to try and get so we could compete offensively. If you had to do it over again, you might ...

"But we were in a no-win situation. We couldn't win the way we won in '82 because those two teams were too good for us. And yet we couldn't get enough better offensively to compete with them."

*After coaching in the WHA, Harry Neale took over behind the Canucks' bench in 1978.* (Graphic Artists/HHOF)

# CAM NEELY

VANCOUVER CANUCKS fans remember Cam Michael Neely as the one who got away.

When the Canucks traded Neely and a first-round pick to the Boston Bruins on June 6, 1986, in exchange for veteran centre Barry Pederson, it didn't look to be a bad deal for either club. In hindsight, it has become commonly referred to as the worst trade in Vancouver history.

Pederson was never quite the same player in a Canucks uniform, while Neely emerged as a superstar power forward playing for an NHL contender in the Boston Garden. He represented the Bruins in five NHL All-Star Games, posted three seasons of 50-plus goals and twice led Boston into the Stanley Cup final. To make matters worse from Vancouver's perspective, the draft pick the Canucks threw in with Neely turned out to be defenceman Glen Wesley, who would also develop into an all-star.

"I always thought [Neely] would turn out to be one of the top-notch players, but I never thought of him becoming a 50-goal scorer," former Canucks coach and general manager Harry Neale once told the Vancouver *Sun*.

"But he developed that talent in Boston. He changed as a player with the Bruins because he went with a better hockey team, while we already had two right wings in Stan Smyl and Tony Tanti on power plays, so Cam never got to play on our top lines. In Boston he did, and he got to play their power play."

Neely's is a classic case of a player developing and maturing once he is put in the right environment.

A native of Comox, British Columbia, he spent some of his childhood in Moose Jaw, Saskatchewan, and Maple Ridge, B.C. After scoring a hat trick in the Memorial Cup final to lead the Portland Winter Hawks to the junior championship in 1983, he was selected ninth overall by the Canucks in that June's entry draft.

But Canuck coaches Harry Neale, Bill LaForge and Tom Watt didn't see Neely as an impact offensive player, choosing instead to play the 6'1", 185-pounder on the third and fourth lines. Under the microscope of skating in his home province and being asked at times to fill the role of a tough guy, Neely didn't exactly set the NHL on fire during his three seasons with Vancouver, posting 31, 39 and 34 points respectively.

"Tom Watt misjudged Neely badly," says Canucks play-by-play man Jim Robson. "Watt put him on the fourth line, had him playing tough, and even put Dave Lowry ahead of him on the power play."

When the trade came, Pederson as a restricted free agent was locked in a contract dispute with Boston general manager Harry Sinden and Neely had grown tired of Watt criticizing his play. The Canucks brass also badly wanted Pederson, another B.C. product, who had put up terrific numbers in Boston.

"I don't defend the Canucks. It was not a good trade," Robson says. "But there were a lot of circumstances around that trade that [later] made it look worse than it was, really. Barry Pederson was pretty good here. He led the team in scoring. He played okay, but he wasn't a superstar and he had a weak team around him. And all the toughness that was in the Boston lineup wasn't here."

Meanwhile, the change of scenery suited the 21-year-old Neely and so did the smaller Boston Garden and the superior Bruin lineup. He was paired with the talented Rick Middleton and another former Canuck, Thomas Gradin. Neely played on the power play.

He posted 36 goals and 72 points in his first season with the Bruins and just kept improving from there. The peak of his career came in 1989-90, when the big winger scored 55 times and finished with 92 points and 117 penalty minutes. He added 28 points in 21 playoff games that spring as the Bruins advanced to the Stanley Cup finals.

Much more than simply a scorer, Neely created space for himself on the ice with a willingness to mix it up and a penchant for delivering bone-crunching bodychecks.

"Cam loved Boston and the fans loved him in Boston," Robson says. "He was a big, tough kid, who crashed around in a smaller rink. He became an all-star and great player. I think it was a great thing for Cam Neely that he got out of town and got to Boston."

*The Canucks gave up too early on Cam Neely, who became an NHL superstar for the Boston Bruins.* (Robert Shaver/HHOF)

Neely retired in 1996 at age 31, after hip and knee injuries plagued the final years of his career. But during his 13 NHL seasons he had become one of the best power forwards the game has ever seen. In January of 2004, the Bruins retired his number 8 jersey. Less than two years later, he was inducted into the Hockey Hall of Fame, becoming the first honouree who skated for the NHL Canucks during his career.

Perhaps Harry Neale put it best when he described to the *Sun* the player he let get away in this manner: "There aren't many who will score 50 goals and go out and threaten your life."

A major celebrity in the Boston area, Neely has appeared in several Hollywood movies, including *D2: The Mighty Ducks* and *Me, Myself and Irene*. He also helped to launch the Cam Neely Foundation for Cancer Care in 1995, after losing his mother and father to the disease. The non-profit Boston foundation helps cancer patients and their families during treatment.

# ROGER NEILSON

HE NEVER WON a Stanley Cup but, if wealth is measured by the number of friends one accumulates, Roger Neilson lived a rich life.

At his memorial service, which in June 2003 gathered 1,500 friends and relatives in Peterborough, Ontario, Neilson was eulogized as "the most loved man in hockey." He certainly had earned a special place in the hearts of Canuck fans, coaches and players, particularly after guiding an unlikely Vancouver team into the Stanley Cup finals in 1982.

Assistant coach Neilson had taken over the Canucks that spring only because head coach and good friend Harry Neale had been suspended for going after a fan in the stands at Quebec City just before the end of the regular season. But once Neilson assumed control, it was obvious that something special was going on.

"Roger came behind the bench and we seemed to take off from that incident, for whatever reason," recalls then captain Stan Smyl.

Neilson will be forever remembered in British Columbia for igniting "towel power," the emotional frenzy that had the Pacific Coliseum awash in white amid a deafening roar and helped propel those Canucks farther than anyone had expected them to go.

During Game 2 of the conference finals in Chicago, a contest Vancouver would lose, Neilson chose an interesting way to protest the penalty calls of referee Bob Myers. He draped a white towel over one end of a hockey stick, then waved it at the official in mock surrender. For that bit of sarcastic showmanship he was fined US$1,000 by the league, but the expenditure would prove well worth it.

When the teams skated out into the Pacific Coliseum for Game 3 back in Vancouver, the stands were jammed with fans waving white towels. The visual effect was striking and so was the emotional effect on the Canucks, who didn't lose the rest of the series, dispatching the Black Hawks in five games.

Although Neilson's towel tactic struck an emotional chord with those Canucks, he wasn't a rah-rah coach. A teacher before taking up coaching full-time, he was more the professorial type in his approach to the game, always meticulously prepared and constantly breaking new technical ground. He pored over hours of video footage, looking to exploit his opponents' weaknesses and give his own team an edge.

"He was a very technical guy," Smyl says. "He wanted everyone to play our system. That was it. There was no other way. This is the way we're going to do it. And he showed us, night after night, when we did not have success, some of the things that we should be doing. When we had success, he showed us why. And every day, no matter what, he was showing us little things, good and bad, within our game so that we could have success.

"That part about it compared to Harry [Neale] was a little different. You know, they called Roger 'Captain Video' and there was a lot of video. But it was for the better of us as a team and individual players."

Neilson was a master technician as a coach and straightforward in his approach with players, Smyl says. A religious man, Neilson didn't curse in the manner of many hockey coaches, preferring to use the softer phrase "for crap's sakes."

"He had his little [inspirational] sayings, but he wasn't a guy who jumped up and down on the benches or anything like that," recalls Smyl. "Everything was under control with Roger and I think that kind of flowed with our team, too."

Defenceman Doug Halward played for Neilson in Peterborough and in Vancouver and says: "I just really appreciated Roger Neilson's coaching, especially at the pro level. Roger was kind of an innovator and really taught you how to play the game. Probably, today, all coaches have the teaching aspect in it, but back then that was a little different. He gave you responsibilities and you knew exactly what was expected of you."

Whatever he did, it worked during that playoff run. But all the preparation and towel power in the world wouldn't have been enough for the Canucks to beat the superior Islanders over a best-of-seven series.

Neilson was back on the Canucks bench the next season, when Vancouver compiled a 30-35-15 record before losing in the first

*Coach Roger Neilson, who took over for the suspended Harry Neale, ignited "Towel Power" during the 1982 playoffs.* [Paul Bereswill/HHOF]

round of the playoffs. Part way through the 1983-84 season, he was fired by then general manager Neale as the Canucks tried desperately to live up to the huge expectations they had set for themselves.

During his NHL head-coaching career, Neilson would work 1,000 games with eight different teams. He served as an assistant coach with four franchises, including the Ottawa Senators, with whom he was working when he finally succumbed to skin and bone cancer on June 21, 2003, at age 69, after a four-year battle. He had spent 25 years as an NHL coach and scout, and he was inducted into the Hockey Hall of Fame less than a year before he died.

He was honoured during his memorial service as a man who had no pretensions, who showed genuine interest in and caring for anybody he encountered. Neale remembers Neilson as a friend who was tremendously dedicated, hard-working and, above all else, passionate about hockey and the people he coached.

"For anyone who played for Roger or coached with him or even coached against him and got to know him that's the one quality that stood out beyond anything else," Neale says. "He loved the game, and it was pretty obvious that his passion for the game made him coach 1,000 games and have an excellent career with a lot of teams. And, you know, you can say, well, he got fired six times or whatever it was — but he got rehired seven ... I think that's a compliment to Roger's coaching ability."

# BARRY PEDERSON

LIKE MANY FANS of the Canucks, Barry Pederson was excited about what would eventually become known simply as "the trade" in the lore of Vancouver's NHL franchise. It was June 1986 and Pederson was coming home to play for the Canucks after a contract dispute with the Boston Bruins. Going the other way was Cam Neely, a strapping forward from Maple Ridge who had struggled to reach his potential with his home-province team.

Pederson was a proven sniper with two seasons of 100-plus points in the NHL under his belt. He was the player Canucks boss Arthur Griffiths felt could help turn the tide for a floundering franchise.

It didn't work out that way. Although he played decently, Pederson never regained the form he had shown playing with Rick Middleton in Boston. Meanwhile, Neely blossomed into an NHL superstar.

"They weren't as good as what I was capable of and that was always a disappointment to me," Pederson says now of his three-plus seasons in Vancouver. "I don't think I did as much there as I thought I was capable of, and from that standpoint I understand wholeheartedly what those [negative] comments about that trade are all about."

Pederson was born in Big River, Saskatchewan, but spent the majority of his youth in Nanaimo, British Columbia, just a short ferry ride from the home of the Canucks. Despite that, he grew up a big Boston fan, drawn in by the brilliance of Bobby Orr. "I grew up with the Orr era and, like a lot of kids growing up watching him, you were kind of pulled in by the big bad Bruins of the early '70s."

After a standout junior career with the Victoria Cougars, including a trip to the Memorial Cup, Pederson was thrilled to be selected by Boston, going 18th overall to the Bruins in the first round of the 1980 draft.

The 5'11", 185-pound centre took almost no time to adjust to the NHL, scoring 44 goals and adding 48 assists in his first season

skating with Middleton and the Bruins. In the process he became only the fifth NHL rookie to score more than 40 goals and was runner-up to Dale Hawerchuk for the Calder Trophy.

Pederson followed that with 107- and 116-point seasons, before being limited to just 22 games in his fourth NHL campaign by a broken knuckle and then by a much more serious health scare.

A benign growth was removed from his shoulder that winter. Doctors removed a four-by-six-inch portion of his shoulder, but he bounced back with 29 goals and 47 assists during the 1985-86 season.

A restricted free agent at that point, Pederson and the Bruins were locked in a contract dispute and the Canucks were eager to sign him. Instead, the two sides worked out a trade under which Pederson went to the Canucks and Neely and Vancouver's 1987 first-rounder went the other way.

Pederson joined the Canucks with high hopes: "When it happened, I was very excited about it. For me, that was going home to the West Coast. I grew up in Nanaimo and then played junior hockey not only in Nanaimo but also in Victoria. We had successful teams there and I had a lot of good friends there."

He didn't have Rick Middleton there, however, and he didn't have the same strong team around him that he had enjoyed in Boston. Pederson put together back-to-back seasons of more than 70 points, but he wasn't the same force he had been with the Bruins.

"I was never really, I don't think, the same after that, looking back on it," he says of his shoulder surgery. "But at the same time, I don't necessarily believe the physical aspect of it was the only aspect of it. I think the mental part was [a factor], for whatever reason."

His production dropped to 41 points in his third season with Vancouver, as he was limited by injuries to only 62 games. Just 16 games into the 1989-90 season, he was traded to Pittsburgh.

"At that time, I think it was time for me to move on," he says now. "I think it was pretty obvious that I wasn't getting

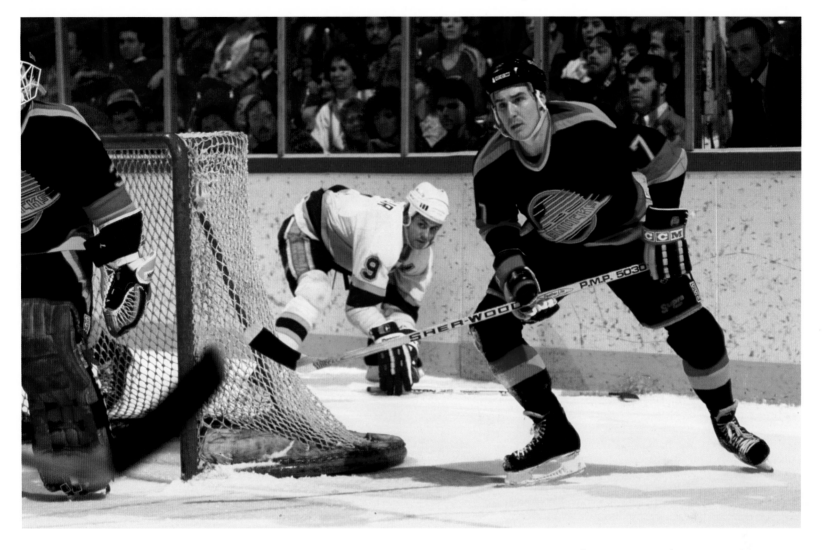

*Barry Pederson was the player the Canucks received in exchange for Cam Neely in June of 1986.* (David Klutho/HHOF)

it done there, myself. I think the organization and me, we kind of came to a mutual understanding that it was probably a better time to move on."

By then he was in the twilight of his playing career. But he enjoyed his two seasons in Pittsburgh, during which he was part of a 1991 Stanley Cup championship team led by Mario Lemieux.

After playing five games for the Hartford Whalers in 1991-92, Pederson was moved back to Boston and finished his NHL career there after that season. He and his family continue to live in the Boston area, where he is an institutional equity broker and also

works for NESN television as a studio analyst for some Bruins games. His partner for some of those telecasts is none other than Cam Neely.

"Even though they were frustrating years for me individually and for the team in Vancouver, I still look upon the Vancouver years as a real change in my life," Pederson says now. "I think it made me grow up a lot.

"I think that [adversity] made me a better person. I think it makes me a better coach and hopefully a better parent and husband."

# PAUL REINHART

HIGH-SCORING DEFENCEMAN Paul Reinhart saw the Canucks of the 1980s from both sides — as a divisional rival and as a member of the Vancouver team himself when the decade drew to a close.

Reinhart was a supremely talented rearguard for the Calgary Flames, whom the 1982 Canucks swept in a best-of-five series to begin their magical run to the Stanley Cup finals. Six years later Reinhart became a Canuck, playing for two productive seasons in Vancouver before retiring from hockey in 1990.

The smooth-skating native of Kitchener, Ontario, remembers that '82 Canucks team vividly. "They were a good, honest, hard-working team. They had four lines that just worked incredibly hard — nothing spectacular, but they worked incredibly hard and, of course, Richard [Brodeur] was just unbelievable. They also had a very big defence. I seem to recall that you couldn't get second shots. I just remember them being very, very tough to play against."

Reinhart was himself pretty difficult to play against. He posted five seasons of 60 or more points on the Calgary blue line, including a career-best 75 points in 1982-83, and he represented the Flames in the 1985 NHL All-Star Game. In 1986 he counted 18 points in 21 playoff games, helping Calgary to the Stanley Cup finals, where the Flames lost to the Montreal Canadiens in five games.

But injuries hampered Reinhart's career, particularly a herniated disc in his back suffered in 1984. He was limited to only 27 games that season, 32 games in 1985-86 and 14 in 1987-88.

"It was on and off," he says of his serious back problems. "And, of course, if you had that same injury today with what we know about core training and physical fitness, I don't think it would have been an issue at all. I'd probably just be hanging up the skates now."

Instead, the Flames decided that Reinhart was no longer in their plans and traded him to Vancouver with Steve Bozek on September 6, 1988, for a third-round pick in the 1989 NHL entry draft.

"I was happy to come to Vancouver — it's a beautiful spot," Reinhart says. "I was a little disappointed [with the trade initially], because I felt I was going to not only have to come back and play more minutes per game than I thought that I was capable of at the time, I was also going to have to go back to face a very big, strong, rugged Calgary team eight times."

Calgary went on to win the Stanley Cup in 1989 without Reinhart. But the Flames underestimated how much hockey he had left. He managed back-to-back 57-point seasons for the Canucks, playing at least 64 games each campaign and representing Vancouver in the 1989 NHL All-Star Game.

He arrived at the same time big changes were happening with the Vancouver franchise. General manager Pat Quinn and his assistant, Brian Burke, were rebuilding the team. They brought back defenceman Harold Snepsts, who took some of the pressure off Reinhart. They drafted Trevor Linden, a future cornerstone of the franchise.

Meanwhile, Reinhart was already comfortable with the advice of Dr. Ross Davidson, the Canucks' orthopedic surgeon who had helped him with his back even when he was with the Flames. The Canucks "treated me incredibly well," he says. "I was thrilled."

Reinhart was immediately paired with hard-rock defenceman Garth Butcher and the two were a successful duo. "Paul moved the puck great," Butcher says. "He was at a point in his career where he had some back problems and I kind of took pride in seeing that he wasn't hit. So that combination worked out really well."

Reinhart retired in 1990 due both to his back problems and business opportunities that were available. A shrewd investor during his playing days, he continued in that field afterward and, for a brief period, owned part of the Vancouver Ravens of the National Lacrosse League.

*Defenceman Paul Reinhart recorded back-to-back 57-point seasons in a Vancouver uniform.* (Paul Bereswill/HHOF)

# DARCY ROTA

DARCY ROTA remembers the moment he got the news as if it were yesterday, though more than a quarter century has passed.

It was the day he found out he was going to play professional hockey in his home province. It was February 8, 1980, and at the time he was a member of the Atlanta Flames.

The Flames' bus had just pulled into the Westin Hotel in Edmonton, where the team would play the Oilers. Rota's road roommate, Ivan Boldirev, had been seeking a trade, so it wasn't a surprise when Atlanta head coach Al MacNeil pulled Boldirev aside to talk as he got off the bus.

As he was getting the key to their hotel room, Rota was approached by David Poile, Atlanta's assistant general manager. Rota assumed Poile would simply be asking him to help his good friend Boldirev come to grips with a trade. He was in for a surprise.

"We've just traded you to Vancouver with Ivan," Poile told the player.

"I said: 'What?'" Rota recalls.

The news came as a shock to the British Columbia kid who had grown up in Kelowna, Vancouver and Prince George. He immediately phoned his parents, who happened to be in Edmonton for the Flames' game. They were ecstatic and so was Rota. After six seasons with the Chicago Black Hawks and a brief stint with the Flames, he was going home.

"It was really, really thrilling," he says. "To me it was a privilege to play in the National Hockey League and a privilege to play in Chicago, and Atlanta was a fun place to play for the 11 months I was there. But playing in Vancouver, I think, really was where I experienced the highlights, individually and for sure team-wise."

He did indeed. The left-winger would enjoy with the Canucks five strong seasons that included a sterling 42-goal, 81-point performance in 1982-83, part of which came playing on a potent line with Thomas Gradin and Stan Smyl.

That line, thrown together in March, went on a tear to finish the season. "I was having a decent year and then the three of us just got red-hot that month," Rota says. "That month of March, it seemed everything we touched was going in. It was unbelievable."

His 81-point output stood as a Canuck team record for a left-winger until broken by Markus Naslund in 2001-02 and it easily marked the best production of Rota's 11-year NHL career. Still, he posted 40 points or more in each of his four full seasons with the Canucks.

"He was courageous in front of the net," recalls Jim Robson, the team's longtime broadcaster. "He was a competitive guy. It was a good hockey team so there was depth, so there wasn't a case of other teams being able to key on Darcy."

Rota contributed six goals in 17 games to help Vancouver reach the Stanley Cup finals in 1982. He rates that playoff run as easily the most exciting part of his hockey career.

"You know, you can talk about scoring 40 goals and I played in an All-Star Game [1984] and you score hat tricks and you do things individually," he says. "But when you accomplish something as a team like we did — and it was the first time ever for the Canucks to go that far — whether we were underdogs or whatever it was thrilling, and people still talk about that Stanley Cup run with great passion. Whether I see moms or dads or grandparents, even young kids will have heard about it — it's by far the highlight of my hockey life."

His hockey life had rather slow beginnings. He didn't make a minor-hockey all-star team until his second year of bantam in Prince George. But the late bloomer went on to an outstanding junior career with the Edmonton Oil Kings.

"I say this to parents: with the Western Hockey League draft today, I would never have been drafted," he says. "I was a guy who was good, but I was never an all-star. I was always like this near-miss guy who couldn't make the team. So I always say that you just never know with kids."

His NHL career was cut short by a neck injury that occurred in February 1984 when he was caught with a hard, "absolutely clean"

*Left-winger Darcy Rota was thrilled in 1979 when he was traded by the Atlanta Flames to his home-province Canucks.* (Paul Bereswill/HHOF)

hit from Los Angeles defenceman Jay Wells. The hit ended Rota's season, requiring spinal fusion that summer. Although he seemed to progress well through extensive rehabilitation, when he returned to practice the physical contact caused him discomfort. After consulting medical and training staff, he decided to retire in 1984.

Rota has never left the game, however. He worked for the Canucks in various capacities, including as a colour analyst and media relations director. He spent two years in New York as a special assistant to then NHL president John Ziegler. In recent years he has been heavily involved in the B.C. Hockey League, and he is now "part owner, president, governor, general manager and chief bottlewasher" with the Burnaby Express of the junior circuit. The Express won both the BCHL and Canadian Junior A titles in the spring of 2006.

Married, with a son and daughter, Rota lives in the Lower Mainland, not far from where his junior team plays. "The nice thing," he says, "is I've always been involved in the game of hockey in some capacity."

# JIM SANDLAK

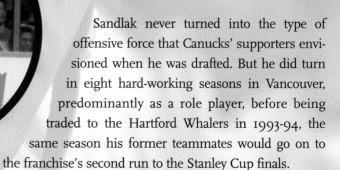

WITH 20 YEARS to reflect on it, big Jim Sandlak agrees that the weight of expectation was probably a little more than a 19-year-old kid from Kitchener, Ontario, was comfortably ready to handle.

It was 1985 and Sandlak had been selected fourth overall by the Canucks from the Ontario Hockey League's London Knights. When Vancouver fans saw his 6'4" frame, his 40-goal season in the OHL and his two world junior championship medals, they had visions of a hulking power forward who could lift their struggling team to greatness.

"The team had really gone downhill when I joined them," Sandlak says. "When I first got there, we were lucky to get 5,000 people in the stands."

In 1986, Sandlak turned in an impressive performance at his second consecutive world junior tournament, when he captained the silver-medal Canadian team and was named outstanding forward of the competition. In retrospect, expectations were likely a little high for the bruising forward who had led the world tournament with 12 points.

"There was pressure [in Vancouver] because they were expecting all this out of a young player," Sandlak says. "You're forced into that adult role right away. Suddenly, you're not playing with teenagers any more, you're playing with men who have wives and kids at home, so it's a big-time adjustment that way. That was the biggest adjustment — in the first two years."

Sandlak, who patterned his game after John Tonelli of the dynasty-era New York Islanders, produced a promising 15 goals and 36 points in his first full NHL season. In the process, he became the first Canuck to ever earn a postseason honour when he was named to the NHL's all-rookie team.

But he regressed somewhat as a sophomore, spending 24 games in the minors the next winter.

He scored 20 goals and 20 assists in 1988-89 and turned in perhaps his best statistical year in 1991-92, when he again posted 40 points — but also threw around his 219-pound frame often enough to earn 176 penalty minutes.

Sandlak never turned into the type of offensive force that Canucks' supporters envisioned when he was drafted. But he did turn in eight hard-working seasons in Vancouver, predominantly as a role player, before being traded to the Hartford Whalers in 1993-94, the same season his former teammates would go on to the franchise's second run to the Stanley Cup finals.

Surprised by the trade, he took solace in the fact that he was rejoining former Canuck executive Brian Burke, then general manager in Hartford. However, Burke left the Whalers to join the NHL head office and Sandlak recalls feeling "stuck, floundering in Hartford."

He says the Canucks tried to reacquire him from the Whalers in time for their playoff run in 1994, but he was recovering from a broken left heel and NHL rules prohibit trading injured players.

After playing parts of two seasons with the Whalers, Sandlak did eventually return to Vancouver as a free agent. He played 33 games with the Canucks in 1995-96 before breaking vertebrae during practice when his skate was caught in a rut; he ran into one of his teammates and crashed into the boards backwards at full speed.

He returned for the playoffs in 1996, skating on the top line as Vancouver lost to eventual Stanley Cup champion Colorado in the first round. But after that he decided it was time to hang up the skates.

"I figured that while [my back] was strong and healthy and I could still function 100 percent — I had two young boys, I had a wonderful career, I got my pension — I figured, why risk it any longer?"

He returned home to London, where he joined his brother-in-law in the grocery business. Aside from a brief return to the game with a German first-division team in 1997-98, he has served as an assistant manager at their Food Basics store in London.

He looks back proudly on his career and calls himself "100 percent" a Canuck.

"I think at first they wanted more scoring from me," he says of his nine seasons in Vancouver. "But when it all boiled down to it, for my overall career, I think they were happy with me."

# PETRI SKRIKO

ONE OF THE MOST exciting players to have worn a Canucks' uniform, Petri Skriko deserved a more fitting send-off from Vancouver.

The Finnish flash, who scored 30 or more goals in four of the six full seasons he skated in Vancouver, was benched, humiliated and finally shuffled out of town for a second-round draft pick in 1991.

The 5'10", 170-pounder from Lappeenranta produced amazing numbers for a player who wasn't selected until the eighth round of the NHL draft, 157th overall, by Vancouver in 1981.

Skriko served a 10-month stint in the Finnish army before joining the Canucks. As a 22-year-old rookie he scored 21 goals in the 1984-85 season, before rolling off four straight winters of 30 goals or better, including a career-best 38 goals and 78 points in 1985-86. His eye-popping moves and skating skill earned him the nickname "the Streak."

But when Skriko slumped to 15 goals and 33 assists in 1989-90, he fell out of favour with Canucks head coach Bob McCammon. Skriko requested a trade over the summer of 1990, but it wasn't granted right away and he became a frustrated, forgotten man in the Canucks organization.

After scoring just four goals during the first 20 games of 1990-91, he didn't see the ice again for Vancouver. For eight weeks, he didn't play. Near the end, he wasn't taken on road trips and he was even left to practise alone, coaching himself through skating drills as he tried to stay in shape.

Finally, Canucks general manager Pat Quinn ended the high-profile standoff by dealing Skriko to the Boston Bruins in exchange

for a second-round pick, which turned out to be forward Mike Peca.

"It's something that I expected for a long time and I'm happy it finally happened," a relieved Skriko told the Vancouver *Sun* upon learning about the trade of January 16, 1991. "It was a terrible thing to take so long. It got very personal and I thought it couldn't go on much longer."

He was excited about going to Boston and envisioned a lengthy stay with the Bruins. But things didn't work out that way. He put up 19 points over his first 28 regular-season games as a Bruin and then added eight points in 18 playoff games as Boston made the Eastern Conference finals. But after scoring just once in nine games during the 1991-92 season, Skriko was dealt to the Winnipeg Jets.

He had only five points in 15 games before being released by Winnipeg. A subsequent attempt to stick with the San Jose Sharks the following season lasted 17 games and he returned to Finland.

Skriko's NHL career numbers were impressive, with 405 points in 541 games, including 365 points for Vancouver. He played six subsequent seasons with the Danish club Herning before taking over as the team's head coach. Most recently, he has coached in Finland.

A member of the Finnish Hockey Hall of Fame, Skriko played for his country at the 1984 and 1992 Olympics as well as in the 1987 and 1991 Canada Cups. In 1984 at Sarajevo, he scored 10 points to lead the Finns to a sixth-place finish.

# STAN SMYL

THE NICKNAME has been with him for more than 30 years, ever since Stan Smyl was a smallish, teenage rookie with the B.C. Hockey League's Bellingham Ice Hawks.

Smyl had just laid another in a series of crunching checks on much older and larger opponents when one of his teammates turned to him on the bench and said: "You're like a steamer out there." The nickname fit. From that day on he was Stan "Steamer" Smyl, a moniker that holds the highest place in the 35-year lore of the Canucks.

The nickname without question suited the playing style of the tireless Smyl, whose all-out effort and unwavering work ethic powered him through 13 seasons with the Canucks, a record eight as team captain.

The native of St. Paul, Alberta, is the only Vancouver player to have had his number — 12 — permanently retired and hanging in the rafters of General Motors Place, signifying his importance to the Canucks organization.

Smyl remains a vital part of that organization. After retiring as a player in 1991, he stepped immediately into the coaching ranks and is now the team's director of player development. In the money-first, modern-day hockey world he is a throwback, a man who has been with one organization his entire career, a man who defines the Canucks.

"It has been, in this day and age, very unusual, especially as a player," he says. "You know, to play 13 years with one team is quite an accomplishment. And then just staying within the organization also, over the years, is something special for me. Definitely, I've been very lucky. But I always believed you work for your luck."

Work has never been a problem for Stan Smyl, who came to the rink wearing his hard hat every day and who played as if every shift might be his last.

"If you look at how many nights he just worked and worked and worked and the team wasn't a winning team," says Glen Hanlon, who broke in with the Canucks at about the same time as Smyl and is now head coach of the Washington Capitals. "It's easy to do it when you're winning, but Stan just worked and worked

and worked, so how could you not admire that? He deserved to win a Stanley Cup. He really did."

Over those 13 NHL seasons Smyl scored 262 goals — most of which, he once cracked, came with "my butt in front of the goaltender" — and added 411 assists for 673 points. But he prides himself most on his consistency as a player over 896 NHL regular-season games.

"You know what?" he says.. "In the 13 years that I played [in Vancouver], I always felt like I had to prove myself at training camp. I never really believed I had a job and I went to training camp in that frame of mind every year. I don't think there was one year that I felt really comfortable or that I was here to stay."

Smyl left St. Paul when he was 13 years old, knowing he had to challenge himself if he wanted to make hockey a career. Friends of his played for the New Westminster Bruins of the Western Hockey League, so he tried out there.

"I look at my 13-year-old now and it is something that's kind of amazing," he says. "But I played so much hockey [as a kid] and really thought at that time that I wanted to see how good I could get and whether I could play at a high level. And I knew I wasn't going to get that in my hometown playing minor hockey ... I kind of hit it off from the start and never looked back."

Too young for the rigours of the WHL, Smyl was sent to Bellingham, Washington, where he spent two seasons and helped the Blazers to a B.C. Hockey League title in his second year. That spring, he was picked up by New Westminster for the Bruins' run to the Memorial Cup national major junior tournament.

Over three subsequent seasons with the Bruins, Smyl emerged as an impact player for legendary coach Ernie "Punch" McLean and his Bruins, who made it to the Memorial Cup each year, winning the national championship in Smyl's final two seasons.

Smyl's work ethic and dedication were at least partially instilled by McLean, who insisted that his players leave everything on the ice every night. Attention to detail and little things such as wearing suits and ties to the rink and sporting close-cropped haircuts when

*Stan Smyl is the only Vancouver Canuck to have his number — 12 — officially retired by the NHL club.* [Graphic Artists/HHOF]

*Stan "Steamer" Smyl posted seven straight seasons of at least 60 points and 100 penalty minutes. (Robert Shaver/HHOF)*

and, you know, I could never stretch myself any taller than that. But that's just the way it was and I believed in the work ethic and beating the guy across from me night after night. I think that had a lot to do with it, because I didn't have the skill quite as much as some of the other players at that age."

Playing junior in the Vancouver area also helped. Smyl was already well-known and well-liked by local fans and he and his Bruins teammates had gone to plenty of Canucks games, scrounging standing-room tickets to watch the NHL team in the Pacific Coliseum.

"I knew what the Canucks were about," he says, "and I strongly believed in myself that I could help them in certain areas of the game, so that was a bonus. I wasn't going to a strange city, I wasn't going to a city where people didn't know me as a player. So I felt very comfortable in that situation. I know a lot of players are intimidated when they go to other cities and in major cities like Philly and New York, but I felt very comfortable with my surroundings going into training camp."

Smyl, Fraser and talented Swedish centre Thomas Gradin all joined the Canucks at the same time. They were quickly thrown on a line by coach Harry Neale and the combination paid immediate dividends.

As a rookie, Smyl posted 14 goals and 38 points in 62 games. His numbers took off the next season, when he had 31 goals, 78 points and 204 penalty minutes to truly arrive as a Canucks star. It was the first of seven straight seasons when the dependable, rugged winger would score at least 60 points and collect at least 100 minutes in penalties.

He assumed the team's captaincy for the 1982 playoffs, after captain and defenceman Kevin McCarthy was injured and couldn't dress. Smyl held the "C" for eight more seasons.

"He was a born leader," says Harry Neale. "He was the heir apparent, when he got some experience, to be the captain of the team and he really personified what you'd call a perfect captain. He was popular with the players and leading by example was one of his skills. And yet he always had an ear and kind of a feeling and an outlook for the coach and his problems handling 20 players."

Smyl's best numbers came in the 1982-83 season, when he had a career-high 38 goals and 88 points. But he is likely best remembered for his all-out play leading the Canucks into the Stanley Cup finals the previous season. That was the highlight of his playing career as far as Steamer himself is concerned.

"I think as a player a lot of things stick in your mind — obviously, your first NHL goal, playing in your first NHL game, those sorts of little highlights," he says. "But the one that really sticks out the most for me is 1982 and I think because it was such a team effort from all of us to get to that level.

players from other junior teams were wearing the shaggy manes of the day also defined those Bruins as a team, as did their intimidating, roughhouse style on the ice.

"All those little things Punch made important off the ice came with us on the ice," Smyl says. "And the thing he really stressed is it's all about work ethic and to do it night after night. He could really get that out of a lot of players who were limited-skill-type players. He got the best out of them."

In his final year with New Westminster, Smyl piled up 29 goals, 76 points and an eye-opening 211 penalty minutes. But pro scouts considered the feisty right-winger's lack of size and skating speed a detriment and he wasn't selected by the hometown Canucks until the third round of the 1978 draft. Smyl went 40th overall, behind Billy Derlago, whom Vancouver took in the first round, and Curt Fraser, the team's second-round pick.

"Getting drafted in the third round by the Canucks, I had to prove myself all the time as a player," Smyl says. "Everyone was looking for six-foot players; I wasn't that size. I was five-[foot]-eight

*Captains Stan Smyl of the Canucks and Bob Gainey of the Montreal Canadiens were character players for their respective teams. (BCSHF)*

"There were some players who were a little bit better skilled than others, but we all knew that in the end the success we were going to have as a team is that we were a team that was going to have to outwork the other teams. One of the players from the Islanders told me a couple of years later, their coach had written on their board: 'You're meeting Vancouver. You better come here to work, because that team does work.' That was our label and that's the way we got success."

One could say the same thing for Stan Smyl, who has carried that work ethic to the coaching and management ranks, first as an assistant with the Canucks, later as head coach of farm teams at Syracuse, Kansas City and Winnipeg and now as director of player development. In overseeing the young players in the Canucks system, he is helping them to develop and deciding whether they should be kept on.

When asked whether he would have kept a fearless 5'8" winger with lots of heart and a catchy nickname, Smyl laughs. "I think I would say he's a little too small to play."

# HAROLD SNEPSTS

MANY OF THE hundreds of players who have skated for the Vancouver Canucks during the last 35 years possessed more talent than Harold John Snepsts. But few, if any, had a greater passion for the game than the big defenceman who played 781 games over 12 seasons during two separate stints in Vancouver. And few, if any, were more popular with fans or teammates than the Edmonton native with the rock-solid blue-collar work ethic.

"I think he was truly one of the big strongmen of the game," says fellow defenceman Paul Reinhart, who played both with and against Snepsts. "And when I say strongmen, I'm talking about how he played a good, strong game. He wasn't just a big, tough-guy fighter. He was a good, strong, honest player."

Snepsts believes he was given a chance to make it in the NHL because of the Philadelphia Flyers, who were busy attempting to beat up the rest of the league in the mid-1970s. He went to the Canucks as the 59th overall draft pick of 1974, after a second season with the junior Edmonton Oil Kings in which he had compiled 49 points and 239 penalty minutes.

"It was at that time when the Broad Street Bullies were trying to intimidate in the league and everybody was looking for someone to combat that," Snepsts says. "And I just happened to come at the right time."

He racked up 1,446 penalty minutes with the Canucks, so he certainly didn't shy away from the rough going. But he also worked hard to learn the tough trade of NHL blueliner. He used his 6'3" frame and his penchant for physical contact to his advantage, but he also mastered the art of defensive responsibility.

During his first 10 seasons with Vancouver, he was named the club's top defenceman four times. He represented the Canucks in the NHL All-Star Game in 1977 and 1982 and he was a central figure in the team's run to the 1982 Stanley Cup finals.

"The first time I played with Harold, the first thing he said to me was: 'If you can establish yourself as a reliable person in your own end as a defenceman, there will always be a job for you,'" says former teammate Doug Lidster, one of two other Canucks to be named the club's top defenceman on four separate occasions.

Snepsts remembers being overwhelmed by the idea of playing in the NHL when he was first drafted by the Canucks. But he quickly adjusted, playing 27 games for Vancouver in the 1974-75 season as the team stunned hockey observers by capturing the Smythe Division title and making the playoffs for the first time in the franchise's history.

"Being a real big hockey fan, I was in awe coming to the NHL," he recalls. "I used to read hockey books and magazines. Players like Gary Smith and Andre Boudrias and Leon Rochefort and Tracy Pratt — those were players who had been in the NHL for quite a while. And if you played in the NHL, I was in awe of you, and you didn't have to be a superstar. I felt that if you were in the league for a while, you were a star."

Goaltender Gary Smith, the undisputed star and free spirit of that 1974-75 Canucks team, remembers the rookie Snepsts a little differently.

"I knew Harold was going to be a good player the first day of training camp in Victoria," Smith told the Vancouver *Province* in 1992. "We had two practices that day and, after the first, we were walking back to the hotel and he was telling me where he played junior and stuff. When we got there, he went straight into the beer parlour. I knew anyone doing that after their first pro practice was going to be around a while."

Snepsts certainly was. He played 17 seasons with the Canucks, Minnesota North Stars, Detroit Red Wings and St. Louis Blues before retiring after the 1990-91 season, having wrung every last bit of potential out of his body.

He remains one of the most loved Canucks of all time, not only by fans but by his fellow players. Asked to name his most memorable teammate, forward Rick Blight didn't hesitate. "Definitely Snepstsy," he said. "He was a lot of fun to be around."

*Popular Canucks' defenceman Harold Snepsts is nailed by the St. Louis Blues' Harvey Bennett. Snepsts was never shy of the rough going.* (London Life-Portnoy/HHOF)

"He was a favourite and rightfully so," adds Lidster. "Everybody pulled for him because of his smile and his laugh. But he always instilled that pride and work ethic and respect for doing the right thing. That was another word that was big for him — respect. He was a guy who played within his limitations, within his abilities, and took pride in that."

Snepsts was a huge factor for Vancouver during the 1982 playoffs, when he played 17 games to help the Canucks reach the finals against the New York Islanders. The team had lost blueliners Rick Lanz, Kevin McCarthy and Jiri Bubla to injuries,

so the rest of the crew had to step up.

"There were times, I remember in Los Angeles, when there were three of us probably playing the last 10 minutes or more of the games," Snepsts says. "I lost about 15 pounds [during the 1982 playoffs]."

Unfortunately for Snepsts, he will be forever associated with an overtime giveaway in Game 1 of the finals against the Islanders, when he laid a would-be clearing pass on the stick of sniper Mike Bossy, who scored the game-winning goal with just two seconds left in the first extra session.

*Harold Snepsts came to Vancouver as the 59th overall pick in the 1974 draft.*
(O-Pee-Chee/HHOF)

"I was hurt [emotionally] when I left," he admits. "For the first part of my career, I was always insecure, thinking I was going to get cut or traded. That feeling probably lasted most of that 10 years, and I had just started getting comfortable that maybe I was going to play there my entire career in Vancouver when the trade happened. I was shocked.

"But in hindsight, probably it was the best thing they could have done. It lengthened my hockey career. Vancouver at the time was a struggling hockey club. And being up in age, I just got a new life going to a different place."

After one season with the North Stars and three with the Red Wings, Snepsts landed back in Vancouver, signing as an unrestricted free agent in 1988. He played two seasons in Vancouver before being shipped with Rich Sutter to the St. Louis Blues, where he skated for one more season before retiring.

One of the last NHL players to play without a helmet, Snepsts became a comforting, familiar sight for fans in the Pacific Coliseum over his career in Vancouver, giving them a thrill with his unique skating stride and dark hair flowing behind him whenever he found some open ice that let him move.

Not surprisingly, given his effect on teammates, Snepsts went into coaching following his playing days. He was a head coach in the International Hockey League and the Western Hockey League as well as an assistant with the Blues.

From 2000 to 2005 he worked for NHL Central Scouting, evaluating players across North America. Prior to the 2005-06 season, he was hired as an amateur scout by the Canucks. Snepsts lives in Vancouver. Why does he think he was so popular as a Canuck? "Passion," he says. "I just loved this game. I would just hope, maybe, that I showed that I cared about winning and losing and not for individual stats.

"And I think people can relate to kind of a blue-collar person."

The visiting Canucks had probably deserved to win that first game against the more talented Islanders. But after they lost it, the series lasted only three more games.

"They always talk about Harold's giveaway," says former Canucks broadcaster Jim Robson. "They don't say that he was tremendous in the playoffs that year. He played game after game and was great."

Snepsts' first stay in Vancouver lasted until June 1984, when he was traded to Minnesota for Al MacAdam. The deal came as an unpleasant surprise to the big defenceman, who had just begun to believe that he might spend his entire NHL career with the Canucks.

## Sniper Snepsts

*Harold Snepsts didn't score a lot of goals in his NHL career, finding the net just 38 times in 1,033 games. But he made the most of his opportunity on February 2, 1980, when he became the first Canuck defenceman ever to be awarded a penalty shot. Snepsts cashed in on the chance, scoring on Minnesota goaltender Gilles Meloche.*

*Shown here in pursuit of Chicago star Denis Savard, Harold Snepsts was a huge factor for the Canucks in the 1982 playoffs. (Paul Bereswill/HHOF)*

# PATRIK SUNDSTROM

HIS FORMER LINEMATE and roommate on the road describes Patrik Sundstrom as "very shy, very quiet." Nevertheless, the gifted Swedish centre's statistics spoke loudly during his time with the Canucks, when he skated alongside Tony Tanti on the team's most potent line.

Sundstrom still holds franchise records for most points by a centre: the 91 he recorded in 1983-84; most assists in a single game; and most points in a game. The latter two records came during a February 29 game in Pittsburgh in 1984, when he had one goal and six assists against the Penguins.

But that's not even his best one-night effort as a National Hockey Leaguer. The six-foot, 205-pound native of Skelleftea went one better as a member of the New Jersey Devils in an incredible eight-point game during the 1987-88 playoffs against the Washington Capitals. With his three goals and five assists that day, he shares the NHL single-game postseason record with Mario Lemieux.

"You have to be pretty lucky to score seven (or eight) points in one game," Sundstrom chuckles over the phone from Umea, Sweden, where he is now head of the school's hockey program.

Those who watched the smooth-skating Swede during his 10-season NHL career believe skill had much more to do with his success than luck. Vancouver was extremely fortunate, however, to pick him up for next to nothing, taking him in the ninth round, 175th overall, in the 1980 entry draft.

"Back then, to be honest, I didn't even know that I got drafted because it wasn't a big thing here in Europe," Sundstrom says.

He served a two-year hitch in the Swedish army and helped his country win its first world junior championship gold medal in the 1981 tournament. He remembers speaking with Canucks general manager Jake Milford after playing for silver-medal-winning Sweden in the 1981 world senior championships in Goteborg.

"They watched me play there and they talked to me a bit, but I told them I wanted to stay another year in Sweden," he recalls.

After playing for the fourth-place Swedish team in the 1982 world tournament in Finland, "we talked some more and I ended up in Vancouver."

Adjusting to the NHL wasn't difficult socially because the Canucks had five Swedes in the lineup and the 20-year-old Sundstrom had learned English in school.

"Looking back, I think the hardest thing to adjust to was the amount of games in the NHL," he says. "In Sweden, they only had about 36 games during the regular season. In the NHL, there were twice that many and all the travelling."

Still, it didn't take long for him to start feeling comfortable. Partway through the Swede's rookie year, Tony Tanti joined the Canucks in a trade with Chicago. The two men were quickly thrown together on a line, a combination that would turn out to be magical.

Sundstrom finished his rookie season with 23 goals and 46 points. The next year, playing with Tanti and often Tiger Williams, he exploded for career-highs of 38 goals, 53 assists and 91 points.

"He's very shy, very quiet," Tanti says of Sundstrom. "But he was so unselfish. He would way rather pass than shoot, which was great for me." Tanti scored 45 times the next season while skating with the talented Swede.

"Yeah, it felt good right away," Sundstrom recalls of the combination. "We had some kind of chemistry, I think. He had a good knack for getting open and I could get him the puck."

Sundstrom wasn't able to replicate those heady numbers later, but he did turn in 68-, 66- and 71-point seasons before being traded to the New Jersey Devils in a deal that would help shape the Canucks for their run to the 1994 Stanley Cup finals. Vancouver traded Sundstrom and two draft picks to the Devils on September 10, 1987, in exchange for goaltender Kirk McLean, forward Greg Adams and a second-round pick that turned out to be Leif Rohlin.

"It was a two-way feeling," Sundstrom says of the trade, "because I knew they were going to make changes in Vancouver. And coming to New Jersey, it was a young team and an upcoming team. And playing on the East Coast meant a lot less travelling.

"I wouldn't have minded to stay in Vancouver, but that's what happened, so ... I don't feel bad about it, because I had a good time in New Jersey, too."

*Swedish centre Patrik Sundstrom says the most difficult adjustment to playing in the NHL was the number of games per year.* (Robert Shaver/HHOF)

Sundstrom played parts of five seasons for the Devils and was named the team's most valuable player in 1988-89, when he had 69 points in 65 games. He also scored 20 points in the playoffs after his first season in New Jersey, when the Devils advanced to the Eastern Conference finals before losing to Boston in a seven-game series.

Sundstrom decided to retire after being limited to 17 games for the Devils in the 1991-92 season due to a painful calcium deposit in a thigh. "I didn't even know if I could keep playing after that, so I decided to go back to my hometown and play there for a year or two and just to retire [from the NHL]."

Of his time with the Canucks he says, "It's tough to say exactly what was the highlight. But looking back now on my five years in Vancouver, I really enjoyed it and I had a really good time there."

He now works with young hockey players between ages 13 and 17 through the school program in Umea.

# TONY TANTI

THE FATHER IMMIGRATED to Canada from the Mediterranean country of Malta never having seen a snowflake. The first-generation-Canadian son would become proficient at the quintessential Canadian winter sport.

At age 16 Tony Tanti chose to pursue hockey over soccer, the game preferred by his father and uncle. It was a fortunate decision for him and for the Canucks, who benefited from the diminutive winger's scoring touch and hockey sense during eight sparkling seasons in the 1980s.

Tanti grew up in Mississauga, Ontario, where his father worked at the Neilson's chocolate factory. As a youngster Tony idolized the Leafs and he would have loved to play professionally in Toronto, but instead he was drafted by the Chicago Black Hawks, who took him twelfth overall in 1981.

As a junior hockey rookie, the 5'9" Tanti had scored an eye-popping 81 goals for the Oshawa Generals to break the Ontario Hockey League record held by Wayne Gretzky. Over 154 major junior games, Tanti totalled an amazing 177 goals and 338 points.

In what remains one of his finest hockey memories, he scored his first NHL goal for Chicago against the Maple Leafs in Toronto, beating Mike Palmateer with a deke and shot to the top corner as his proud family watched from the stands in Maple Leaf Gardens.

But Tanti wasn't a Hawk for long. After appearing in just three regular-season NHL games and then playing for Canada in the world junior tournament, his rights were shipped to Vancouver on January 6, 1983, in exchange for veteran winger Curt Fraser.

"Chicago was going for the Cup and they had to trade one of their prospects and it happened to be me," Tanti says today.

The spring before, he had travelled with the Black Hawks as insurance against injury during the conference finals against the Canucks, so he was familiar with Vancouver. "We stayed down at the Westin Bayshore and I just thought: 'Oh my God, what a beautiful city this is.' I said I could live here any time — and the next year I was here."

The trade proved an excellent one for the Canucks and Tanti.

He finished his rookie season with 16 points in 39 games, providing a hint of what was to come.

"Even though I only played half that year, I had a lot of chances," he recalls. "I still remember hitting a lot of posts and always being around and getting a lot of chances — I just had to work on the finishing. So I came back the next year with a lot of confidence and the puck just started going in and it just kept going in."

It certainly did. Tanti burst into prominence during his sophomore NHL campaign by scoring a then team-record 45 goals in 1983-84 and adding 41 assists. That was just the first of five straight seasons in which he would hover around the 40-goal mark, cementing his place as one of the most prolific offensive players in Vancouver franchise history.

Tanti formed a terrific combination with quiet and gifted Swedish centre Patrik Sundstrom and the tenacious Dave "Tiger" Williams, who dug out the puck and provided physical support for his smaller linemates.

"Patrik was a playmaker — very, very, very unselfish," Tanti says. "Dave was a grinder and got the puck to us, so it was good combination. Really, I give credit to Patrik and to Tiger because they were the ones who were getting me the puck."

Fans gave plenty of credit to Tanti, naming him the Canucks' most exciting player in five consecutive seasons. Many of his goals came on tip-ins due to his deft hands and his ability to anticipate precisely where to be.

"I think a lot of it was just anticipation," he says now, "knowing where to be, trying to think ahead of the play and be where other guys aren't. I'd just go to the net and try to anticipate and either get rebounds, deflections or nice passes from Patrik or, of course, Tiger."

Tanti played parts of eight seasons with the Canucks before being traded to the Pittsburgh Penguins with Barry Pederson and Rod Buskas in return for Dan Quinn, Andrew McBain and Dave Capuano on January 8, 1990.

*Sniper Tony Tanti enjoyed five straight seasons in which he hovered around the 40-goal mark.* (Robert Shaver/HHOF)

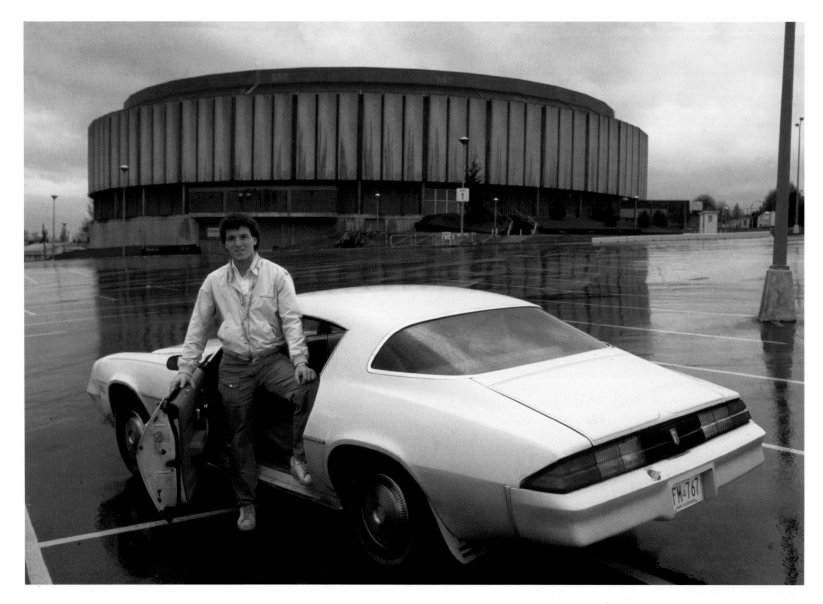

*Posed here with his car in front of the Pacific Coliseum, Tanti was a driving force for the mid-1980s Canucks.* (Paul Bereswill /HHOF)

"I didn't want to leave Vancouver, absolutely," Tanti notes. "But I always had a house here and I married a Vancouver girl so I knew I'd come back."

After injuries hampered him during parts of three seasons with the Penguins and Buffalo Sabres, he left the NHL in 1992 and headed overseas. He said goodbye to a big-league salary of about US$400,000 per year in the process, but the sacrifice was negligible. In Berlin, he made nearly US$300,000 tax-free and had to play far fewer games.

"I was the type of player who couldn't shy away from the body contact," he says of his reasons for leaving the NHL. "If you look at the penalty minutes during my career, they're also up there. It's just one of those things; I paid the price to score goals. After 10 or 12 years, it takes its toll on you.

"We had a young daughter who was three at the time. We just thought playing 30 or 40 games [in Europe] was a lot easier on your body. And at that time NHL salaries weren't nearly what they are now. We just wanted to see the world. We had young kids and it was a nice opportunity."

After the 1998 season Tanti and his family returned to West Vancouver, where he now operates a flooring company.

"Once I retired, I didn't even follow hockey for a couple of years," he says. "In the last [few] years I've become a fan again, playing and going to games."

His parents were both born in Hamrun, Malta, and his uncle was a member of the Maltese national soccer team. Tony Tanti remains the only person of Maltese descent to play in the NHL, a distinction in which he takes great pride.

## For the Record:

*Only twice in 35 years has a Canuck lineup included eight or more players who scored at least 20 goals in the season. Both of those teams played in the 1980s, and Stan Smyl and Thomas Gradin recorded more than 20 goals on both.*

*Reaching that mark for the 1980-81 Canucks, who lost in the opening round of the playoffs that spring, were Smyl, Gradin, Tiger Williams, Bobby Schmautz, Ivan Boldirev, Curt Fraser, Darcy Rota and Per-Olov Brasar.*

*Hitting the milestone for the 1984-85 Canucks were Smyl, Gradin, Tony Tanti, Patrik Sundstrom, Peter McNab, Moe Lemay, Cam Neely, Blair MacDonald and Petri Skriko. Despite spreading around the scoring nicely, that lineup did not make the postseason.*

*Although only 5'9", Tony Tanti was a pure scorer. He had 81 goals for the junior Oshawa Generals. (David Klutho/HHOF)*

131

# TIGER WILLIAMS

JUST BEFORE Dave "Tiger" Williams' first game as a member of the Toronto Maple Leafs in January 1975, he was given a piece of advice by the legendary Francis "King" Clancy.

"Don't be coming into this league as a crusher and think you're a rusher and then end up being an usher," Clancy told the 20-year-old forward from Weyburn, Saskatchewan.

Williams took the advice to heart. He never forgot that it was toughness, a willingness to scrap and get physical, that earned him his shot in the NHL.

Fourteen seasons and 962 games later, Williams retired as the NHL's all-time leader in penalty minutes with 3,966. Sure, he could score when given the opportunity, as shown by the career-high 35 goals he potted for the Canucks in 1980-81, but he was always ready to go to war.

"It's so true, that statement," Williams says of Clancy's advice. "Because that's what happens to guys. As they mature as players and get used to the pro lifestyle, they kind of want to look like their bank book. They want to be a little more dignified, but there's no job for them in that area.

"They forget what got them there and they're not around very long."

Williams was part of a different tough-guy era in the NHL. He and players such as Al Secord, Dave Semenko, Terry O'Reilly and Bob Probert carried a regular shift along with their duties as club policemen.

"It's changed a little bit lately, because guys now, that's all they ever do, [fight,]" he says. "You think of all the guys who play that same role today — all of them, on 30 teams — they don't score 30 goals [combined]."

Williams was a rare player who proved he could fight as well as score when given the opportunity. As a junior with the Swift Current Broncos, he compiled back-to-back seasons of 100-plus points playing on a line with future Islanders star Bryan Trottier while racking up 310 penalty minutes in his final year alone.

That was enough for the Leafs to take him in the second round, 31st overall, of the 1974 NHL draft. After 39 games with the Oklahoma City Blazers of the Central Hockey League, Williams made the jump to the Leafs and never looked back.

He averaged 20 goals and 295 penalty minutes over five full seasons with Toronto before being traded to Vancouver, with Jerry Butler, for Rick Vaive and Bill Derlago in February 1980.

"As a team, the Leafs [afterward] were in the tank for four years, five years, which is really unfortunate," Williams says of the fallout from the trade. "And out here [in Vancouver], we probably did a little bit better than they expected us to do."

No kidding. In his first full season with the Canucks, Williams led the team in scoring with 35 goals and finished with 62 points, while still compiling 343 penalty minutes. He became the first Vancouver player voted to start in an NHL All-Star Game, getting the chance to skate on a line with Wayne Gretzky and Mike Bossy.

The additional grit provided by Williams was a big contributor to the Canucks' much-improved team performance, as well. After the team lost in the first round of the playoffs in his initial season in Vancouver, he contributed 10 points and 116 penalty minutes in 17 playoff games as they advanced to the 1982 Stanley Cup finals.

Williams' overtime goal won the second game of the opening-round series against Calgary in those 1982 playoffs. He added the series-clinching goal as the Canucks got past the Flames in three straight.

"We really improved from the first game I played here to the last game," he recalls. "We really improved our character base. And during the '80s here in Vancouver, that was their strength as a franchise — character. That's proven out 10 and 20 years later by the accomplishments of those individuals, what they do in their lives now."

Williams never again approached the points production he had enjoyed during his first two seasons as a Canuck and, after two more years, he was dealt to Detroit. During the previous off-season,

*Rugged Tiger Williams added plenty of grit, character and some timely scoring to the 1982 Canucks' playoff drive.* (Robert Shaver/HHOF)

## Riding High

*Hockey lore has it that Dave "Tiger" Williams routinely rode his hockey stick like a wild stallion down the ice after scoring big goals. But Williams says he actually did that as a pro only once, after scoring for the Canucks in his first game back in Toronto after being traded by the Leafs to Vancouver. "It's just perception that I did it all the time."*

## For the Record:

*The Canucks of the 1980s had their share of tough players, evident by the fact that four of the franchise's top five all-time career penalty leaders played during that decade.*

*Gino Odjick, who skated in Vancouver in the 1990s, leads the penalty parade with 2,127 career minutes as a Canuck, but players from the 1980s occupy the next four spots, led by defenceman Garth Butcher at number 2 overall with 1,668 minutes.*

*Longtime Canuck captain Stan Smyl sits at number 3 with 1,556 minutes, Harold Snepsts is fourth at 1,446 and Tiger Williams fifth at 1,324.*

*Forward Tiger Williams retired as the NHL's all-time penalty-minutes leader with 3,966 in 962 games. (Robert Shaver/HHOF)*

he had told Canucks general manager Harry Neale that incoming coach Bill LaForge would be a disaster and that he didn't want to play for the man. With the trade, he didn't have to.

After playing less than a season with the Red Wings, he was traded to Los Angeles, where he enjoyed two full seasons with the Kings before being sent to Hartford, a team he says "was the exact reason why some people shouldn't be allowed to have franchises." He retired in 1988 after scoring 241 goals and 513 points over 962 games.

Williams learned his hockey in the south Saskatchewan town of Weyburn, where the value of doing what your team needed most was instilled in him. He was given the fitting nickname "Tiger" by a minor-hockey coach when the boy was just five years old.

"The way that we were brought up to think was: If you're the best man for it, then do the job, and it doesn't amount to any more than that," he says. "We were taught that bullshit, and some of us bought into it."

At 5'11" and 190 pounds, Williams wasn't big even by the standards of the day. But he was fearless and he knew being a tough guy was a service he was capable of providing.

"Does anybody want that job?" he asks today. "Anybody who says yes, you know the guy's an idiot. You just do what you do. And then again, you get in that lane and you better stay in that lane, or you won't be in any lane."

Asked if he considers his 35-goal season the best of his career, Williams offers an emphatic no. "It just becomes the way [your team] plays you," he says. "And as a player, the only things you have control over are two things: your mental state of mind and your physical condition ... So, if they put you in an offensive situation and you respond, you'd hope that they'd keep you there.

"With a lot of great players, you'll always hear the knock, 'Well, defensively, he's not any good.' Do you know why? Because he doesn't want it to be known that he's any good at it. It's by design.

"But for other guys, that's not the way they are. If they're asked to do something, they just do it. But unfortunately, they get pigeonholed and they stay there forever."

Although he earned his reputation as a tough guy, those who know Williams will tell you there's more to him than that. "Dave is really hard on the outside," says Tony Tanti, who benefited from Williams' protective nature, particularly during road games. "But once you got to know him and once you stood up to Dave, then Dave had more respect for you.

"Dave and I became good friends and we're still good friends. On the inside, he's a really, really good guy. It's just that's Tiger Williams. That's the way he's perceived and he's made a living out of it and he's just a great guy."

*Dave "Tiger" Williams liked to mix it up, but he also had a team-high 35 goals in 1980–81. (Robert Shaver/HHOF)*

Williams has fashioned a successful post-hockey career; he is heavily involved in the oil and gas development business in the Northwest Territories and northern British Columbia and has widespread logging interests across B.C. He lives in West Vancouver.

He says he enjoyed playing in Toronto, Vancouver, Detroit and Los Angeles, but as to which team he identifies with in retirement, "It's like my kids say to me: 'Well, which one do you love more?' What is the answer?

"My perfect scenario is to have Toronto and Vancouver be in the finals and the team that just does everything consistently better wins; whether it is Toronto or Vancouver I wouldn't be disappointed, because I love my Canucks and I love my Leafs."

# TOWEL POWER

*British Columbia embraced a pack of underdogs with a passion for hard work*

## by Tony Gallagher

*"The artist is nothing without the gift, but the gift is nothing without work."*

THE WORDS OF French novelist Emile Zola sum up at least part of the story of the very successful 1981-82 edition of the Canucks. The word "artist" may be stretching things a little, and only Thomas Gradin, Jiri Bubla and the late Ivan Hlinka might be considered gifted, but over a bizarre season this team certainly developed a passion for hard work.

This was the team that began the white-towel waving and perfected the art of relying on a brilliant goaltender while waiting for scoring opportunities. This was the team that flushed out the true passion the city of Vancouver has for its professional hockey club, the team that spurred normally docile citizens to show what the game meant to them.

Initially this was a team coached by Harry Neale; it was known all season that he would succeed Jake Milford that summer as general manager. When Neale was suspended, during the long playoff run it was assistant coach Roger Neilson who directed from behind the bench. It was Neilson whose droll waving of a white towel drove Canucks fans into a frenzy.

This season had begun and appeared to be continuing to go pretty much the way the previous 11 NHL seasons had gone for this hapless franchise: poorly. In an era when only the blind and lame didn't make the watered-down NHL playoffs, this collection of players was expected to finish well down the overall standings, play their one round and depart without a whimper in their usual manner.

But one night, late in the season, something happened to this group that caused them to come together like no previous Vancouver club had managed, and it was triggered by Dave "Tiger" Williams in Quebec City. A man who a year earlier had referred to fans of the Montreal Canadiens as "Frogs," Williams was anything but popular in the beautiful city along the St. Lawrence. And when during the third period he began to rough up the Nordiques' legendary star Peter Stastny along the boards, it was too much for a fan named Pierre Fournell to stomach. He reached over the glass

and took a couple of pokes at Williams, who was by then being pinned by Wilf Paiement near the Vancouver bench.

Coach Neale decided his player needed help and waded into the stands to halt such fan interference. Not to be outdone, players Doug Halward, Curt Fraser and, you guessed it, Marc Crawford followed their coach into the stands and, by the time the NHL had finished its kangaroo court, Neale was suspended for 10 games, leading to one of his many great quotes over the years: "I guess I should have hit the referee instead," he said, referring to the fact that Philly's Paul Holmgren had hit referee Andy van Hellemond and received just a five-game suspension.

Enter Neilson, beginning one of the greatest stretches in Canuck hockey history. The team won 10 of its last 12 games and smoked the Calgary Flames in three straight playoff contests, essentially winning the series in the first eight seconds. In the opening game Gradin made a great play to Stan Smyl, who scored and, at the faceoff following the goal, Calgary's Willi Plett squared off with Fraser, who with one punch deflated the entire Flames team by knocking their enforcer right off his feet, to the delight of Vancouver fans.

Williams, whose mischief had led to Neilson's elevation to head coach, scored the winning goal in overtime in Game 2 and a second game winner in Game 3 to clinch the best-of-five opening series.

Throughout the playoffs, "King" Richard Brodeur was brilliant in goal for Vancouver. The Canucks also benefited from one of the greatest NHL comebacks of all time, the so-called "Miracle on Manchester" in the first round of the playoffs, when the Los Angeles Kings in their LA Forum on Manchester stunned the up-and-coming Edmonton Oilers. The Oilers were tough foes who later would win five Stanley Cups, so the Kings were spent by the time they were pitted against the Canucks in Round 2. Vancouver trampled them in five games despite a string of injuries on the Canucks' defence. With Bubla, Halward, Rick Lanz and Kevin McCarthy hurt, the "Four Horsemen" Lars Lindgren, Neil Belland, Colin Campbell and the legendary Harold Snepsts played almost the entire series.

Brodeur, the portly goaltender who was unshakeable

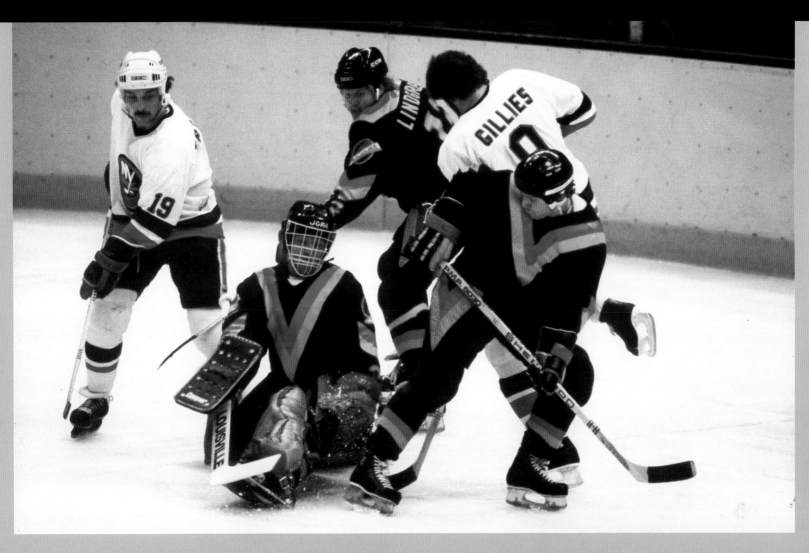

Goaltender Richard Brodeur found himself plenty busy during the 1982 Stanley Cup final against the Islanders. (Paul Bereswill/HHOF)

throughout, spawned one of the great fan-held signs during the playoffs; it borrowed from an old song to read HE AIN'T HEAVY, HE'S R. BRODEUR.

The masked man from Longueuil saved his greatest performance for Game 1 of the semifinals at the old Chicago Stadium. That night he made 46 saves, at least 20 of them otherwise certain goals, with Jim Nill scoring in double overtime to win it 2-1 and get the Canucks off and rolling. In Game 2, the Black Hawks roared back to tie the series on some calls by referee Bob Myers that Vancouver didn't think were appropriate, and in the third period Neilson picked up a towel from the bench, stuck it on the butt end of Gerry Minor's stick and hoisted it overhead in mock surrender.

Myers flew into a rage and so did the league. Neilson was fined US$1,000 but he had set towel sales sizzling, the fans waving them like crazy when the series returned to Vancouver. Thus one of the better NHL traditions, which has spread to many other cities, was born.

That first Chicago loss was a killer to the Hawks and they fell in five games, the Canucks winning the series in Chicago and going straight to Long Island to face the vaunted Stanley Cup-defending Islanders in the final.

The first game was close, but Mike Bossy ended up scoring on

the famed Snepsts giveaway at 19:58 of overtime. The over-matched Canucks were thrown into a skid from which they could not recover. They lost again in New York and flew back trailing in the series 2-0, but they were met by thousands of fans at the airport in one of the greatest outpourings of emotion in Vancouver sporting history.

A Stanley Cup final game had not been played in Vancouver since 1925, and when a local funeral parlour sign read GO CANUCKS GO, ISLANDERS DROP DEAD you could understand even this darker enthusiasm. Alas, the Canucks were finished off in four straight, with Islander sniper Bossy scoring seven goals in the final series alone to tie the NHL record held by Jean Beliveau, winning the Smythe Trophy as playoff MVP in the bargain.

The loss did nothing to dampen Vancouver's enthusiasm for this team, lavished as it was with the gift of embracing hard work. Thousands of fans lined the streets for a parade sponsored by the city, prompting captain Smyl to say: "We didn't think anyone would come to this parade."

They've been coming ever since.

*Tony Gallagher is a sports columnist for the Vancouver* Province *newspaper. He has covered the Canucks for more than three decades.*

# the **roaring nineties**

O f the Vancouver Canucks' first three decades in the NHL, the 1990s were easily the
most successful. The decade began with the hope of general manager and head coach
Pat Quinn's rebuilding effort and ended as the seeds of another Canuck era were being care-
fully sowed by Brian Burke.

Five times during the '90s, Vancouver finished with a .500 or

better record. If that does not seem overly impressive, consider

the team's history: in the 1970s and 1980s combined,

the Canucks posted a grand total of two winning seasons.

Perhaps more important, Quinn's Canucks made the

playoffs in each of the first six seasons of the '90s,

four times winning at least one postseason series.

And in the spring of 1994 they made their second

trip to the Stanley Cup finals in franchise history,

coming just short of winning it all against the

New York Rangers.

Facing page: *An exhausted Trevor Linden and Kirk McLean embrace after a game
in the memorable 1994 Stanley Cup playoffs.* (Doug MacLellan/HHOF)

Above: *Pavel Bure and Jyrki Lumme were key players for the Canucks of the early
1990s.* (BCSHF)

*After fan support dipped in the late-1980s, Pat Quinn's leadership provided something more to cheer for in the early 1990s.* [David Klutho/HHOF]

After taking over as "superboss" in 1987, Quinn quickly began remaking the Canucks, mostly through trades but also through two key draft picks — the 1988 selection of Trevor Linden, second overall, from the Medicine Hat Tigers and the drafting of Russian star Pavel Bure with the 113th pick one year later. Other core players brought in by Quinn through various trades or other means included Jyrki Lumme, Dave Babych, Dana Murzyn, Kirk McLean, Gerald Diduck, Greg Adams, Geoff Courtnall and Cliff Ronning.

The rebuilding effort paid off with a dramatic improvement in the standings between the 1990-91 season, when the Canucks finished at 28-43-9, and the following winter, when they sported a sparkling 42-26-12 record.

The Canucks won the Smythe Division regular-season title in 1991-92 and again in 1992-93, when they finished with a franchise-record 46-29-9 mark. Overnight, or so it seemed, they had gone from hockey's outhouse to the penthouse.

"During my first year we probably changed at least 10 guys on the team," recalls defenceman Jyrki Lumme, whom Quinn obtained from Montreal in 1990. "It was kind of weird. We all just kind of came together and, all of a sudden, we had such a fun time off the ice and then obviously on the ice we started to play better. Those three, four years we had from 1992 to 1994 or 1995, it was a blast."

Those Canuck teams played for each other, with nobody willing to let down the teammate beside them or their general manager. Defenceman Robert Dirk, who moved to the Canucks from the St. Louis Blues along with Courtnall, Sergio Momesso and Ronning in March 1991, remembers a common feeling in that newly assembled group: everybody had something to prove.

"The way we looked at it is, we were all sort of cast-offs that other teams didn't want and it brought us together," Dirk says. "We all brought something to the table and you threw it into the pot and it made a good stew."

While the stew simmered nicely for a couple of regular seasons, the real spice for hungry fans came in 1994, when the Canucks went on their greatest playoff run. After snoozing through a surprisingly lacklustre regular season in which they finished barely above .500 at 41-40-3, they became the springtime darlings of the NHL for the second time in their history.

That magic spring very nearly didn't happen, however. After beating Calgary in their first-round series opener at the Saddledome, the Canucks dropped three straight to the Flames and their sizzling goaltender, Mike Vernon. Calgary headed home for Game 5 needing just one win to eliminate Vancouver.

But that one win proved elusive for the Flames. In Game 5, Geoff Courtnall sped down the left wing and fired home the winner over the outstretched glove of Vernon just over seven minutes into the extra session to keep the Canucks alive. In Game 6, Vancouver twice overcame Calgary leads to once again force overtime. Late in the extra session the Flames were penalized for having too many men on the ice and Vancouver responded with Trevor Linden backhanding home a rebound on the power play.

That set up Game 7, another contest in which the Cardiac Canucks had to engineer a dramatic comeback. Trailing 3-2 late in the third period, Greg Adams tied it up for Vancouver with a backhander. In overtime, goaltender Kirk McLean made what still stands as arguably the greatest save in Canuck history when he slid over on both pads to foil Robert Reichel, who had been staring at an open net after being set up on a rush by Theo Fleury.

Less than three minutes into the second overtime, Bure completed the Canucks' stunning series comeback by taking a perfect breakaway pass from defenceman Jeff Brown, going in alone on Vernon and scoring with a crafty deke.

Once back from the near dead, the Canucks took on the aura of a team of destiny.

"That year was kind of weird," recalls Sergio Momesso, a physical winger on that team. "We didn't play that well during

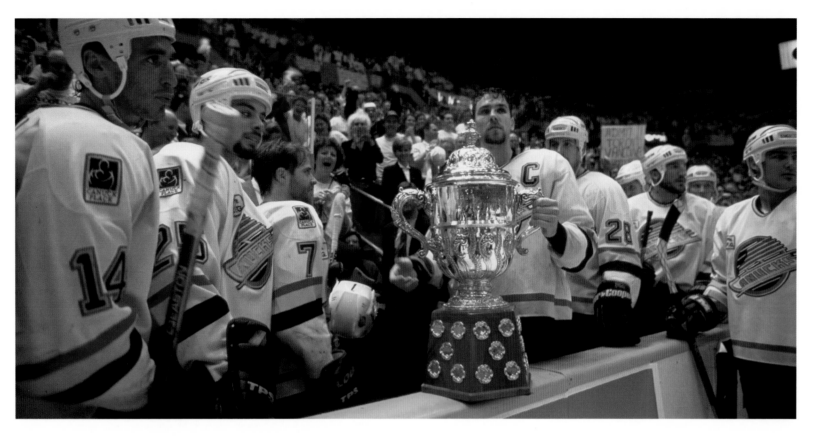

*Trevor Linden and the rest of the Canucks with the Clarence Campbell Bowl after winning the West in 1994.* (Chris Relke/HHOF)

the season and did the opposite [in the playoffs]. We'd had all the ingredients, as we were finishing first in our division for a couple of years, but we didn't really get to that next level in the playoffs. I think in '94 ... we knew that there are only so many chances that you get when you're going to be [kept] together. We thought: 'We can't just lose in the second round again.'"

The next two rounds proved easier for the Canucks than extinguishing the Flames had been. While Dallas and Toronto were no pushovers, Vancouver had clearly captured momentum in a bottle and needed only five games in each series to advance.

It dodged a second-round playoff bullet when the upstart San Jose Sharks stunned the favoured Detroit Red Wings in the first round, leaving Vancouver to play the Dallas Stars. The key in that series was Game 2 in Texas, when Bure seemed to set the tone by scoring twice and levelling Dallas tough guy Shane Churla with a high elbow.

Vancouver's third-round opponent was Toronto, and things got off to a rocky start when Peter Zezel gave the Leafs a 1-0 series lead with an overtime goal in the opener at Maple Leaf Gardens. But the Canucks then rolled off four straight victories, including two shutouts by a masterful McLean.

The Canucks clinched a spot in the final on home ice, but they needed to dip into double overtime in Game 5 against the Leafs to secure that honour. Seconds into that session, Greg Adams knocked in a rebound off defenceman Dave Babych's shot from the point to give Vancouver a 4-1 series victory.

The Stanley Cup final against New York was a classic, considered among the best in NHL history. The Rangers, led by charismatic veteran Mark Messier, were trying to end a 54-year Cup drought, while the Canucks were vying for their first sip from the silverware.

Vancouver drew first blood in the series, winning 3-2 in overtime in Madison Square Garden on another goal by the gutsy Adams, his second straight extra-time winner. Kirk McLean made 52 stops on the night in perhaps his best performance in an already outstanding playoff run.

New York took Game 2 by a 3-1 score, sending the series back to Vancouver, where fans in the Pacific Coliseum had been whipped into a white-towel-waving frenzy. The Rangers put a damper on the celebrations, however, winning 5-1 in Game 3 and 4-2 in Game 4 to head back to Manhattan with a seemingly commanding 3-1 series lead.

But the Canucks had come too far to fold. In New York they grabbed a 3-0 lead in Game 5, only to see the Rangers claw back to tie the score in the third. Goals by Bure and Courtnall, each their second of the game, powered Vancouver to a 6-3 win and a trip back to Vancouver for Game 6.

Buoyed by 16,150 fans and two goals by Courtnall, the Canucks prevailed 4-1 in Game 6, a strange contest that saw video review used three times, once to disallow a Rangers goal and twice to prove Vancouver goals in fact had crossed the line. The series was headed back to the Garden for Game 7.

The Canucks found themselves behind from the start, when Brian Leetch and Steve Larmer gave the Rangers a 2-0 first-period lead. Trevor Linden countered with a Herculean effort in which he wound his way through the entire New York lineup, but Messier's goal late in the second frame gave the Rangers a 3-1 lead heading into the third.

Once again, Linden put some life in the Canucks, scoring on a goalmouth power-play feed from Courtnall less than five minutes into the third. Vancouver continued to furiously press for the equalizer, but New York goaltender Mike Richter was brilliant. A shot from Canuck forward Nathan LaFayette that would have tied it with less than three minutes remaining rang tantalizingly off the post.

The Rangers hung on to the 3-2 lead until both the period and the game expired. They had captured the Cup, expunged their supposed curse and broken the hearts of the Canucks and thousands of B.C. hockey fans.

"It was a total deflation," recalls Kirk McLean. The goalie who had played so brilliantly in that playoff run was on the bench when the final horn sounded, after being pulled for the extra attacker.

"You have to sit and watch this go on, [New York] guys jumping around and the fans going nuts, and they have to get out of their little huddle so we can shake hands," McLean recalls. "You get into the locker room and I think you could have heard a pin drop. It was a pretty big downer and certain guys — Murray Craven, you know, that was his third chance at [the Cup] — you look at guys like that and you feel for them. It was a pretty quiet plane ride on the way home."

"It was a horrible feeling," adds Dave Babych of losing that seventh game. "Coming close, it's like kissing your sister ... We were so tired and beat — and I'm sure New York was also — that at first it's just sheer disappointment because you see those guys jumping around and, by the time you shake hands, all of a sudden the Stanley Cup's out and they're already starting to get ready to parade it around. It was pretty much a sickening feeling —

you're skating off the ice never to know what it would be like to hoist the Stanley Cup."

Fans in downtown Vancouver rioted after the game, putting a further damper on what was a crushing outcome for the province's hockey fans. But a more appreciative and mature crowd of several thousand greeted the Canucks when they arrived at the airport, and an estimated 45,000 people showed up at B.C. Place two days after Game 7 to properly honour the team that had captured their imagination for two exciting months.

By then, the spirits of many of the Canucks had improved. They were a relatively young, talented bunch and they would be back for another shot at the Cup, they reasoned. "I was young and naive then," recalls Gino Odjick. "I thought we'd get a chance to go back every year."

They didn't. The following year, an NHL labour lockout shortened the season to 48 games, Pat Quinn relinquished the coaching duties to Rick Ley and the Canucks didn't recapture their magic of the previous spring. Vancouver finished with a dead-even 18-18-12 record and bowed out rather quietly in the second round of the 1995 playoffs.

Moving into brand new General Motors Place the next year, the Canucks were desperate to improve and play a more offensive brand of hockey. Management brought in sniper Alex Mogilny from Buffalo, and the thought of having two talented Russians in the lineup made fans salivate. The big-ticket addition didn't make much difference, however. Mogilny potted 55 goals during his

*The mid-1990s Canucks had high hopes for their Russian duo of Alex Mogilny and Pavel Bure. (Chris Relke/HHOF)*

first year in Vancouver, but Bure played only 15 games due to a serious knee injury. The team struggled on the ice, prompting Quinn to fire Ley and go back behind the bench. Still, the Canucks slipped below .500, finished with a 32-35-15 record and lost in the first round of the playoffs.

The worst was yet to come. Quinn hired former national team program coach Tom Renney to go behind the bench for the 1996-97 season, but it didn't help. The Canucks went 35-40-7 and missed the playoffs for the first time in seven years.

By then, new owner John McCaw was growing restless watching his investment depreciate. Having failed to lure Wayne Gretzky to Vancouver, McCaw courted Mark Messier, landing the veteran free agent for a US$20-million deal over three years. The splashy move was meant to put Vancouver back into the upper echelon of the NHL, but it didn't. Messier turned in decent statistics during three seasons with the Canucks but, well past his prime and hampered by injuries and an organization that was floundering, he couldn't make the difference himself.

Chaos reigned during the 1997-98 season, Messier's first with the Canucks. With the team struggling out to a 3-11-2 start, Quinn seemed poised to fire Renney and once again assume the coaching duties. But on November 4 the owners stunned Canucks fans by instead firing Quinn. An era had come to an end.

"It was obviously devastating when Pat was fired," says Kirk McLean. "I can remember we were in Washington and we found out and it was like a kick in the groin. All of a sudden our leader, our mentor, is gone. So you kind of look at each other and you go: 'Okay, well, you know somebody's coming in to clean house.' So it was just a matter of time."

Indeed, it was. Renney lasted only another nine days and was replaced by "Iron" Mike Keenan, the hard-nosed coach who had guided Messier and the Rangers past Vancouver in the 1994 Stanley Cup final. The dismantling of the Canucks then swung into full gear.

Within a few months, core Canucks such as McLean, Odjick, Martin Gelinas and even captain Trevor Linden had been traded. But the slide continued: the Canucks finished 25-43-14 in 1997-98 and out of the playoffs for the second straight year.

Just when things seemed at their worst, another rebirth began. Brian Burke, a former protege of Pat Quinn who had helped build the early-'90s team, was hired as Vancouver president and general manager in June 1998. Keenan would survive as coach only until January before being replaced by Marc Crawford, a highly regarded coach who had won a Stanley Cup in 1996 with the Colorado Avalanche.

Things seemed more stable immediately, but the Canuck ship didn't get turned around right away. A messy holdout by superstar Pavel Bure during the 1998-99 season ended up with Burke trading him to Florida in January. The Canucks continued to struggle on the ice, finishing with a 23-47-12 record in 1998-99, their fourth straight winter of losing more games than they'd won and their third consecutive year out of the playoffs.

But the troubled franchise was on the upswing. The Canucks had landed key building blocks Ed Jovanovski and Todd Bertuzzi, and smooth Swede Markus Naslund was beginning to find his scoring touch.

The following season, Messier's last in Vancouver, the Canucks began turning the corner. They went on a tear at the end of the season, finishing 1999-2000 with a 30-29-15-8 record and narrowly missing a playoff berth. As a new decade dawned and with Burke running the team in decisive fashion, things were finally looking up again in Canuckville.

### BEST OF THE DECADE

This is an easy one. For a team that has had only two appearances in the Stanley Cup finals, the 1994 playoff run has to be judged the best of the 1990s and indeed the highwater mark in franchise history.

### WORST OF THE DECADE

There is a lot to choose from in this category, but the biggest disappointment was Pavel Bure's exit from Vancouver. The hockey heartthrob who gave fans two 60-goal seasons and countless thrills never gave them a good reason why he wanted to leave a city that loved him.

### TOP CANUCKS OF THE DECADE

**Goal:** Kirk McLean

**Defence:** Doug Lidster, Jyrki Lumme

**Right wing:** Pavel Bure

**Left wing:** Geoff Courtnall

**Centre:** Trevor Linden

# GREG ADAMS

GREG ADAMS scored a total of 375 NHL regular-season and playoff goals but none quite like the one that came in late May 1994 against the Toronto Maple Leafs.

When Adams backhanded a rebound past Toronto goaltender Felix Potvin early in double overtime, the emotion that poured out of Canucks fans shook the foundations of the Pacific Coliseum in Vancouver. Car horns and hollering echoed down Renfrew Street late into the night.

That goal capped a dramatic comeback from a three-goal deficit and sent the Canucks into the Stanley Cup final for only the second time in franchise history. It was the winner in Game 5 against the storied Leafs, and it moved the Canucks into the NHL's championship series against the New York Rangers.

"I think that one against Toronto was probably the biggest one I ever scored," Adams says now.

"It was start of the second overtime and I remember just being exhausted by then. The faceoff was at centre, and somehow we got it in their zone and I think Trevor [Linden] carried it in. He got the puck back to [Dave] Babych and Babych just took a shot on net. It wasn't a real hard shot, but the rebound came out and there was no one in front of me. I saw the rebound come straight out from Potvin and I just went to the net and I was able to backhand it by him."

Adams vividly remembers the dynamic feeling in the Coliseum after that goal. The building was literally shaking, and reporters trying to file stories on deadline were having trouble getting through on telephone lines.

"That whole playoff year, after our first series against Calgary, I've never been in a building that was more electrifying than what it was there," he says. "Every time we stepped on the ice to start a game, the noise level was amazing. It was so exciting. You couldn't help but just get goosebumps on the back of your neck."

That 1994 run, as it did for many of his teammates, marked the pinnacle of Greg Adams' pro hockey career. The 6'2", 185-pound left-winger was a major force for the Canucks that spring,

scoring six goals and adding 14 points in the playoffs as Vancouver advanced to Game 7 of the finals before falling to the Rangers.

Skating on the Canucks' top line with Linden and Pavel Bure, the rugged power forward known to teammates as "Gus" also scored the overtime winner in the opening game of the finals in New York.

"Without a doubt that was the most exciting time in my career," he recalls. "You know, we had a kind of character on that team. Other than Pavel, we had a bunch of guys who worked hard, who sacrificed, and it was just a contagious thing. One guy's out there throwing himself in front of slapshots, another guy's taking big hits for the win. And it's just something — there was no way you weren't going to do the same thing.

"It was a close team and it was probably the biggest time I felt where a team had come together, where I really understood what that meant."

He grew up in the picturesque Kootenay town of Nelson, British Columbia. He wasn't a big fan of the Canucks, though, preferring to cheer for the dynasty New York Islanders of the era and for his favourite NHL player, Bryan Trottier.

Adams played two seasons with the Kelowna Buckaroos of the B.C. Hockey League before accepting a scholarship to Northern Arizona University, a small independent National Collegiate Athletic Association school. The move wasn't as common then as it would be today for a B.C. hockey player with his eye on the NHL.

"I was more of a late developer, I guess," says Adams, who took business classes while at Northern Arizona. "That was part of the reason for my decision to go to college. A big part of the reason is I wanted to get my schooling. I wanted to have some kind of backup to hockey."

He played two seasons of college hockey and in his second, when he scored 44 times in 26 games, he caught the eye of the New Jersey Devils, who offered him a free-agent contract.

"I felt like this was an opportunity that I couldn't let go,

*Greg "Gus" Adams scored one of the biggest goals in Vancouver history to eliminate the Toronto Maple Leafs from the 1994 playoffs.* (David Klutho/HHOF)

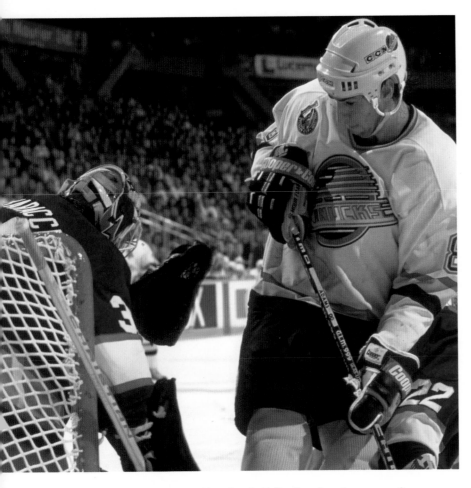

*Forward Greg Adams was shipped to the Dallas Stars less than a year after Vancouver's 1994 run to the Cup final.* (David Klutho/HHOF)

"I think the thing that stuck out in my mind was that Pat Quinn was there and I kind of had a feel for him, what kind of hockey person he was. He had coached me in the world championship two years before that, so I knew what kind of hockey man he was and knew that this was a place that had the opportunity, with him controlling it, to make things a lot better."

Adams produced instant dividends for the Canucks, scoring four times in his first game. That hot start led him to a career-high 36 goals and 40 assists in his opening season in Vancouver and a place in the NHL All-Star Game. In six full seasons with the club, he reached the 30-goal mark three times.

Despite being one of the team's core players, he was traded less than a year after Vancouver made its playoff run in 1994. He was sent to the Dallas Stars on April 7, 1995, in a deal that delivered speedster Russ Courtnall to the Canucks.

"That was the lockout year and we had kind of just got back [playing]," Adams says. "And to hear [trade] rumours, you know, in a short season like that, and after coming off a Stanley Cup contention, it was a bit of a shock.

"Being traded was a disappointment, but I had been there for eight years and maybe it was almost a good thing in a way to get out of Vancouver, because it had been a long time and it was kind of a breath of fresh air to start over for me. It was hard, though. At that time, I was very dejected and upset about being traded."

After more than three seasons with the Stars, Adams found himself on the move again. The Phoenix Coyotes signed him as a free agent in the fall of 1998 and he spent two seasons in the desert, before finishing his NHL career with a single season with the Florida Panthers.

After retiring from the NHL, Adams went to Germany and played a season in that country's elite league with the Frankfurt Lions, then quit the game for good in 2003.

He lives in the Victoria area, where he is one of several former hockey players who are partners in the Bear Mountain golf course and housing development.

because I probably wouldn't have gotten that opportunity again," he says of the decision to leave school.

He made the most of his chance, splitting his first pro season between the Devils and their American Hockey League affiliate Maine Mariners. He joined the Devils full-time the next season and had an impressive 35-goal, 42-assist campaign.

After one more season in New Jersey, Adams was initially disappointed to learn that he had been packaged with goaltender Kirk McLean in a trade to the Canucks.

"I had a bunch of good friends in New Jersey and I felt comfortable there," he says. "I had had personal success, so being traded, I really didn't know how to take it. You know, you feel like someone doesn't want you, but on the other hand another team does. But your first reaction is: 'Why don't they want me here?'

"After a day or so, when things settled down and I realized I was coming as close to home as I can get, I was really excited and my family were excited as well."

Although he was going from one struggling franchise to another, the leadership in Vancouver was reassuring to the 24-year-old.

*Greg Adams describes the 1994 Stanley Cup playoff run as the most exciting time of his NHL career.* (O-Pee-Chee/HHOF)

# DAVE BABYCH

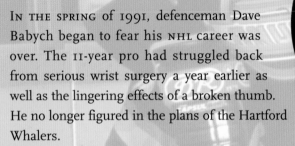

IN THE SPRING of 1991, defenceman Dave Babych began to fear his NHL career was over. The 11-year pro had struggled back from serious wrist surgery a year earlier as well as the lingering effects of a broken thumb. He no longer figured in the plans of the Hartford Whalers.

Babych was claimed by the Minnesota North Stars in a league dispersal draft. But the Stars quickly flipped him to the Vancouver Canucks, where his career was reborn.

"I had the wrist fused," he says. "The people in Hartford thought I was faking it but, you know, the doctor said it was the most serious wrist surgery that you can get other than chopping your hand off. They [Hartford] didn't want to know about it.

"Luckily, Pat Quinn took a chance on me and I ended up seven years in Vancouver."

The injury limited Babych to eight games in his final season with the Whalers but he bounced back in Vancouver, playing 75 games in 1991-92 and contributing five goals and 29 points. Previously an offensive-minded defenceman, his game became more defence-oriented and he proved to be a steady, veteran component on a rising team.

Today he says the injury was partially responsible for the change in playing style. "You couldn't stickhandle the same way, you couldn't move the puck the same way, you couldn't shoot the same way. So you knew if you didn't change your game you were kind of hooped.

"I was excited [about going to Vancouver]. I mean, I was excited to go anywhere, because the year before, going through an injury and just kind of sitting out most of the year and not getting a good feeling from the management in Hartford because of what their thoughts were ... I knew something was going to change, and I didn't know if it was going to end my career or not. So just to get another opportunity, it worked out great."

The big defenceman with the trademark bushy moustache went on to play seven seasons with the Canucks, including a 32-point campaign in 1993-94. In the playoffs that season he played all 24 games, scoring three goals and adding five assists as the Canucks reached the 1994 Stanley Cup finals. While in Vancouver he formed a reliable defensive pairing with Gerald Diduck.

"Pat [Quinn] basically told me: 'Babs, I don't care if you get a point or score a goal. I really don't care. I just want you to play solid hockey.' Of course, I threw in a few points here and there, but we had such a strong defensive corps at that time that anyone could score at any time.

"Maybe old Robert Dirk, he might not have been as good around the net as some of the other guys," Babych laughs, "but it was such a solid group that everyone could contribute in a lot of ways. That's why we ended up having such a good team."

He grew up in Edmonton with his brother Wayne, who was three years older. Both were good enough hockey players to carve out lengthy NHL careers, and they played together in Hartford for a little more than one season.

Dave had been a standout junior defenceman with the Portland Winter Hawks, recording 79- and 82-point efforts in two full Western Hockey League seasons. Scouts loved his 6'2", 220-pound frame and his skating and offensive abilities enough that he went second overall in the 1980 NHL draft, to the Winnipeg Jets.

Babych remembers going to Winnipeg to sign his first contract and being asked by the coaching and scouting staff how he felt about going to training camp.

"I'm nervous, I just hope I make the team," the 19-year-old Babych answered.

"If you don't make the team, we're all f——in' fired," came the reply.

He made the team, and it didn't take him long to become a standout with the Jets. In just his second NHL season, he posted a team-high 61 assists on his way to a career-best 74-point season. He represented Winnipeg in the NHL All-Star Game that winter and the next. After a 44-point season, he posted four straight campaigns of at least 57 points.

*A wrist injury prompted Dave Babych to switch from being an offensive-minded defenceman to more of a stay-at-home type.* (Chris Relke/HHOF)

Traded to Hartford in November 1985, he played parts of six seasons before winding up in Vancouver. After seven seasons with the Canucks, he was part of Mike Keenan's house-cleaning effort in 1998, when he was traded to the Philadelphia Flyers.

"I knew it was coming," Babych says now. "Keenan called me in about a month before the deadline and said: 'If we don't make the playoffs, you're out of here. We're getting rid of all you old buggers.'

"I know he liked me," adds Babych, who saw a lot of ice time under Keenan. "He just had a different way of showing it ... He would never make you feel comfortable. He just didn't know the proper way of telling people nicely. And you know what, I learned a lot from him of what *not* to do. But I did learn a lot from the guy."

Babych played parts of two seasons with the Flyers, his ice time severely curtailed by a broken foot that wasn't properly diagnosed

at the time by Philadelphia. Traded to Los Angeles in March 1999, he played eight games for the Kings before retiring from the NHL.

Two years later he sued the Flyers for failing to properly inform either him or the Kings of the broken foot. In October 2002 he was awarded US$1.37 million in damages for lost wages and pain and suffering.

"I had no choice," he says of the lawsuit. "What do you teach your kids if you don't stick up for yourself?"

Still bothered by the foot, he believes that the legal action may have prevented him from getting coaching work in the tight-knit NHL fraternity.

"I would like to [coach]," he says. "But my first inquiries weren't too [welcomed] and I think it's because of the lawsuit. And that's fine. There will come a time. I'm not holding my breath for an NHL job, but I would sure like to get involved, because I have a lot to offer."

# DONALD BRASHEAR

DURING HIS HALF-DOZEN NHL seasons in Vancouver, designated tough guy Donald Brashear left countless opponents lying vanquished on the ice. But his tenure with the Canucks will be remembered most for the night of February 21, 2000, when Brashear himself was the fallen victim of one of the ugliest assaults in pro hockey history.

With just three seconds remaining in a home game against Boston, Brashear was struck viciously across the head by the stick of Bruins enforcer Marty McSorley, who appeared to be attempting to provoke a fight with his Canuck counterpart.

The 6'2", 235-pound Brashear dropped to the ice, his helmet popped off and he was knocked out, suffering a serious concussion. The attack dominated the hockey world for several days and resulted in McSorley being charged with assault with a weapon. It was the first criminal charge in 12 years against an NHL player as a result of an on-ice incident.

McSorley would be convicted eight months later and face 18 months of probation, though with no jail time or criminal record. The 37-year-old, who had played 12 years in the NHL, never again skated in hockey's highest league.

After several weeks of recovery, Brashear rebounded to play 79 games and record 145 penalty minutes the following season with the Canucks. In court later, he testified to having no memory of McSorley's attack.

The incident had come near the end of Brashear's term with the Canucks, a stint that began in the fall of 1996 when he was traded to Vancouver by Montreal after a verbal dispute with Canadiens head coach Mario Tremblay during practice.

In Vancouver, Brashear blossomed as a tough guy who could wheel, particularly after longtime Canuck enforcer Gino Odjick was traded by Mike Keenan. In each of his first three seasons in Vancouver, Brashear recorded at least 200 penalty minutes, including a single-season franchise-record 372 in 1997-98. That total was one minute higher than the former team record, set by Odjick the previous season.

Brashear displayed some limited offensive skills while with the Canucks, earning a career-best 28 points in 2000-01 after the McSorley incident. But the following December he was traded to the Philadelphia Flyers for Jan Hlavac and an exchange of draft picks. He recorded 212 penalty minutes for the Flyers in 2003-04.

During the NHL labour dispute of 2004-05, Brashear signed for a reported Can$300,000 with Radio X of the Ligue Nord-Americaine de Hockey, a semi-pro Quebec circuit. However, in December 2004 he was suspended for the remainder of the season after repeatedly punching a Thetford Mines player who was already down.

Brashear made the NHL after a difficult upbringing. Born in Bedford, Indiana, he was the only one of three siblings given up to foster care by his mother. Shuttled to three different foster homes by age eight, the African-American youngster endured racial taunts while attending school in Quebec City, and that often led to fighting.

Hockey provided a path for the young man, who played junior with Longueuil and Verdun of the Quebec league before signing as a free agent with the Habs in 1992. "I was always just happiest when I was on the ice," he told the Philadelphia *Daily News* in a compelling 2003 feature story in which his generous work with foster children also was brought to light.

While Brashear might be happiest on the ice, one can't say the same for his opponents. During his first 11 NHL seasons he posted 1,999 penalty minutes, more than half of those while he was in a Vancouver uniform.

# JEFF BROWN

OFFENSIVE DEFENCEMAN Jeff Brown played a brief but pivotal role in the history of the Vancouver Canucks. A power-play specialist who also excelled at moving the puck and making the long pass out of his team's zone, Brown may well have been the extra ingredient that propelled the Canucks into the 1994 Stanley Cup finals.

The talented 6'2", 204-pound rearguard was obtained from the St. Louis Blues on March 21, 1994, along with Bret Hedican and Nathan LaFayette, by Vancouver general manager and coach Pat Quinn in exchange for centre Craig Janney. The trade was a timely one. Brown proved a huge contributor during that 1994 playoff run, with a gambling offensive style and capable power-play quarterbacking that helped him earn 15 points in 24 postseason games.

His most memorable play in a Vancouver uniform came in Game 7 of the opening round, when he sent speedster Pavel Bure in alone on Calgary goaltender Mike Vernon with a perfect tape-to-tape breakout, setting up the dramatic series winner in overtime.

In the following season, which was shortened by the NHL labour lockout, Brown posted 31 points while playing just 33 games. But after signing a lucrative contract with the Canucks, things began to sour for him in Vancouver. By the time the 1995-96 season began he found himself feuding with Rick Ley, the assistant who had taken over for Quinn behind the bench in the summer of 1994.

Initially, Brown criticized the Canucks for not moving more quickly to re-sign captain Trevor Linden. Then in October, after being benched by Ley for two straight games, Brown went public with his displeasure over the coach, saying the hard-nosed former NHL defenceman didn't have the guts to sit out other players on the roster if they were slumping.

The rift between Brown and Ley became too big to heal and on December 19, 1995, the Canucks dealt Brown to the Hartford Whalers for Frank Kucera and Jim Dowd in a trade that many thought offered far too little in exchange for the talented defenceman.

"I don't think they were the only two reasons [for the trade]," Brown told the Vancouver *Province* as he departed for Hartford. "I'm sure they contributed to it. It's cost me as a result."

Following the trade, Ley criticized Brown as not having played hard enough after signing his new deal with Vancouver. He added that Brown didn't possess the character required to play for the Canucks.

Although the Canucks now have an outstanding defensive rotation, they have never fully replaced the skill level and vision Brown provided as a point man on the power play.

Drafted by the Quebec Nordiques in 1984 from the Sudbury Wolves, Brown quickly developed into a solid offensive defenceman, posting 52 and 68 points in his second and third NHL seasons, respectively. After a trade to St. Louis in 1989, he continued to shine during five seasons with the Blues, including a career-best 78-point output in 1992-93. Following his time with the Canucks, Brown skated in Hartford, Raleigh, Toronto and Washington before retiring after the 1997-98 NHL season.

While with the Leafs in 1998, Brown was hit by a form of necrotizing fasciitis, or flesh-eating disease. Only the quick action of the Toronto training staff, who took him to a clinic rather than let him go back to his hotel room, enabled him to fully recover.

Over 747 NHL games, the native of Nepean, Ontario, compiled 583 points, including 154 goals.

# PAVEL BURE

IT HAD ALL THE ELEMENTS of a classic love story — a hint of mystery, a breathtaking beauty, a full-on infatuation, a serious communication breakdown and, finally, a messy divorce. Such was the tumultuous relationship between Pavel Bure and fans of the Vancouver Canucks.

The most exciting player ever to have donned the team's uniform was also the franchise's most misunderstood, and when "the Russian Rocket" finally blasted off in 1999 he left the province and its hockey faithful feeling like jilted lovers.

Bure was Vancouver's first professional-sports superstar, a player capable of lifting fans out of their seats on a nightly basis; a player who made the increasingly outrageous price of NHL game tickets seem worth it. Five times he was named the team's most exciting player, and he played in four NHL All-Star Games during his seven seasons with the Canucks.

That the Russian Rocket was a special player was evident from the first night he pulled on a Vancouver jersey. Bure didn't score a goal in his debut on November 5, 1991, a tie against the visiting Winnipeg Jets, but the 20-year-old rookie electrified the Pacific Coliseum with a trio of rushes that tantalized star-starved fans and teammates alike by providing an unmistakable hint of what he could deliver.

"You couldn't help but notice that he was going to be a great player," said former Canucks defenceman Dana Murzyn. "It wasn't so much surprising as it was really encouraging. It was like: 'Holy cow, look what else we have now!'"

Indeed, the Canucks had in Bure a player with blazing speed and the ability to cut and dipsy-doodle at nearly impossible angles. He wasn't big, at 5'10" and 180 pounds, but he was strong, with a goal scorer's sense and an edge to his game that reminded veteran hockey watchers of an earlier Rocket — Maurice Richard.

Bure "was probably the most explosive player I've ever played with," Murzyn says. "I've never seen anyone [else] who, in a three-stride start, would be as fast as he was going to be. He's the only player I've ever seen who could go at full steam and basically cut at a 90-degree angle to the net behind a guy."

Bure's incredible skills, speed and determination helped him capture the Calder Trophy as the NHL's rookie of the year in 1991-92. In doing so, he became the first Canuck ever to win a major postseason award, finishing the year with 34 goals and 26 assists in 65 games. His goal total was the most ever for a Canuck rookie and his point output equalled the previous team record set by Ivan Hlinka.

But the baby-faced Moscow native, whom Vancouver had stolen with the 113th overall choice in the 1989 NHL draft, was just getting started. Bure scored 60 goals in each of his second and third seasons, becoming the first Canuck to reach even the 50-goal barrier. As a sophomore in 1992-93, he finished with 110 points and an impressive plus-35 rating. En route to those gaudy numbers, Bure was voted as a starter for the NHL All-Star Game.

After a slower start to his third season, he turned in the most brilliant period of his Canucks career. During the final 40 games of the 1993-94 campaign he scored 40 times, including 19 goals in March alone. On the season, he finished fifth among NHL point-getters, higher than any player in Vancouver history to that point.

That superb finish set the scene for the 1994 playoffs, a time to shine for both Bure and the Canucks. In 24 postseason games, the 23-year-old right-winger had 16 goals. Among them was a crucial series winner against the Calgary Flames in Game 7 of the opening round.

If there were any doubters, Bure also proved himself physically during those playoffs by smoking Dallas Stars tough guy Shane Churla with a high elbow in Game 2 of the Western Conference semifinal. He was fined US$500 by the NHL for the hit, but it served notice that Bure was not a stereotypical soft European who could be pushed around.

By the time the 1993-94 NHL playoffs were over, he was widely recognized as one of the league's finest players. Most felt he was easily the NHL's most exciting performer. He collected 31 points in playoff prime time as the Canucks advanced to Game 7 of the Stanley Cup finals before losing to the New York Rangers.

*From his very first game as a Vancouver Canuck, fans and teammates knew Pavel Bure was a special player.* (Doug MacLellan/HHOF)

*Shown here flying through the air after being tripped up, Pavel Bure was one of the NHL's most exciting players to watch.* (Chris Relke/HHOF)

"I got caught watching him sometimes, some of the things he used to do out there," admits Greg Adams, who often played on the same line with Bure. "You know, he uses his imagination and he has the ability to make things happen out there where other players don't have that ability. It was exciting playing with him. You never knew what he was going to do."

Former Canucks tough guy Gino Odjick, who often rode shotgun for Bure during his years in Vancouver and became his closest friend on the team, said Bure's secret ingredient was conditioning. His father, Vladimir, a former Olympic medalist swimmer for Russia, was most responsible for that.

"Pavel told me a lot of times that he would have probably been a good NHLer, but working out extremely hard with his dad, six days a week, twice a day, brought him over the edge," Odjick says now. "It made him a great player ... What he had over everybody else was that extra step where he was able to get around a guy and get a shot or get a step on you and get a breakaway."

Bure had more than that, too. His angelic good looks and air of mystery made him a heartthrob. But beneath that choirboy exterior lay a fierce determination. He relied on his powerful legs and upper body strength to beat opponents, but he also relied on a will that, time and again, drew comparisons with the fiery Rocket Richard.

"I played with a lot of other players with great talent," says former teammate Jyrki Lumme. "I think the one thing with Pavel, though, is he wanted to score and he'd do anything to score. There are probably some other guys who might have better talent, but he worked so hard. I don't think there's another

guy in the league who works as hard as he did."

Or as former Canucks captain Stan Smyl once told the Vancouver *Sun:* "If you could zero in on him when he has an opportunity to go to the net, you would see the determination on his face. He smells blood."

In the spring of 1994, Bure and the Canucks appeared in the midst of a golden decade. But that point would prove to be the zenith for both the Russian Rocket and his first NHL team.

The following season, the NHL and its players slogged through a labour dispute and, once the season did resume, Bure did not find his form, putting up a respectable 43 points in 44 games but scoring just 20 times. Then, in 1995-96, he tore the anterior cruciate ligament in his right knee after being hit by Chicago's Steve Smith. The injury wiped out the rest of Bure's season.

A player who relied heavily on acceleration and cutting, he struggled to recover from the ligament damage and posted just 55 points in 63 games the following season. But he bounced back in 1997-98, with 51 goals and 90 points and, once again, Canuck fans fell in love.

This is where the relationship began to get messy, however. After leading Russia to a silver medal at the 1998 Winter Olympics in Nagano, where he was selected as the tournament's top forward, Bure stunned the Canucks and their fans by vowing in August not to play for the team again and demanding a trade. True to his word, he never wore a Vancouver uniform again, exiting the Canucks stage in as mysterious a fashion as he had entered.

Still, former teammates stick up for Bure, saying he was misread by angry fans who felt he had betrayed the city.

"I think he really was misunderstood," Murzyn says. "I really believe there's a huge adjustment for the Russian players and some of the European players when they come over. You're coming into a new environment, a new society and everything else. And I never questioned his heart as a teammate at all. I know he always played as hard as he could for us. And I think that people got so spoiled at how good he was that if he didn't have success they thought he wasn't trying."

Lumme says he "would play with [Bure] any time, anywhere."

"A lot of stuff happened [in Vancouver] because he's a really private guy," Lumme adds. "Especially when he first came over, his English wasn't the best. He never really felt comfortable doing all the stuff he had to do. And I think, just at the end, it just got to be too much. But he was definitely a good guy, a quiet guy who minds his own stuff. He's not a guy who goes in front of TV cameras and shows his house every week to a different paper. He's not that type of guy. And you know how media works: if you don't give them what they want, then they can get on a guy."

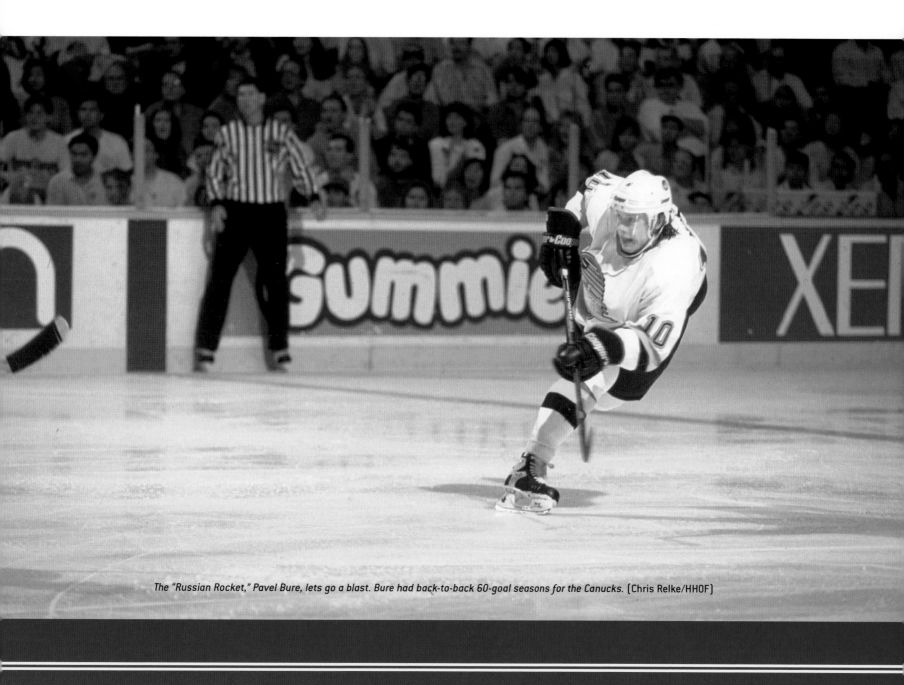

The "Russian Rocket," Pavel Bure, lets go a blast. Bure had back-to-back 60-goal seasons for the Canucks. (Chris Relke/HHOF)

## We Have Liftoff

One of the toughest goodbyes in Canucks history came on January 17, 1999, when general manager Brian Burke sent Pavel Bure, along with Bret Hedican, Brad Ference and a draft pick, to the Florida Panthers. The move ended a controversial five-month holdout during which "the Russian Rocket" refused to play for Vancouver and demanded a trade.

Bure never revealed a precise reason for wanting to leave Vancouver, although the Canucks were in upheaval at the time and he seemed to have grown weary of both losing and living in the fishbowl of a Canadian hockey city. He and the Canucks had also haggled over his salary during the lockout season and he wasn't fond of the heavy travel required of west coast teams.

The trade brought Vancouver a quality building block in return, with 22-year-old defenceman Ed Jovanovski coming to the Canucks as part of the package.

Although Bure managed 58- and 59-goal seasons with the Panthers, his post-Canuck career was plagued with recurring knee injuries. After two mediocre seasons with the New York Rangers, he retired in 2005 and served as general manager of the Russian team which finished fourth at the Turin Winter Olympics.

# BRIAN BURKE

IT'S DOUBTFUL that any general manager could have done more to help his NHL club than Brian Burke did during his half-dozen years at the helm of the Vancouver Canucks.

Burke inherited a mess when he took the job in the summer of 1998. The club's season-ticket base sat at only 7,000; the team was bleeding millions of dollars in financial losses a year; players and management from the 1994 Stanley Cup final team had been run out of town; and the organization seemed completely devoid of direction.

But Burke rolled up his sleeves and went to work, getting soaring costs under control by reducing payroll and increasing revenue. He tirelessly promoted the Canucks across B.C. and sold his ideas for the rebuilding of the franchise to both players and fans. He laid out a plan and he stuck by it while enduring and openly battling both skeptics and critics.

Within two seasons, the Canucks once again sported a winning record. By his fifth season, the team had been transformed into an NHL powerhouse with a franchise-record 104 points. Burke's accomplishments were noted outside Vancouver as well, as he was named NHL executive of the year by *The Sporting News* in 2001.

Best of all for the long-term security of NHL hockey in Vancouver, the Canucks were making money. After losing more than US$100 million over his first six seasons as a Canucks owner, John McCaw was finally realizing a profit.

In 2003-04, the Canucks were busy recording their second-straight 100-point season and their 86th consecutive sellout of GM Place. Not only that, but they were icing one of the NHL's most exciting lineups, playing an uptempo, offensive style and boasting stars such as Markus Naslund, Ed Jovanovski and Todd Bertuzzi, each of whom Burke had signed to long-term contracts.

It seemed a given that the Canucks ownership would sign their president and general manager — the man most credited with turning around a terrible situation — to a long-term deal himself.

But as the 2003-04 season dragged on, and with Burke's contract due to expire in the summer of 2004, no signing occurred.

In February, Orca Bay Sports and Entertainment chief executive officer Stan McCammon let it be known that the team would wait until the end of the season to decide Burke's future, effectively rendering him a lame-duck general manager.

Speculation raged that McCaw might actually do the unthinkable and jettison Burke. That was confirmed on May 3, when McCammon called a press conference to announce that Orca Bay would not be renewing Burke's contract, meaning that the team had essentially fired the most successful general manager it had ever employed.

Worse yet, nobody could provide a solid reason for Burke's dismissal, leading to the inevitable conclusion that an irresolvable rift had developed between Burke and McCaw and the Orca Bay management headed by McCammon.

"It's my belief that we're better served by looking at the future and saying we're prepared to move on," McCammon told reporters as he announced that Burke would not return.

"We're comfortable in our assessment. Obviously, Brian has done a good job and I think everybody would agree that this franchise has improved immeasurably both on-ice and off-ice. I think what we need to focus on isn't so much what we've done but where we believe we need to go. That's really what's at the heart of our analysis and what's at the root of the decision."

Burke did not take part in the press conference. He was informed of his dismissal during a morning meeting with McCammon, a session on which Burke walked out.

The decision not to retain Burke left NHL fans, media and even hockey insiders scratching their heads.

Phil Maloney, a former general manager of the Canucks who was fired after the 1976-77 season, was one of those mystified. "When the Canucks fired Brian Burke for being financially responsible and for producing a very competitive team and getting the players involved in the community and making personal appearances and making money for the team, it showed me [that in hockey decisions aren't always fair]," Maloney says.

*Posing for this light-hearted photo are (from left) Pat Quinn, Brian Burke and Bob McCammon. All three had previous connections to the Flyers.* (Vancouver Canucks)

Burke has a quick temper and a sometimes bristly attitude, which makes the possibility of a personality conflict easy to understand. But in terms of how he handled the hockey and business operations of the Canucks, it is difficult to see what more he could have accomplished.

The way the Canucks were going before Burke took over, with the team losing tens of millions of dollars a year and headed downward in both the standings and at the gate, the franchise could easily have been moved south by McCaw, much as the Seattle businessman did when he sold Vancouver's NBA Grizzlies to ownership that eventually relocated the team to Memphis.

But with the Canucks shown capable of being profitable — not to mention wildly popular — it would be difficult to imagine McCaw or any other owner justifying such a move to Vancouver fans.

In many eyes, Burke saved NHL hockey in Vancouver. He took a sad-sack franchise that was going nowhere despite the presence of highly paid stars such as Alex Mogilny, Pavel Bure and Mark Messier, and improved that on-ice product by 46 points over five years. He initially reduced payroll by US$8 million and, even after signing his key young stars to new deals, the total was identical to the US$36 million when he took over. He handled difficult situations such as the Bure holdout and the decision to end the Messier experiment without alienating his fan base.

The latest tour was Burke's second with the Canucks. He was a key part of the early-1990s turnaround engineered by Pat Quinn. Hired as Quinn's vice-president and director of hockey operations in 1987, he worked in contract negotiations and with the team's scouting and minor-league systems before becoming

*Brian Burke (right) and Mike Keenan, shown here watching Canucks training camp, didn't last long together in Vancouver.* (Chris Relke/HHOF)

general manager with the Hartford Whalers in 1992.

"Brian wasn't with us in '94 [for the Stanley Cup run], but Brian Burke was a big part of that success of that team," says Stan Smyl, an assistant coach on that squad.

Burke stayed with the Whalers for only a season before moving to the NHL head office in New York; where he was senior vice-president and director of hockey operations for five years, during which time he handled league discipline.

One of 10 children born to an Irish-American family, Burke didn't begin playing hockey until he was 13, after the family moved to Edina, Minnesota. Although far from naturally gifted at the game, his work ethic helped him develop into a varsity high school player and, eventually, into a walk-on captain of U.S. college hockey's Providence Friars.

He was an outstanding student and gained entrance to Harvard Law School, but he put his legal education on hold for a year to pursue a minor-pro contract with the Philadelphia Flyers organization. After one season of chasing his dream on the ice, he attended Harvard, from which he graduated with a law degree. Burke worked as an NHL player agent until he was hired by Quinn and the Canucks in 1987.

While serving his second stint with the Canucks, Burke met and married Vancouver radio and television journalist Jennifer Mather. They have a daughter, Mairin, born in 2004.

A year after being dumped by the Canucks, Burke was hired by the Anaheim Mighty Ducks as executive vice-president and general manager. The Ducks, who finished six games under .500 and failed to make the playoffs in the season before Burke arrived, qualified for the post-season with a 43-27-12 record in his first year at the helm and made the Western Conference finals.

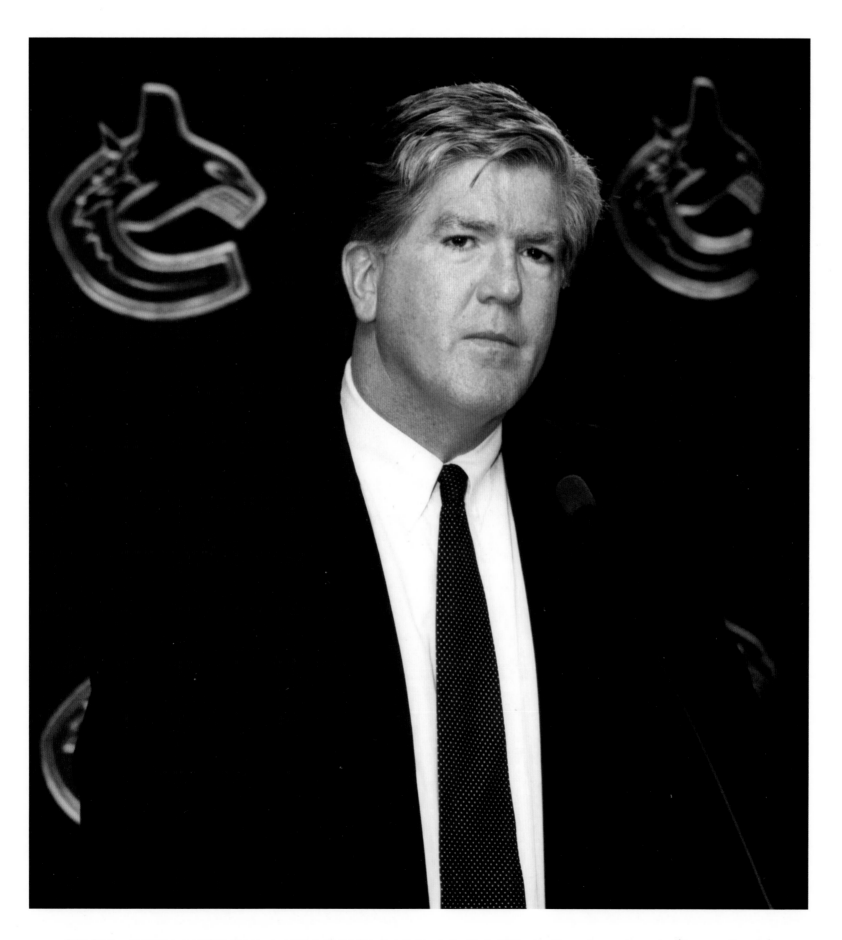

*Brian Burke was highly successful in Vancouver, which made the Canucks' decision to fire him in 2004 subject to much second-guessing.* (Vancouver Canucks)

# GEOFF AND RUSS COURTNALL

IT LASTED ONLY 13 regular-season games and two playoff rounds, but for brothers Geoff and Russ Courtnall the chance to play together on the same NHL team was something to savour for a lifetime. Making the experience even richer was the fact that it came while they were wearing the uniform of the Vancouver Canucks and playing home games just a short ferry ride from their hometown of Victoria.

Both Courtnalls were well into long and prosperous careers in which they would eventually become the first pair of brothers to each play 1,000 games in hockey's highest league. Geoff was already a well-established mainstay on left wing with the Canucks when the trade for Russ occurred late in the 1994-95 season; Russ, a centre turned right-winger, was having contract troubles with the Dallas Stars.

One hour before the NHL trade deadline, Russ received the news: he had been traded home to Vancouver to play with his brother. It was only the second time in their organized hockey careers that Geoff, three years senior, and Russ had been able to skate on the same team; the first had come in Geoff's final year of junior hockey with the Victoria Cougars.

"I was so fired up. It was like draft time again. I was just so excited," Russ recalls now. "Geoff had mentioned to Pat [Quinn] that things weren't going very well in Dallas and that I would love to come and play in Vancouver and so they started discussing the possible trade and [Stars general manager] Bob Gainey knew that it would be a good fit for me and that it was close to home."

Russ met the Canucks in Calgary, where coach Rick Ley initially put him on the same line as Geoff. In their first game together, the brothers combined to each draw an assist on a goal by Jassen Cullimore.

"For pretty much our entire careers we were always talking about it," Russ says of playing together. "When it happened, it was just great, great fun. I really enjoyed playing with him. You know, he'd changed a lot as a player from when we were junior players and I guess I had, too, and so it was neat to see

how he had evolved in the locker room."

Both Courtnalls evolved nicely as NHLers, though each took a distinctly different career path.

Geoff didn't begin playing the game until age nine and was a late bloomer once he did. He went undrafted as a key member of a talented Cougar junior team, but after posting 41 goals and 73 assists as a 20-year-old in the Western Hockey League he was signed as a free agent by the Boston Bruins.

After some seasoning in the minors, he played four winters with the Bruins before being traded to Edmonton in the spring of 1988. Once there he helped the Oilers' dynasty team, including Mark Messier and Wayne Gretzky, win the Stanley Cup.

He established himself as a timely scorer and pesky opponent during stints with Washington and St. Louis. With the Capitals, he posted a career-high 42 goals in 1988-89.

In the spring of 1991, Geoff was a key component in what was seen as the defining trade for the 1990s Canucks. Vancouver dealt Garth Butcher and Dan Quinn to the Blues in exchange for three British Columbia hockey products — Courtnall, Cliff Ronning and Robert Dirk — along with Sergio Momesso.

In parts of five seasons with Vancouver, Geoff was one of the Canucks' key players, combining scoring ability, speed and an aggressive style that tended to infuriate opponents. He had 31 goals and 77 points, and 167 penalty minutes, in 1992-93 and added 70 points and 123 penalty minutes the following season.

But Geoff was at his best in the playoffs, showing a knack for timely goals and producing extremely well under pressure. In the Canucks' 1994 playoff run, he scored nine goals and 19 points and had the overtime winner against Calgary in Game 5 of the first round to keep Vancouver's fading hopes alive.

Inexplicably, the Canucks allowed Geoff to leave as a free agent during the summer of 1995, ending the brothers' brief stint as NHL teammates. Geoff rejoined the Blues in St. Louis, who were offering a far more lucrative contract.

"It was probably the biggest marketing faux pas ever in Canuck

*The Brothers Courtnall: Russ, left, and Geoff were able to play together briefly for their home-province team in 1995.* (Chris Relke/HHOF)

history, because we'd had very good careers and neither one of us had ever had the media attention ... until we played together, and then it just became like we were a rock group," Russ says. "We were in every magazine and newspaper and TV show and radio show in Vancouver and, because we were from Victoria, they treated us like hometown boys.

"Mike McPhee, who was kind of handling [contract negotiations] for Pat Quinn at the time, didn't think that Geoff was going to command the dollars that he got. He was about a million dollars wrong a year."

Geoff remained with the Blues until the end of his career, which was cut short by post-concussion syndrome during the 1999-2000 season. He played 1,049 games in 17 NHL seasons, collecting 799 points and finishing with a positive plus-minus rating in 13 of those years. As a Canuck playoff scorer he was particularly effective, notching 61 points in 65 games, including six overtime winners.

Russ Courtnall, a speedster who was drafted seventh overall by the Toronto Maple Leafs in 1983, played a total of 1,029 NHL games over 16 seasons, scoring 744 points. He was also a prime

playoff performer, collecting 83 points in 129 postseason games and helping the Montreal Canadiens reach the Stanley Cup final in 1989.

Russ also had NHL stops in Minnesota, Dallas, New York and Los Angeles and played in the NHL All-Star Game in 1994. He represented Canada during the 1984 Winter Olympics in Sarajevo as well as in the 1991 Canada Cup.

Russ's stint with the Canucks didn't last long. He posted 26 goals and 65 points in 1995-96, his only full season with Vancouver, before being traded to the Rangers after 47 games the next year. Married to former actress Paris Vaughan, the daughter of legendary jazz singer Sarah Vaughan, Russ retired after the 1998-99 season.

The Courtnall brothers live near each other in the seaside Victoria suburb of Oak Bay. Both are active in business and with a family charity foundation that has raised funds for a psychiatric emergency services unit named for their late father, Archie Courtnall.

# GERALD DIDUCK

THE CANUCKS of 1994 had one offensive superstar, terrific goaltending, some surprising contributions from virtual unknowns and a coach capable of coaxing the most out of his troops.

The team also had more than its share of rock-solid "character" veterans who provided the combination of skills, experience and background leadership necessary to make a spectacular run, and defenceman Gerald Diduck was that kind of player. He could take care of his own end, handle any physical challenges and kill penalties, and the 6'1", 216-pound Edmonton native was quite content to make keeping the puck out of the Canucks' net his top priority.

"I used to have some offence in juniors, but Al Arbour got that fixed on me real quick in my early days," chuckles Diduck, who was drafted by head coach Arbour's New York Islanders 16th overall in 1983. "He either cost me a lot of money or made me a long career, and it's probably the latter."

Diduck was paired with Dave Babych for most of Diduck's five seasons in Vancouver, and the two veterans formed a reliable combination.

"Because of our size, it was nice," Diduck recalls. "We just kind of split the ice down the middle, let [goaltender] Kirk [McLean] stop the first shot, and then turned the puck in and out and around and gone. You never had to worry about your partner being outmuscled or anything else like that."

Diduck himself was rarely outmuscled during a 17-year NHL career that began with the Islanders and included stops in Montreal, Chicago, Hartford, Phoenix, Toronto and Dallas. Over those years he had hundreds of teammates, but never quite experienced the chemistry he felt with the Canucks.

"The best thing about playing in Vancouver was the mix of guys while I was there," he says. "It was probably the most cohesive team, as far as personalities went, that I played with in my entire career. We all got along, yeah, but most importantly, when push came to shove, everybody was there playing for each other. There weren't guys out playing just for themselves when it got down to the real nitty-gritty."

Diduck went to the Canucks from the Canadiens in a 1991 swap for a fourth-round draft pick. He had spent only 32 games in Montreal and wasn't seeing eye to eye with coach Pat Burns after being traded to the Canadiens by the Islanders due to a contract dispute just a few months earlier.

"Leaving the situation [in Montreal] was great," he says. "Getting to Vancouver was a little different in that the team was not a good team at that point at all. It was very much at the bottom of the pile and didn't look like it was going anywhere. But I found really quickly that playing under Pat Quinn was a pleasure."

Diduck was a staple in Quinn's remixing of the Canucks. Over parts of five seasons, he scored a modest 72 points in 265 games and his best statistical year came in 1991-92, when he accumulated 27 points and a career-high 229 penalty minutes. But the finest experience of his career came when he played all 24 playoff games in the spring of 1994.

"From my position and how I played my game, there were not a lot of highlights on an individual basis," he says. "All my glory or non-glory came through however the team did. So by definition, that would be the highlight of the career."

Unfortunately, the low point came less than a year later when Diduck was dealt to the Chicago Blackhawks at the trade deadline. The Canucks weren't interested in paying what he would eventually command as a free agent. "It's professional hockey, which means you are trying to get paid the most you can for your services," he says.

In all, he played 932 games with eight NHL teams. He and his family now reside mainly in his final playing stop, Dallas, where he has a real estate company and coaches minor hockey.

"My disappointment is I didn't get my 1,000 games, but it is what it is," he says. "My kids are healthy and the cheques don't bounce, so life's good."

# ROBERT DIRK

FOR EVIDENCE that professional hockey can be a cruel game, one need look no farther than defenceman Robert Dirk.

The stay-at-home blueliner was part of the Canucks' team turnaround of the early 1990s. But after three seasons in Vancouver and with the franchise finally poised to make a Stanley Cup run, he was traded away to the Chicago Blackhawks on the NHL trading deadline in March 1994.

All he could do was watch as his former Canucks teammates rolled all the way to Game 7 of the Cup finals before losing to the New York Rangers.

"I was devastated when that trade happened," Dirk says now. The Canucks "had made a deal earlier in the day with St. Louis to get [Jeff] Brown and [Bret] Hedican and [Nathan] LaFayette, so there was [an] excess of defencemen and they had to move somebody ... But I was devastated to get traded, because for three years we were such a close group. We went from doormats to the penthouse with those guys. So they were my friends and my buddies, and they got on a roll and went to the playoffs and went to the finals."

The Blackhawks lost in the first round of the 1994 postseason, so he was back in Vancouver as the city was steadily whipped into a frenzy by the Canucks, and the experience brought out a range of difficult emotions in the veteran.

"I was happy for the guys and happy for Pat and [assistant coach] Ricky Ley and the whole organization and the Griffiths," he says. "But a part of me was very, very sad as well. I remember I was in downtown Vancouver with my wife and friends, having supper, and we beat Toronto in Game 5 to go to the Stanley Cup and I basically broke down and cried, right there."

Within two days of that victory, staying in Vancouver became too difficult for Dirk "because it was breaking my heart not being a part of it." He left on a two-week vacation to Hawaii, but even then he couldn't keep away from the television.

"Every day during those finals, at one o'clock Hawaii time, I was in a bar watching the game, watching the boys playing the Rangers," he says. "In Game 7, when they came up one goal short, I broke down and cried again for the guys."

Robert Dirk didn't always have such an affinity for Vancouver or the Canucks. Growing up in Kelowna, he disliked British Columbia's biggest city because his minor baseball, soccer and hockey teams seemed to perpetually lose to teams from the Lower Mainland.

Born in Regina and raised in Kelowna, Dirk was the junior property of the Regina Pats. He played three full seasons with the Western Hockey League team and was drafted by the St. Louis Blues, 53rd overall, in 1984.

After four seasons split between the Blues' International Hockey League farm team, the Peoria Rivermen, and the big club, he finally seemed to be carving out a place on a Stanley Cup-contender St. Louis lineup in 1990-91 when he became part of one of the biggest trades in Canucks history. He went to the Canucks, along with forwards Geoff Courtnall, Cliff Ronning and Sergio Momesso, in a deal that would go a long way toward shaping the 1994 Stanley Cup finalist Vancouver squad.

"I would say 90 to 95 percent of guys are caught off guard when they are traded," Dirk says. "And the type of person that I am, I had been drafted by St. Louis, it was the only organization that I had been a part of, and it was the only organization at the time that I wanted to be a part of in my whole career. So I was very disappointed in being traded from St. Louis.

"The four of us were all very disappointed, because at the time of the trade St. Louis was in first place overall in the league. And we felt that we had a real legitimate shot at winning the Stanley Cup or getting to a Stanley Cup."

The trade turned out to be the best move of Dirk's career. Under Pat Quinn in Vancouver, the 6'4", 207-pounder became a dependable regular for the retooling Canucks. He never scored more than 12 points in any of his three seasons with the club, but he was reliable on the back end and he was an effective physical presence, totalling more than 100 penalty minutes each winter.

*Defenceman Robert Dirk was heartbroken when he was traded away by the Canucks at the deadline in 1994.* [Chris Relke/HHOF]

He was a nice complement to Doug Lidster, his defensive partner, who was much more offence-minded.

"It was the best thing that happened for me as a person and for my career, getting traded to Vancouver and being part of the Canucks and, more importantly, being tutored under Pat Quinn," Dirk says now.

"In St. Louis, I was more of a spare part, where in Vancouver I became, not a main part, but I was in the lineup every night and Pat looked for me to contribute in my way and he gave me the confidence and the opportunity to do that. I was basically the type of player that he was. He was a tough, stay-at-home defenceman who could play the game but took care of business when business needed to be taken care of."

After being traded by the Canucks in the spring of 1994, Dirk spent time with Anaheim and Montreal and also with Detroit and Chicago of the IHL before retiring in 1997 at age 31 when playing the game stopped being fun. But with the help of Detroit Vipers general manager Rick Dudley he jumped right into coaching.

After three seasons coaching in the United Hockey League and two more in the West Coast league, Dirk served as head coach of the East Coast Hockey League's Texas Wildcatters in 2003-04. His goal is to coach in the NHL and perhaps capture the Stanley Cup that eluded him during 12 professional seasons as a player.

"Being a player is the best thing," he says. "Coaching is the next best thing."

# MARTIN GELINAS

VANCOUVER HOCKEY FANS will always reserve a special place in their hearts for Martin Gelinas, the feisty French Canadian whose nose for the net and gritty play helped the Canucks reach the Stanley Cup finals in 1994.

But what makes the man from Shawinigan, Quebec, unique is that fans in Edmonton, Raleigh and Calgary have all felt the same way about him at one time or another. During a 17-year NHL career he has played for six teams and has made it to the Stanley Cup finals with four of them; the only exceptions have been his home-province Nordiques, with whom he began the 1993-94 season, and the Florida Panthers, his most recent team.

It was the Nordiques who decided to jettison Gelinas after 31 games that winter, putting him on waivers. The left-winger was scooped up by the Canucks on January 15, 1994, in a move that proved to be one of general manager Pat Quinn's shrewdest.

The smooth-skating Gelinas wasted little time proving his value to the Canucks. After producing 16 points over 33 regular-season games, he was particularly effective during the physical warfare of the playoffs, checking effectively and chipping in nine points as the Canucks made it to Game 7 of the finals before losing to the New York Rangers.

Over the next three seasons Gelinas developed into one of the Canucks' offensive stars. He scored 30 goals and 56 points in 1995-96 and then contributed a career-high 35 goals and 33 assists to finish as the Canucks' second-leading point-getter during the 1996-97 season. In each of those three seasons he finished with a positive plus-minus rating.

The son of a Shawinigan barber, Gelinas became known as one of the Canucks' most likeable players and was unfailingly engaging with the media. Nevertheless, he was part of the purge by coach Mike Keenan and was traded to the Carolina Hurricanes along with Kirk McLean on January 3, 1998, in exchange for Geoff Sanderson, Sean Burke and Enrico Ciccone.

It was with Carolina that Gelinas began to develop his reputation for big-time playoff goals. He scored in overtime in Game 6 to allow the Hurricanes to beat Toronto in the 2002 Eastern Conference championship series, sending Carolina to its first Stanley Cup finals appearance, where it lost 4-1 to the Detroit Red Wings.

But Gelinas truly earned the nickname "the Closer" from his teammates in Calgary, where he signed as a free agent in July 2002. During the Flames' remarkable 2004 playoff run he scored three series-clinching goals, two of them in overtime. He also very nearly potted the Stanley Cup winner after TV replays appeared to show a puck hitting him late in Game 6 against Tampa Bay and then crossing the goal line. But the red light did not go on and the play wasn't reviewed. The Lightning survived and went on to win Game 7 at home.

Earlier in those playoffs, Gelinas' overtime goal in Game 7 had eliminated the Canucks in Round 1. In Game 6 of the second round, he banged home a rebound to give the Flames a 1-0 overtime victory over the Red Wings and a berth in the Western Conference final. In doing so, he became the first NHLer to score the overtime winner in three different playoff series.

"It's overwhelming, I was at the right place at the right time," he told the Calgary *Herald* after scoring the overtime winner against Detroit.

Even though he was plucked by Los Angeles seventh overall from the Hull Olympiques in the 1988 draft, Gelinas never played a game for the Kings. Instead, he was packaged in one of the biggest trades in NHL history, going to the Edmonton Oilers with Jimmy Carson, three first-round draft choices and cash in exchange for Wayne Gretzky, Mike Krushelnyski and Marty McSorley on August 9, 1988.

Gelinas had 17 goals and 25 points over 46 games in his rookie season with the Oilers, when he teamed with Adam Graves and Joe Murphy on Edmonton's successful rookie line. He played 20 games, collecting five points, as the Oilers won the Stanley Cup that spring, his only Cup win in four trips to the final.

"My first Cup was my first year and I took it for granted," he would admit to The Canadian Press much later in his career.

# BRET HEDICAN

BRET HEDICAN is probably the only NHL player who is less famous on the ice than his wife.

One of the strongest skaters in the NHL since breaking into the league in 1992-93, Hedican married US gold-medal-winning figure skater Kristi Yamaguchi in Hawaii on July 8, 2000. The pair now live in North Raleigh, where Hedican tours the blue line with the Carolina Hurricanes, but their relationship began getting serious at General Motors Place in 1995 during Hedican's five-year tour with the Canucks.

Hedican is no slouch on the blades himself. The native of St. Paul, Minnesota, finished second in the 1996 NHL All-Star Game's fastest-skater competition, behind only Mike Gartner.

Hedican was part of two of the biggest trades in Vancouver franchise history and also contributed steadily during the Canucks' 1994 Stanley Cup run. The 6'2", 205-pound defenceman was obtained from the St. Louis Blues on March 21, 1994, going to Vancouver with Jeff Brown and Nathan LaFayette in exchange for Craig Janney.

The deal had a major role in shaping the Canucks' playoff fortunes that spring. Brown was the offensive, quarterbacking defenceman Vancouver needed, Hedican was a mobile young blueliner who played all 24 postseason games, and Lafayette a young centre who chipped in a surprising nine points in 20 playoff games.

Although Hedican's overall game never quite lived up to his obvious skating skills in Vancouver, he did evolve into a solid regular on the blue line. His top statistical year with the Canucks came in 1995-96, when he recorded 29 points, including 23 assists, to place second among Vancouver defencemen.

His time with the Canucks was marked by upheaval in the franchise as it tried, unsuccessfully, to recapture the playoff magic of 1994. On January 17, 1999, he was moved out in a blockbuster deal, going to the Florida Panthers with superstar Pavel Bure, prospect Brad Ference and a draft pick. That trade brought all-star defenceman Ed Jovanovski to Vancouver, along with Dave Gagner, Mike Brown and Kevin Weekes.

Three years later Hedican was again dealt, this time to Carolina, where he became part of another unlikely Stanley Cup run. He played in all 23 postseason games and averaged nearly 24 minutes of ice time to help the Hurricanes reach the NHL final, where they lost in five games to the Detroit Red Wings. That June, he signed a six-year contract with Carolina. Hedican helped the Hurricanes capture the Stanley Cup in 2006, notching 11 points and nearly 23 minutes of ice time a night over 25 playoff contests.

Hedican had been selected by St. Louis out of St. Cloud State, where he played three seasons of National Collegiate Athletic Association hockey. In his final year with the Minnesota school he collected 47 points in 41 games. The Blues took him 198th overall in the 1988 NHL draft.

Hedican met Yamaguchi during the 1992 Winter Olympics in Albertville, France, where both represented the United States; Yamaguchi claimed gold in women's singles skating and Hedican played defence for the fourth-place American hockey squad. But the pair didn't begin seeing each other seriously other until after Hedican reintroduced himself to her in 1995, when he was with the Canucks and she was appearing in an ice show at GM Place. In 2003 they had their first of two daughters.

# DOUG LIDSTER

AFTER 10 YEARS in the NHL, Doug Lidster finally tasted champagne out of the Stanley Cup in June 1994.

It was the crowning moment of a fine career for the versatile defenceman, but his emotions were mixed. Down the hall in Madison Square Garden his former team was tasting a bitter, emotional defeat.

Lidster had moved from the Canucks to the New York Rangers before the 1993-94 season. As fate would have it, the Canucks and Rangers tangled that spring in one of the best Stanley Cup finals in history. It was the kind of series in which it seemed unfortunate that one team had to lose. The Rangers, led by Mark Messier, Brian Leetch and Mike Richter, prevailed by a single goal on home ice in the seventh game. The underdog Canucks were denied what many fans had believed was their destiny.

"I remember being interviewed after Game 7 by, I think, it was [*Hockey Night in Canada* broadcaster] Dick Irvin," Lidster says. "He asked me what it was like and I said something like, 'I can really feel for the Canucks.'"

Lidster says it's common for teams to develop respect and empathy for each other over a tough seven-game playoff series, but he felt more than that. Not only had he been a 10-year, career-long Canuck until just months earlier, but he also hailed from Kamloops, British Columbia.

"In this particular case, because it was Vancouver, I *could* really feel for them," he says. "I knew the guys in the Vancouver dressing room better than I knew the guys in my own dressing room. I knew all the sweat and toil that they'd put into it, so yeah, I could feel for them. There were some emotional moments right after that game."

Canucks owner Arthur Griffiths visited the crowded New York dressing room, where he ran into Lidster's wife. "She started crying, and I think Arthur was pretty emotional, too," Lidster says. "Little things like that really made it an emotional experience."

The only thing worse than having to beat your friends and former teammates in the Stanley Cup finals might be reaching that point and not getting the chance to play. That nearly happened to Lidster, who struggled to get into the lineup of head coach Mike Keenan and played in only 34 games for the Rangers that regular season.

The veteran blueliner wasn't playing in the playoffs, either, until a Ranger suspension during the Eastern Conference final created an open spot. He made the most of the opportunity and was able to skate the entire series against the Canucks.

"The year that we won the Cup, it was basically a Tale of Two Cities type of thing," he recalls. "It was the best year, because we won the Stanley Cup, and it was the worst year, because it was so trying. I was relegated to part-time status [by Keenan]. It was a very soul-searching year."

Nevertheless, having his name engraved on the Cup for the first time is something he cherishes. He went on to grab a second Cup ring with the Dallas Stars in 1999.

"It's an experience that's very difficult to describe properly to someone who hasn't been there," he says of winning a Stanley Cup. "When you're involved in it, though, you're so focused on the preparation for the games and then the games themselves you don't really have an appreciation for everything else that's going on. You know that it's there, but your focus is basically on the game."

Lidster was always a focused player during his decade with the Canucks, when he was usually the best defenceman on what was usually a bad team. His best year in Vancouver came in 1986-87 when he posted a career-best 63 points, a Canuck record for a defenceman. Not bad for a player taken in the seventh round, 133rd overall, out of Colorado College.

"The Canucks were not a good team when he was in his prime," recalls former Vancouver play-by-play man Jim Robson. "One year he had the worst plus-minus in the NHL, I think — it was something like minus-40 or 50 — and people would point to that. But he was Vancouver's best defenceman and always played against Gretzky and Messier in the days when Edmonton would

*Winning the Stanley Cup in 1994 with the Rangers brought mixed emotions for Doug Lidster, a Canuck for a decade.* (Chris Relke/HHOF)

get eight, nine goals a night. Doug Lidster would be on the ice 30 minutes against the Oilers and would come out of the game minus-5 or something. In those days they had an unbalanced schedule, so the Canucks played the Oilers more. Lidster's stats, especially the plus-minus numbers, were unfair."

Vancouver fans respected what Lidster brought to the ice every night. He was a quiet leader, who shared the team captaincy during the 1990-91 season with Dan Quinn and Trevor Linden. He was also a proven playmaker, recording 307 points in 666 games with Vancouver.

"I think I was kind of a jack-of-all-trades-type defenceman," he says. "I could do a little bit of everything but wasn't exceptional in any one area."

His most vivid memory of his time with the Canucks is from 1989, when Vancouver took Calgary to the seventh game of the

opening round of the playoffs before losing an overtime heartbreaker. The Flames went on to capture the Stanley Cup that spring.

"I was on the ice, and when they scored it was just like the movies," he recalls. "I couldn't hear the fans. I could see them cheering. I could see guys throwing popcorn in the air, the whole nine yards, and celebrating. But it all was in slow motion and it all was with no sound. And I've never had that experience before or since in my whole life. I don't know how many seconds it lasted. It seemed like an eternity at the time.

"That's not a great memory, but it's a vivid memory."

He could see the end coming in Vancouver during the 1992-93 season. He had contract problems with the Canucks, so he wasn't surprised when he was shipped to the Rangers on June 25, 1993, as the future consideration in a previous deal for goalie John Vanbiesbrouck.

*Defenceman Doug Lidster posted 63 points for the Canucks in the 1986–87 season.* (David Klutho/HHOF)

At first Lidster was wary of going to New York, where he thought it might be difficult to safely raise a family. But he ended up loving the Big Apple and doing two tours with the Rangers, with a stint on the St. Louis Blues sandwiched in between. "Honestly, it was just a fantastic place to play," he says of New York.

Near the end of his NHL career he became a part-time player, even spending a season as a playing assistant coach with Stanley Cup champion Dallas. He also worked for Hockey Canada as an assistant coach.

After retiring in 1999, he spent a season as an assistant coach with the Western Hockey League's Medicine Hat Tigers before going on to work for Hockey Canada, mainly with the national women's team.

Before the 2004-05 season he took a job as head coach of the Saginaw Spirit of the Ontario Hockey League. But he resigned less than halfway through the season after a pre-practice incident in which he argued with goaltender Mike Brown and poked a finger in Brown's chest.

Known by his teammates as "Liddy," Lidster says he cherishes his time as a Ranger but probably identifies his playing career more with the Canucks. Vancouver fans feel the same way.

"The only good thing about the Rangers beating the Canucks in '94," says Robson, "is Doug Lidster got a ring."

*Doug Lidster was a proven playmaker, recording 309 points in 666 games with the Canucks.* (Doug MacLellan/HHOF)

# TREVOR LINDEN

NOBODY SUMMED it up better than former Canucks general manager Brian Burke when it comes to Trevor Linden. "He never looked right in another uniform," Burke told a press conference in January 2003.

That was the day Burke and the Canucks signed Linden to a three-year contract extension worth a guaranteed US$6.3 million, making it seem likely he would finish his NHL career at "home" where it all began.

Linden has played for four different NHL teams, but he left his heart in Vancouver when he was unceremoniously cleared out by Mike Keenan in February 1998. Nearly four years later, after stops in Long Island, Montreal and Washington, he was repatriated to the team and the city where he belongs.

From his first days with the Canucks in September 1988, when a skinny, peach-fuzz-faced 18-year-old from Medicine Hat, Alberta, made an immediate impact, Linden has enjoyed a special bond that few Vancouver athletes engender.

He arrived in British Columbia as a winner at a time when the Canucks were sorely in need of one. Linden had captained the Medicine Hat Tigers to two consecutive Memorial Cup national junior championships and won a world junior title with Canada; Canucks general manager Pat Quinn was looking to build similar success in an organization that had enjoyed precious little.

The Canucks selected Linden number 2 overall in the 1988 NHL draft after he wowed them with his mature attitude during pre-draft interviews. Perhaps Dennis McDonald, general manager of the world junior team on which Linden played, put it best when he told the Ottawa *Citizen* the youngster was a "refreshing delight."

"He's a golly-gee kid, the kind you'd love your daughter to bring home," McDonald said. "He's so genuine."

As a teenaged Canuck rookie Linden roomed on the road with 34-year-old Harold Snepsts, who helped show him the ropes. That winter Linden was billeted in the North Vancouver home of Joanne Hull-Robinson, mother of NHLer Brett Hull. Often, Linden and Stan Smyl shared rides to the Pacific Coliseum,

the captain of the present and the captain of the future.

Linden contributed 59 points and heady play beyond his years to finish second to Brian Leetch of the New York Rangers in Calder Trophy balloting during his rookie season. He continued to progress as a player and a leader, and the Canucks made him a captain in only his third NHL season, at the tender age of 20.

Vancouver soon became his team and, with Linden's leadership, the Canucks developed into one of the NHL's better squads in the early 1990s.

Although he was never a consistently big scorer in the regular season, Linden did all the little things well. He was terrific on faceoffs, a punishing checker, a good penalty killer, tough when he needed to be and responsible defensively. Nevertheless, in six of his first eight seasons with Vancouver he managed to hit the 30-goal mark, and four times during that span he collected at least 70 points.

More important to both Linden and the team, in seven of his first eight years with Vancouver the Canucks made the playoffs. And it was in the postseason that Linden was at his best, a time during which Smyl once described the young forward as a player who "sees things differently. He doesn't panic."

During his first stint with Vancouver, the 6'4" Linden posted 80 points in 79 playoff games.

In 1994 he was the physical and spiritual cornerstone of the Canucks during the greatest playoff run in Vancouver franchise history. He had 25 points in 24 playoff games that spring, including a two-goal effort in Game 7 of the final against the New York Rangers, when the courageous captain nearly pulled his team back from a 2-0 deficit all by himself.

Almost as important, Linden was the consummate good citizen, giving his time to charity and becoming the public face of the team. In 1997 he received the NHL's King Clancy Award for humanitarian contributions to his community. Linden was as popular as an athlete in a laid-back West Coast Canadian city is ever likely to get.

*A fresh-faced Trevor Linden and Canucks general manager Pat Quinn grin for the cameras on draft day, 1988.* (Vancouver Canucks)

He peaked as an NHL scorer in 1995-96, when he had a career-best 80 points, including 33 goals. But the next season injuries limited him to 49 games and his point production slipped to 40.

In the summer of 1997, with the team coming off its first spring out of the playoffs in seven years, the Canucks brought in as a free agent Mark Messier, the so-called greatest leader in team sports. Being the consummate team guy, Linden gave up the captaincy to Messier before the season began.

It was a typically selfless gesture for Linden, but it wasn't rewarded. Less than two months into the 1997-98 season the Canucks fired Pat Quinn, the general manager who had drafted Linden. Coach Tom Renney was next to go and his replacement, the unpredictable Keenan, seemed all too eager to rid the Canucks of any remnants of 1994.

Chief on that list was Trevor Linden, whom Keenan challenged publicly and then seemed to go out of his way to criticize, including

with a between-periods dressing room tirade during a game in St. Louis. It seemed only a matter of time before Keenan pulled the trigger on a trade involving the former captain.

On February 6, 1998, Linden was dealt to the New York Islanders in a trade that gave future star power forward Todd Bertuzzi and mobile defenceman Bryan McCabe to the Canucks.

"It's a difficult day," Linden, then 27, told reporters at a press conference to announce his departure. "I can't say enough about the time I spent here. The people have been tremendous. On the other hand, I knew something was going to happen. It's a chance for me to start again and move forward."

He did move forward, but he did not duplicate the success he had enjoyed with the Canucks. After playing for Canada at the midseason Winter Olympics in Nagano, Japan, he joined the woeful Islanders for the final 25 games of the 1997-98 regular season and posted an encouraging 17 points.

*As captain of the Canucks for seven seasons, no player has had a greater impact on the franchise than Trevor Linden.* (BCSHF)

*Shown here letting a shot go from the wing, Trevor Linden had a career-best 80 points in 1995–96.* (Paul Bereswill/HHOF)

He was quickly named captain of the Islanders, but ownership was unstable on Long Island and the team struggled mightily; it had trouble even getting basics such as proper hockey equipment. Linden earned 47 points in 82 games in that environment the following season before being traded to Montreal.

He played parts of two seasons for the Canadiens, who signed him to a four-year, US$15-million deal and promptly traded him to the Washington Capitals late in the 2000-01 season.

Struggling to get ice time with the Capitals, he played in just 28 games over parts of two seasons before Washington general manager George McPhee, a former assistant to Pat Quinn with the Canucks, made the deal with Burke to send Linden back to Vancouver. "Some players are just a natural fit in a certain city," McPhee told the Vancouver *Sun*.

The move was welcome news to the 31-year-old Linden, who had kept a Kitsilano Beach home during his time away from the city.

Though initially nervous about whether he could live up to expectations created by his return, he has been an effective, steady presence and a complement in the dressing room to current captain Markus Naslund.

Linden is clearly one of the most loved Canucks of all time and his generous charity work is well-known across British Columbia. In a Vancouver *Province* newspaper poll in 2003, he was voted the player fans "most wanted to meet for a beer after a game." In fact, he was so popular that he received votes in 18 of the 20 poll categories.

He also remains highly regarded by his peers. As president of the NHL Players' Association he was integrally involved in ending the labour lockout that pre-empted the 2004-05 NHL season.

## For the Record:

*Trevor Linden became the Vancouver Canucks' all-time points leader on March 8, 2004, when he collected a pair of assists in a home game against the Colorado Avalanche.*

*The two-point night gave Linden 675 points with the team and moved him ahead of former captain Stan Smyl, who collected 673*

*points in his career, all with Vancouver.*

*Linden's big night was overshadowed by a nasty third-period incident, however, when Todd Bertuzzi punched Steve Moore to the back of the head, causing the Avalanche player to suffer a serious injury.*

*In six of his first eight seasons with Vancouver, Trevor Linden hit or passed the 30-goal mark. (Chris Relke/HHOF)*

# JYRKI LUMME

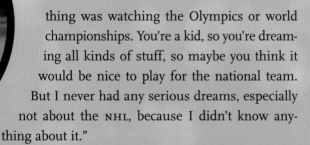

When 19-year-old Jyrki Lumme learned he had been drafted by the NHL's flagship Montreal Canadiens, he didn't have the reaction typical of, say, a North American hockey prospect. Living a world away in Tampere, Finland, Lumme more or less shrugged off the news.

It came in the midst a major Finnish summer holiday and Lumme had just popped home for a quick shower and change of clothes before rejoining his buddies for the festivities.

"Just as I was leaving, the phone rang," he recalls. "There was somebody from the Finnish Hockey Federation who was in Montreal where the draft was being held. He called and said that I had been drafted. And I'm like, 'Okay, so what?' I didn't really know much about it. I didn't know the system because I never read about that stuff in the papers.

"I talked to [then Canadiens assistant general manager] Andre Boudrias on the phone for a couple of minutes, and then off I went again with my friends."

Lumme recalls the draft news being like an afterthought in the midst of the holiday — "It was a big, big weekend" — but during the celebrations he ran into Risto Siltanen, a Finnish player who was already in the NHL with the Quebec Nordiques.

"I told him that I just got drafted and he was like, 'Wow! Great!' Because obviously he knew [what it meant] even if Lumme didn't.

Growing up in Finland in the 1970s and '80s, Lumme had little exposure to the NHL. League news was not as widely available in his country as it is now. He had seen a couple of games at the Forum during a visit to Montreal and Quebec City as a 14-year-old attending a hockey tournament, but even that experience didn't make him pine for an NHL career.

"Those were the only two NHL games I ever saw before I came over [to Canada]," he says. "We had no NHL on TV back then ... Growing up, I never really had any big dreams about playing hockey as an adult. I never thought about it. I just enjoyed playing. I was a kid. I never had any goals or plans. Back then, the big thing was watching the Olympics or world championships. You're a kid, so you're dreaming all kinds of stuff, so maybe you think it would be nice to play for the national team. But I never had any serious dreams, especially not about the NHL, because I didn't know anything about it."

It was not until two years after he was drafted by the Canadiens, in the third round and 57th overall, that he signed a contract. He showed up in North America in time for the 1988-89 season and split it between Montreal and its American Hockey League affiliate, the Sherbrooke Canadiens.

He quickly realized he had to change his approach to the game under Montreal coach Pat Burns.

"I think the biggest change was that I came from a team in Finland where it was all run-and-gun," Lumme says. "It was all offence. When I played for my team in Finland, if I got the puck, I could just kind of go. But with Montreal it was like okay, just get rid of it."

Fifty-four games into his second NHL season he was traded to Vancouver, where the smooth-skating defenceman quickly made an impression. Over 11 games with the Canucks that season, he had 10 points.

Although he had enjoyed being part of the rich Habs hockey tradition, he welcomed the chance to move to the Canucks under Pat Quinn. Bob McCammon was the Vancouver coach when Lumme arrived, but Quinn slid behind the bench the next season.

"I think Pat just let the guys do what he thought that they are the best at," Lumme says. "He wasn't trying to put the guys in different roles. He kind of wanted them to play the way they can. He gave me a lot of confidence, because if I made one mistake he let me play again. In Montreal it was, like, if I screwed up once, I sat on the bench."

For the next eight seasons Lumme grew into one of the NHL's premier offensive blueliners. He and Dana Murzyn formed an effective tandem, with Murzyn's defensive style allowing Lumme to freewheel much more than he had in Montreal.

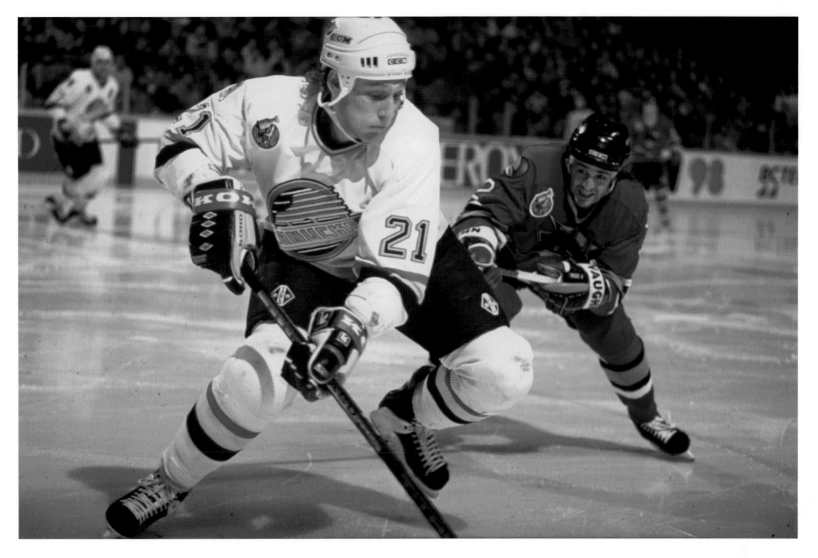

*Finnish defenceman Jyrki Lumme found playing for Pat Quinn a relief after being traded to Vancouver by the Montreal Canadiens.* (Chris Relke/HHOF)

The 6'1", 210-pound Finn improved his point output for four straight seasons after joining Vancouver, with his best year in 1993-94 as he finished with 42 assists and 55 points. During the Canucks' run to the 1994 Stanley Cup finals he was a key ingredient, contributing 11 assists and 13 points in 24 games. He also logged a 54-point season, including a career-high 17 goals, during the 1995-96 campaign.

In four of his eight full seasons in Vancouver he was selected the Canucks' top defenceman. He says he would have finished his career in Vancouver had the Canucks been willing to offer him a no-trade clause as a free agent after the 1997-98 season; they wouldn't, so he signed with the Phoenix Coyotes.

"It was tough. I never wanted to leave," he says. "Our good friend [Mike] Keenan was here. I would have taken a lot less money to stay in Vancouver, but there was no way I would have stayed without [the] no-trade [clause]. So I ended up leaving. It was tough, though. I was here for more than eight years."

Lumme played three seasons in Phoenix, but there he suffered shoulder and back injuries. He ended his career following the 2002-03 season, after stints with Dallas and Toronto, and he moved back to Vancouver. For now that is home, although he does not rule out a return to Finland.

"I just tried to do my best and that's it," he says of his NHL career. "I wasn't a guy who was going to go out there and score 50 goals, so I wanted to play for the team and do everything I could for the team."

# JOHN McCAW

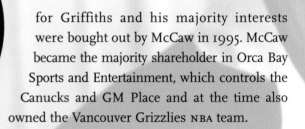

He might have the lowest profile of all owners in professional sports. John E. McCaw Jr. has been the money man behind the Vancouver Canucks for a decade, but he certainly has not been the public face of the NHL franchise.

The Seattle billionaire, who was ranked by Forbes.com in 2004 at number 472 among the world's richest individuals with a net worth estimated at US$1.2 billion, prefers to remain in the background.

The biography of the 55-year-old McCaw on the Canucks website is limited to one paragraph. He is sometimes seen at Canucks games, but he never grants interviews. His official word — if there is one — is passed to the sporting public through press releases or through other administrators in McCaw's Orca Bay Sports and Entertainment.

The Canucks' owner is one of three surviving sons of John McCaw Sr., a cable television magnate who died in 1969. The brothers, who include Craig and Bruce, inherited a company that was crippled by debt but, during the next 18 years, transformed their relatively small inheritance into a US cellular telephone empire.

John McCaw was a co-founder of McCaw Communications and McCaw Cellular Communications Incorporated. The McCaws sold their cellular interests to communications giant AT & T in 1993 for a reported US$11.5 billion. While John did not appear on the Forbes' 2005 list of the world's billionaires, Craig was number 365 with a net worth of US$2.1 billion.

McCaw became involved with the Canucks in 1994 at the request of Arthur Griffiths, who by the early 1990s was running the sports and communications interests founded by his father, Frank Griffiths.

Arthur Griffiths recruited the McCaws, family friends, to help bear the immense costs of building General Motors Place and bringing a National Basketball Association franchise to Vancouver for the 1995-96 season. But the debt load soon became too much for Griffiths and his majority interests were bought out by McCaw in 1995. McCaw became the majority shareholder in Orca Bay Sports and Entertainment, which controls the Canucks and GM Place and at the time also owned the Vancouver Grizzlies NBA team.

McCaw has made several major moves during his Canucks ownership. Early, he and his management team brought in high-priced stars Alexander Mogilny and Mark Messier in an attempt to turn around the team's flagging fortunes. In 1998 McCaw hired Brian Burke, who cut expenses while improving the Canucks dramatically on the ice and at the gate.

In May 2000 McCaw sold the Grizzlies to U.S. businessman Michael Heisley, who moved the team to Memphis one season later. But McCaw did not bail out of the hockey business. At various times, he has shelled out millions to keep stars such as Markus Naslund, Todd Bertuzzi and, most recently, Roberto Luongo, in Vancouver uniforms and, for the most part over the past few seasons, has kept the franchise in the upper echelon of the NHL with one of the most exciting lineups in hockey.

Under McCaw's ownership the Canucks also, surprisingly, fired Burke in the spring of 2004, though as president and general manager Burke had helped push the Canucks to an estimated US$45 million in profit over the previous two seasons.

In November 2004 Vancouver real estate developer Francesco Aquilini became a partner in Orca Bay. He agreed to buy 50 percent of the operation, though day-to-day control remained with McCaw, in a deal estimated to be worth US$125 million.

In a statement released by the club at the time, McCaw described the sale as "an exciting next step for the Vancouver Canucks."

McCaw remains chairman of Orca Bay Sports and Entertainment and represents the Canucks on the NHL's board of governors. He also sits on the boards of several privately owned companies as well as that of Conservation International.

# KIRK McLEAN

THERE IS ONLY one reasonable answer to the question "Who is the best goaltender to have worn a Vancouver Canucks uniform?" Some netminders were brilliant for relatively short stretches, and Gary Smith and Richard Brodeur top this category, but only one man has shown sustained excellence. His name is Kirk McLean.

A stand-up goaltender who could "butterfly" when he had to, McLean became an anchor in the Canucks net after being acquired in 1987 as a little-known prospect from the New Jersey Devils.

A native of Toronto, McLean was captivated early by the position that would become his career. When he was just five years old he took part in a year-long hockey skills camp in Scarborough, Ontario. It so happened that a goaltenders' camp followed his session every day. Young Kirk found himself intrigued by the masked men on the ice.

"I'd always bug my dad to stick around afterward to watch," he says. "I was just kind of fascinated by the goaltenders. Growing up in Toronto, my heroes were Bernie Parent and Jacques Plant, along with Davey Keon and Darryl Sittler and players like that."

As a six-year-old McLean graduated to house league hockey, where he initially played forward. But in his second season the team was short of goaltenders, so "myself and another guy put our hands up and we kind of rotated. I ended up, in a half a season, winning a goalie award. That was all she wrote after that."

He eventually found his way to the Ontario Hockey League's Oshawa Generals, where he won 47 games over his final two seasons. The New Jersey Devils drafted him in the sixth round, 107th overall, in 1984.

In his first full year with the Devils he saw action in only four NHL games; New Jersey's system was loaded with goaltenders, including Craig Billington, Sean Burke, Alain Chevrier and Chris Terreri. So in September 1987 the Devils traded McLean and forward Greg Adams to the Canucks in a deal that saw star forward Patrik Sundstrom head to New Jersey.

"I didn't know that I was traded with Greg Adams," McLean recalls. "Then I get on the plane and I see Greg come walking on."

The trade turned out to be a key in the Canucks' turnaround under Pat Quinn. Adams would prove to be a gritty, effective scorer and the six-foot, 182-pound McLean would emerge quickly as a reliable netminder. To this day, McLean holds team records for most games, victories and shutouts.

Still, he went into his first training camp as a Canuck with considerable doubt in his mind. He was coming off knee surgery and wasn't sure about the club's plans.

"I still didn't know what was up," he recalls. "But I went through training camp, and I was nursing [the knee]. I didn't know what was going to happen. Then I got the call from Cagey [coach Bob McCammon], saying to go find an apartment. That was music to my ears at the time."

McLean joined Brodeur, whose star was already fading in Vancouver, Steve Weeks and Frank Caprice in the lineup. Caprice was eventually sent to the minors and Brodeur was traded as McLean became entrenched as the number 1 goalie.

"Richard was very accommodating," McLean says. "I can imagine what was going through his mind when new brass comes in, with Pat [Quinn] and Burkie [Brian Burke] and Bob [McCammon]. And they'd already traded away one of their high-profile players, basically for an unknown goaltender and a winger who wasn't quite established yet. I thought Richard handled it very well. It was a tough situation for him and he treated me fine."

In his first season in Vancouver, McLean appeared in 41 games and won just 11 for what was still a weak team. The following season he won 20 and tied three in 42 starts, with a 3.08 goals-against average.

His best season came in 1991-92, when he appeared in 65 games and won a career-high 38. He posted five shutouts and an impressive 2.74 average and made the NHL's second all-star team. That season he also played in the NHL All-Star Game, his second appearance in the classic since debuting as a Vancouver representative in 1990.

Canucks' goaltender Kirk McLean was sensational during the 1994
*Stanley Cup playoffs.* (Doug MacLellan/HHOF)

Former Canucks defenceman Dana Murzyn remembers feeling confident playing in front of McLean. "He was a standup goalie. He was just very calm, always in control — you knew what he was going to be doing. Very predictable."

McLean's best regular season was 1991-92, but it was in 1994 that he sealed his claim as the finest goaltender to play for the Canucks. That was the spring when Vancouver shed its reputation as a playoff underachiever and McLean showed he could be a big-money postseason netminder.

After a mediocre regular season in which his record was sub-.500 (23-26-3), he was spectacular over 24 playoff games as the Canucks reached the seventh game of the Stanley Cup finals before falling to the New York Rangers. McLean had 15 wins and four shutouts while posting a 2.29 average.

"I was a pretty confident goaltender," he says. "But you get on that roll like that ... To be honest, some of it becomes a blur, because you do get into this zone and you just roll with it and go."

He was never better than in Game 7 of the opening-round series against the Calgary Flames, when he helped the Canucks cap a comeback from a 3-1 series deficit. His sliding two-pad save on Robert Reichel, who had appeared to have an open net for what would have been the overtime winner, is regarded by many as the greatest stop in Vancouver history. Without it, the team would have gone down as just another postseason underachiever. With it, those Canucks nearly won it all.

"Yeah, I guess that would have to be the biggest save of my career," agrees McLean, who also stopped German Titov, Gary Roberts and Al MacInnis on terrific chances late in the same game. "That one stands out in a lot of people's minds."

He wasn't able to recapture that brilliance over the following three seasons and neither was the team. As the Vancouver lineup was dismantled, the veteran goaltender was traded to the Carolina Hurricanes on January 3, 1998, in a deal that sent Sean Burke to Vancouver.

"When I got the phone call, I was pretty emotional, I was pretty devastated," McLean says. "I don't want to say I didn't recover from it, but it took a while."

He didn't stay long with Carolina, which seemed intent on going with Trevor Kidd as their goalie. McLean asked for a trade and the Hurricanes obliged, dealing him to Florida in March of that year. After appearing in 30 games and posting a 2.74 average for the Panthers in 1998-99, McLean wasn't offered another contract by Florida. He signed as a free agent with the New York Rangers and played two seasons in a backup role before he retired in 2001 and moved back to Vancouver.

McLean remains heavily involved with the Canucks alumni and has been part owner of the junior B.C. Hockey League's Burnaby Express, along with Bill Ranford, Dave Lowry and former Canuck Darcy Rota. He has also served as an analyst on Canuck pay-per-view broadcasts.

Ideally, McLean would like to become more closely involved with the Canucks as a goaltending coach or scout.

*Kirk McLean says he was "pretty devastated" after being traded from the Canucks to the Carolina Hurricanes in 1998.* (Vancouver Canucks)

## A Stand-Up Guy

Kirk McLean was a prototypical stand-up goalie, a style now overtaken in the NHL by kneeling "butterfly" netminders.

"The only time I used the butterfly was if I really had to, but I could do it," McLean says. "But I was a big believer in angles and standing your ground and making the player hit you and using your defence to your advantage as well — taking the pass away and all that kind of stuff, working together with your teammates."

He believes the stand-up style has fallen by the wayside because today's offensive players concentrate on crashing the net: "Everything's

crashing the net now. You never see anybody streaking down the wing and letting the shot go ... Guys just crash the net, wrap around, and you have all that confusion in front of the net. So everybody tries to cover the low part.

"Of course, the goalies are a lot more athletic and bigger and stronger than they ever were. They cover a lot of the net with the paddle down and bigger equipment."

*Goaltender Kirk McLean arrived in Vancouver via a 1987 trade from New Jersey that also brought Greg Adams to the Canucks. (Chris Relke/HHOF)*

# MARK MESSIER

IT WAS ONE OF those big, bold "statement" moves that professional sports franchises occasionally make when they are desperately trying to snap out of the doldrums. Sometimes they work, sometimes they don't. And sometimes the truth lies somewhere in between.

In retrospect, installing 36-year-old Mark Messier in Vancouver as the final piece in a supposed Stanley Cup puzzle now seems a trifle silly. By any reasonable assessment, the future Hockey Hall of Famer was already too old to make the difference by himself and he certainly wasn't worth the more than US$6.6 million per year that Canucks owner John McCaw shelled out in 1997 to lure him away from the New York Rangers.

But McCaw and the Canucks had a nearly brand new building to fill in General Motors Place and a fan base that was growing disenchanted as memories of 1994 playoff glory became more and more distant.

Hindsight is 20/20, of course, which, incidentally, is a better record than the Canucks managed to post during most of Messier's three-year stay on the West Coast.

Vancouver was coming off a dismal 35-40-7 season in the summer of 1997 when they signed Messier as a free agent. Three years removed from their seven-game Stanley Cup loss to Messier and the Rangers, the Canucks had found themselves on a dangerous downward slide.

Messier was brought in to much fanfare, with Pat Quinn describing him as "the best free agent to come along since there's been free agency." Messier was touted as the player who would turn things around with the near legendary leadership qualities that had enabled him to captain two different franchises to Stanley Cups. But it didn't work out that way.

Things got off to a rocky start when the club gave Messier his favourite number 11 jersey, in the process enraging the family of the late Wayne Maki, who thought the franchise had unofficially retired Maki's number.

Then Trevor Linden, for nearly a decade the heart and soul of the Canucks, voluntarily surrendered the captaincy to Messier before the season began, a show of deference that to most observers seemed strange.

Even stranger was the leadership mix on the team, as elder statesman Messier was paired with inexperienced NHL head coach Tom Renney.

By early November, with the Canucks off to a horrid 3-11-2 start, team architect and general manager Quinn was fired. Nine days later Renney was moved out, clearing the way for the abrasive Mike Keenan. In one fall stretch, the Canucks lost a franchise record 10 consecutive games.

Amid all the chaos it was difficult for fans to see any merit in Messier, particularly after the captain declared publicly, following a 25-43-14 campaign, that his first year with the Canucks had been a good one.

He was also blamed in some quarters for quietly engineering the exodus of popular veterans from Vancouver. Enforcer Gino Odjick, dealt to the New York Islanders in March 1998, told reporters that Messier "didn't even break a sweat for the first 10 games and just waited for Quinn to be fired."

As an individual Messier's production in Vancouver was decent, though well short of spectacular. After years of hovering near or above the 100-point mark as the best two-way player in the game, he turned in 60-, 48- and 54-point seasons in a Canuck uniform despite playing on the top line and the power play.

His plus-minus totals slipped in each of his three Vancouver seasons, bottoming out at a then career-worst minus-15 in 1999-2000. In each of his final two seasons with the Canucks, he missed at least 16 games due to injury as his nearly 40-year-old body finally seemed to be catching up to his chronological age.

More important, however, his leadership qualities, much lauded in six different career Stanley Cup victories, were not apparent to fans in Vancouver. "The Moose" simply could not lift the team into the playoffs and he led the Canucks to just one winning season, a 30-29-15-8 mark in 1999-2000, when Vancouver made a valiant second-half charge at the playoffs only to fall four points short.

*The import of free agent Mark Messier to Vancouver didn't have the instant results that Canucks management had hoped for.* (Paul Bereswill/HHOF)

In July 2000, after months of speculation, Messier left Vancouver to rejoin the Rangers and his former Edmonton coach and general manager Glen Sather. The Canucks bought out the final two years of Messier's contract for US$2 million and then offered him another single season at US$3 million. Understandably, he took the Rangers' offer of US$11 million for two seasons.

"I came there [to the Canucks] to do the best I could for the organization," he told Vancouver reporters after signing with the Rangers. "I think I did that and gave it all I had. All I can say is I'm disappointed I didn't see it through. It's just time to move on and I wish everybody well."

His departure saved Vancouver ownership money and cleared room for some of the young Canuck forwards to emerge, most notably Brendan Morrison, who joined the team's top line with Todd Bertuzzi and Markus Naslund.

Survivors of the brief Messier era insist that he had a positive effect on the growth of the Canucks.

"I didn't really know what to expect when we first signed him," Naslund admitted during Messier's final season in Vancouver. "You'd heard all these rumours ... But once you've played with him,

I'd say it grows on you. He is a really tremendous leader. He talks at the right times, but not for the sake of talking."

Those lessons served Naslund well as he took over the captaincy following Messier's departure and developed into one of the NHL's premier players.

Other Canuck players, coaches and managers also insisted that despite the team's lack of success the Messier era paid dividends. One season after Messier departed, the Canucks made the playoffs, and they didn't miss the postseason again until 2005-06. Lessons learned from Messier, both in the dressing room and on the ice, had something to do with that resurgence.

"Mark's best quality is how he carries himself," former Canucks coach Marc Crawford told the Vancouver *Sun* on the day Messier left the Canucks. "Even through the tough times in Vancouver, he carried himself as a champion. We're a better club and the coaches are better coaches and the players are better players because of Mark Messier."

# ALEX MOGILNY

WHEN IT COMES to pure hockey sense and an overall skill package, Pavel Bure might be only the second most remarkable Russian right-winger to have worn a Canucks uniform. Alexander Mogilny could well lay claim to top honours in those categories.

A wily and somewhat enigmatic forward from Khabarovsk, a city on the former Soviet Union's remote eastern border with China, Mogilny had only one season of more than 50 goals for the Canucks. But he scored 76 times for the Buffalo Sabres in his fourth NHL season and he managed two key things that Bure didn't — to remain relatively healthy for a long career and to win a Stanley Cup.

Mogilny is "just an amazing hockey player," says former Canuck linemate Cliff Ronning. "I don't know how to explain it. When I played with him, his brain process of the game was exactly the same as what I was thinking. I knew when he wanted to criss-cross, I knew when he wanted to get the puck, I knew when he didn't want it, so that was fun. A player that stood out in my mind was definitely Alexander Mogilny."

Mogilny defected from Russia as a 20-year-old in 1989. A star with the Russian national junior team, where he had been a line-mate of Bure's, and a standout with CKSA Moscow, Mogilny was selected by the Buffalo Sabres 89th overall in the 1988 NHL draft.

That pick paid off handsomely for the Sabres; Mogilny got word to Buffalo management that he was willing to leave Russia without official consent. He met with then Sabres general manager Gerry Meehan at a Swedish hotel during the 1989 world tourna-ment in Stockholm and was spirited into the United States in time for the 1989-90 season.

The move was a risk for Mogilny, the first Soviet player in his prime to defect. At the time, he was a lieutenant in the Red Army; after he defected, he was tried in absentia and found guilty of trea-son. "I never wanted to be a military man," he told the Vancouver *Sun* in 1995. "I just wanted to play hockey."

While adjusting to a new country and language, Mogilny blos-somed in Buffalo. By his fourth season he had evolved into the NHL's most dangerous sniper, scoring those league-best 76 goals and adding 51 assists to finish with 127 points in 1992-93.

But injuries hampered him over the next two seasons and his point total dropped dra-matically. After putting up 47 points for the Sabres in 44 games in 1994-95, he was traded to the Canucks, who were seeking star power to fill their brand new General Motors Place. Vancouver gave up Mike Peca, Mike Wilson and an exchange of draft picks to reunite Mogilny with his former Russian junior teammate, Pavel Bure.

Mogilny paid instant dividends for the Canucks, scoring 55 times in 1995-96 to become only the second Vancouver player after Bure to break the 50-goal barrier. But that would be his peak as a Canuck as the franchise began to hit hard times. His goal total slipped to 31 in his second season in Vancouver, 18 in his third and 14 in his fourth. He was criticized by fans and the media for what was perceived as a lack of commitment to the game, a perception he rejected.

"Hockey is everything in my life," he said during a 1999 training camp interview in Kamloops. "Because of hockey, I am where I am, you know. I live a comfortable life and it's because of hockey. I'm not some entrepreneur or businessman. Hockey got me where I am."

The Canucks received value in return for Mogilny on March 14, 2000, when they traded him to the New Jersey Devils in exchange for centres Brendan Morrison and Denis Pederson. Morrison, born in British Columbia, would go on to become the Canucks' top-line centre.

Mogilny has prospered since leaving Vancouver. After being traded, he helped the Devils to a Stanley Cup title that spring. The next season, he scored 43 goals, had 83 points and added another 16 points in the playoffs as the Devils again reached the Cup finals. Perceived by some as an individualist on the ice, he savoured the feeling of team victory at hockey's highest level.

"Seventy-six goals were very special," he told the Toronto Maple Leafs' *Game Day Magazine* in a 2004 interview. "I'll never forget that.

*Alex Mogilny had an impressive 55 goals for the Canucks during the 1995–96 season.* (Chris Relke/HHOF)

It was a lot of fun, but the Stanley Cup is a different experience. It's more a team accomplishment instead of 76 goals, which is an individual accomplishment. When you're raising that Cup above your head it's amazing ... When you experience it once, you want to make sure you share it with the people who have never experienced it. It's a great joy and it's a real team accomplishment.

There's no one individual award that can overshadow winning the Stanley Cup. It's incredible — it really is."

Mogilny left the Devils as a free agent, signing with the Leafs and reuniting with former Canucks general manager Pat Quinn in July 2001.

# SERGIO MOMESSO

THESE DAYS, Sergio Momesso offers tasty breaded veal sandwiches and Italian sausage in his suburban Montreal restaurant, Momesso's Cafe. But a decade ago he was serving up stiff body checks to opponents of the Vancouver Canucks as a hard-hitting NHL left-winger.

Momesso had a valuable supporting role on the 1994 Canucks team that went to the Stanley Cup finals. He rode shotgun for Cliff Ronning and Martin Gelinas on Vancouver's second line that spring.

"We had size, we had speed, we had Cliffy with the skill, and Marty is a gritty player and he's quick," he recalls. "We seemed to gel well."

Momesso and Ronning played a lot of hockey together, first in St. Louis and then in Vancouver, after they were part of a huge trade that helped shape the future of the early 1990s Canucks. On March 5, 1991, Momesso, Ronning, Geoff Courtnall and Robert Dirk were sent by the Blues to Vancouver.

"I was playing a lot with Cliff, even in St. Louis, so we were used to each other, and my part was to work the corners and get in front of the net and create room for Cliff to do his moves and work hard and be kind of his big brother, I'd say, on the ice — to take care of him, too," Momesso says now. "That's what I was asked to do — play physical and tough and stick up for my teammates."

He felt the trade did little to help St. Louis, a team believed to be a Stanley Cup contender before the deal. But it helped turn the Canucks into a powerhouse in the early 1990s.

"We filled in the holes that they [Vancouver] needed [plugged]," he says. "The trade seemed to add players to the guys that they already had. You fill in a hole here, a hole there — that's how you make a team. Then, with the arrival of Pavel Bure the next year, we started to become a good team."

Momesso put up solid numbers, in terms of scoring and in the penalty box. In his first full season in Vancouver, the 6'3", 200-pounder posted 20 goals and 43 points, along with 198 penalty minutes. The next year he had 38 points and a career-high 200 minutes in the penalty box.

"We were very close on and off the ice," he reminisces. "We did a lot of things together. You know, we used to go out to dinner together a lot, even with the wives, not just the players. We were all around the same time when everyone was starting to play the best hockey of their career. I think that one year we had about seven or eight guys who had around 20 goals. Everyone was contributing, so it was a good feeling all around and everyone — other than, say, Pavel Bure, who was the so-called star player — we were all in the same boat. It wasn't like big star/little guy. We were all around the same level, so we got along well."

Momesso, who had posted 130- and 146-point seasons as a junior star with the Shawinigan Cataractes, never found anything close to the same scoring touch as an NHLer. His best statistical NHL season came in 1989-90, when the big winger scored 24 goals and added 32 assists for the Blues.

While Momesso didn't wow fans as a pro scorer, Canuck coach Pat Quinn used him in a variety of ways, at times even on the power play, and he contributed seven points and 56 penalty minutes in the 1994 playoffs as the Canucks reached the Stanley Cup finals.

Momesso found himself caught up in the club's rebuilding process less than a year after the dramatic playoff run. He was traded to the Toronto Maple Leafs following the lockout that shortened the 1994-95 season.

Originally selected by his hometown Canadiens in the second round of the 1983 NHL draft, played one season in Toronto before ending his career with brief stints with the Rangers and the Blues. He capped his NHL career after the 1996-97 season and then played four winters in the German elite league.

Returning to Canada, he became involved in the restaurant business his parents have operated for three decades. The original Momesso's Cafe founded by his parents is operated by his brother in downtown Montreal; Sergio and his wife own and operate a second restaurant, in suburban West Island.

# DANA MURZYN

HE WON THE Stanley Cup while playing in his hometown. For a professional hockey player it doesn't get much better than that. But a close second, if you ask Dana Murzyn, is coming within a goalpost or two of winning another Stanley Cup with a bunch of guys who have accomplished more than most thought they could.

Murzyn was a young but key defenceman with the Calgary Flames when they captured hockey's top prize during the spring of 1989. Five years later he was in the finals again, this time with the Vancouver Canucks, though he watched from the press box after injuring a knee late in the first round.

"Well, team-wise, for sure that was the highlight of my career," Murzyn says of his trip to the finals with the more fortunate Flames. "Personally, I started to play a lot more in Vancouver. And I took more of a leadership role and whatnot once I got there. But, yeah, winning a Stanley Cup would have to be a highlight."

Murzyn was raised in Calgary and played junior hockey in the southern Alberta city for the Western Hockey League Wranglers. In his final WHL season the 6'2", 200-pounder impressed the scouts enough to be selected fifth overall by the Hartford Whalers in the 1985 NHL draft. After breaking into the big leagues as an 18-year-old, he made the NHL all-rookie team with a season that included 26 points and 125 penalty minutes.

After improving to 28 points in his sophomore season, he was traded by Whalers general manager Emile Francis to the Flames 33 games into the 1987-88 season. But a triumphant homecoming wasn't prominent in Murzyn's mind when he learned of the deal.

"Well, you know what? When you get traded that's not really your first thought," he says. "Your first thought at that age — I was only 21 — was: 'Why are they trading me? I must have done something wrong.'

"But once I got to Calgary and started playing with the team and realized how good it was for me, and how good our team was, it worked out great."

It did. He eventually paired up with veteran Flames standout Al MacInnis and helped a Calgary lineup led by Lanny McDonald,

Mike Vernon and Gary Suter to the Stanley Cup. "Once I got to Calgary, it was pretty much spelled out for me that they wanted me to play a defensive role because we had some really talented offensive defencemen — you know, guys like Al MacInnis and Gary Suter."

Just one season removed from their league championship, the Flames brought in Doug Risebrough as general manager. The writing was on the wall for Murzyn.

"Calgary started to struggle a little bit. Doug Risebrough had taken over and, for whatever reasons, he just didn't feel I belonged there any more," Murzyn recalls. "I think it was a good time to leave and I came to another team that was on an upswing."

That was Vancouver. He arrived in the spring of 1991 as Pat Quinn retooled the Canucks and it was a key move, as Murzyn provided strong leadership and a steady hand on the blue line.

With the Canucks for parts of nine seasons, he never scored more than 20 points. In fact, his two best offensive seasons remain the years with Hartford. But he was valuable in Vancouver all the same and with Jyrki Lumme formed one of the NHL's longest-serving defensive pairs; they lasted together for more than six seasons.

"I guess he was obviously a lot more physical and maybe he was more stay-at-home," Lumme says now, reflecting on why the pairing worked so well. "But I think the biggest thing was that we cared for each other. We wanted to help each other. We would do anything for each other. We were roommates off the ice, on the road. We spent a lot of time together. He's just a great guy."

The feeling is mutual. Murzyn speaks fondly of his time playing with the flashy Finn: "I just think that we complemented each other so well. We became very, very good friends, so I think it was a pride thing for us, too, how we played every night together. And we never wanted to let each other down. And Jyrki being a lot more offensive-minded and a lot more skilled than I was, it was a good complement, similar to what I was doing with Al [MacInnis] in Calgary. It just worked really well. We kind of knew where everybody was going to be all the time."

*Defenceman Dana Murzyn formed an effective pair with the more offensive-minded Jyrki Lumme for the Canucks in the 1990s.* (Chris Relke/HHOF)

Murzyn retired in the spring of 1999 after coming back from knee reconstruction surgery. He'd been playing for Mike Keenan, but by the time he returned Marc Crawford was running the Canucks bench.

"He basically just played me two games and told me I didn't fit into his vision of the Vancouver Canucks and that was it," he says of Crawford. Still, in an NHL career that spanned 838 games Murzyn clearly relishes his time with the Canucks.

"We had a great bunch of guys for a lot of years in Vancouver. It's one thing to have some of the best players on your team in the league [as was the case in Calgary], but it's another thing to watch players develop into them. And I think we all got a chance to do that in Vancouver."

Murzyn now lives with his family in Calgary, where he is a partner in a pair of wine and spirit stores.

# GINO ODJICK

FAR MORE TALENTED hockey players have worn the uniform of the Vancouver Canucks, but few if any have endeared themselves to fans or their teammates more than Gino Odjick.

During his more than seven years with the Canucks, chants of "Gino! Gino!" regularly rained down from the seats in the Pacific Coliseum and General Motors Place. The 6'3", 215-pound "Algonquin Enforcer" grabbed their attention with his fists and earned their respect with the heart he showed on every shift, not to mention the fact that he was capable of staying in the same time zone as close friend and sometime linemate Pavel Bure.

"I think Gino is one of those guys you'd refer to as an ultimate teammate," says former Canuck defenceman Dana Murzyn. "He really, honestly cared about his job, which at that point in time was one of the toughest jobs in the NHL. I don't think anyone can ever underestimate that. Gino had no problem in going out there and taking on the toughest guys in the league, two or three times a game. He took a lot of pride in it and, like most of the enforcers that I've known, once you take off the skates, he's one of the nicest guys you'd ever want to be around."

On the ice, it was a different story for opponents. Odjick piled up a franchise-high 2,127 penalty minutes in seven and a half seasons with Vancouver. More important, he created some security for offensive stars such as Cliff Ronning and, particularly, for Pavel Bure.

Bure and Odjick were unlikely pals, a quiet Russian from Moscow with superb skills and a gangly kid from a Quebec First Nations reserve who had a better knack with his knuckles than for nailing the net.

"What he did was, he got Pavel a lot of space," Murzyn says. "That's important."

Odjick created a lot of space for all his teammates between the time he was selected 86th overall by the Canucks in the 1990 NHL draft and when he was traded away to the New York Islanders in March 1998.

He credits Canucks coach and general manager Pat Quinn

with helping him develop into an 11-year NHLer and a better person.

"He basically said that I wouldn't make it on fighting alone and that I had to work on my game," Odjick recalls being told as a rookie by Quinn. "He wanted to have 20 guys on his bench that he would feel comfortable putting on the ice at any time. I don't think he likes to carry a person on the roster who can't play at least 10, 12 minutes a night for him on any given night. That doesn't mean that we played that every night, but some nights he needed us to play 15 minutes and we'd have to be ready for that.

"It's fun as a hockey player when you go to the rink every night knowing that you'll be given a chance to make a difference in the game, whether it's a big goal or a big fight or a big assist or a big hit."

Odjick scored 137 points during a 605-game NHL career. His finest scoring season was in 1994 when, often skating with Bure, he had 16 goals and 29 points and was plus 13.

Gino Odjick didn't have much to learn about the other part of his role, that of a top NHL enforcer. He grew up on the Kitigan Zibi reserve near Maniwaki, Quebec, about one and a half hours north of Ottawa, and the experience served him well.

"I had good years growing up," he says. "I never missed a meal. Certainly, we weren't a rich family, but my dad worked hard and we all worked with him in the bush, too. We never missed out on anything and we had whatever we needed.

"But when I grew up in the '70s and the '80s there was a lot of friction between the people of the community in Maniwaki, who were non-native, and Kitigan Zibi on the reserve. We learned to stick together as a family from the get-go, and we thought that we would be okay if we stuck together, and if anybody picked on one of us then they'd have to pick on all of us. That's how we got by, so that's where I learned how to fight.

"It just came naturally to me [to fight on the ice]."

Odjick played two seasons of major junior hockey and in two Memorial Cup tournaments with the Laval Titan, piling up 558

*Gino Odjick wasn't a big offensive producer but he was one of the most popular players in Canucks history.* (Chris Relke/HHOF)

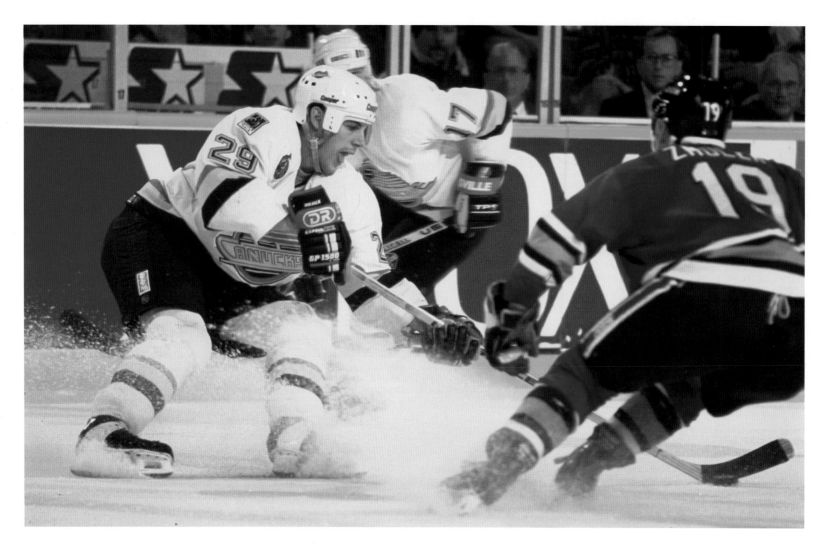

The "Algonquin Enforcer," forward Gino Odjick created plenty of space on the ice for his Canuck teammates. (David Klutho/HHOF)

penalty minutes along the way. In his second season with Laval, he scored 38 points to go along with his 280 penalty minutes to prove he could play a little, too.

He put on 20 pounds of muscle and quickly adapted to the NHL tough-guy circuit, needing just 17 rookie games with the International Hockey League's Milwaukee Admirals before he was called up by the Canucks. He racked up 296 NHL penalty minutes in only 45 games in his first season and it quickly became evident that he and the Canucks were a good combination.

"I was happy to go anywhere, to be totally honest with you, but for me it ended up being a perfect fit," he says. "There were a lot of First Nations communities [in British Columbia] ... where I grew up in a First Nations community, a lot of times we used to walk around with our heads down and kind of feel a little bit inferior to people who were non-natives. And I was happy one day when Pat told me to walk with my head high and look people in the eyes,

and that I was a part of society and a part of the Vancouver community. It really did a lot for my self-esteem and changed the way I looked at things."

Odjick had NHL stints in Philadelphia and Montreal before retiring in 2002. He was unhappy to leave Vancouver as a player, but he has returned as a business partner of the Musqueam Indian Band in the Musqueam Golf & Learning Academy, located across the Fraser River from Vancouver International Airport.

He remembers the feeling that came from hearing his name chanted by thousands of Canucks fans. "It was great. It was really motivating and it pumped you up. It really made you want to go out and make something happen. I really respected that and enjoyed it a lot.

"Even nowadays when I meet people on the street, they still say thanks for the great memories."

## One-Two Punch

When asked to name the enforcers whom he respected the most during his 11 years in the NHL, former Vancouver tough guy Gino Odjick lists Dave Brown and Tie Domi.

"Dave Brown, when I first started out in the league, was one of the toughest guys that I fought — a big, strong, left-handed player who could hurt you with a punch," Odjick says.

"The person that I respected the most was probably Tie Domi, because of his size — you know, 5'10", 200 pounds and fighting everybody night in and night out and still doing it at his age. You have to respect the job he's doing."

*Tough guy Gino Odjick posted 137 points over a 605-game NHL career. (Paul Bereswill/HHOF)*

# PAT QUINN

NOTHING lasts forever in professional sports, even if you're a winner. That point was driven home on November 4, 1997, when the Vancouver Canucks fired president and general manager Pat Quinn.

A charter member of the Canucks franchise as a tough, lunch-bucket defenceman in 1970-71, Quinn is much better known as the man who finally brought sustained NHL respectability to Vancouver in the late-1980s and early '90s.

His Canuck teams won a pair of division titles and reached the Stanley Cup finals in 1994. But more impressive than the on-ice record was the enduring loyalty he instilled in his players, both as a coach and general manager. When he was fired by Vancouver's new ownership, the Canucks lost the closest thing to a father figure that the franchise had ever experienced.

"Once he was gone, it was like a morgue in that dressing room until everybody got traded," recalls former Canucks tough guy Gino Odjick.

"Pat was a big part of our lives for the whole '90s here, a person that you looked up to and respected. He was a person who you learned to love and who made you the best hockey player that you could be and also, maybe, a better human being."

Talk to almost any of the players Quinn assembled during his tenure in Vancouver and the comments are similar. The big Irishman with the ever present cigar clearly had a huge impact on those who played for him.

"I look up to the man and respect everything he taught me at a young age," says former Canuck Jim Sandlak.

"I was only 22 years old when Pat first came in. That was only my first year of marriage and he sort of settled me down and helped me along and I've used all his influence in my life today. He came in, took the bull by the horns and said, 'This is the way we're going to do it.' He is a man's man, a player's coach. Not only were you playing, obviously, for the team and the organization, but the way I felt as a person, I played for Pat."

Adds former Vancouver goalie Kirk McLean: "You just wanted to win for him and do well. If we didn't, you felt like you let him down."

Perhaps Quinn inspired such strong loyalty and emotion in his players because he played with his heart on his sleeve himself. Not blessed with loads of talent or much mobility, he was a steady defenceman who could take care of his own end and the physical aspects of the game, earning him the nickname "the Irish Enforcer" during his nine-year career as an NHL journeyman.

The eldest son of a Hamilton firefighter who briefly considered a career in the priesthood, Quinn spent five years in hockey's minor leagues, during which time he began working toward his law degree. He was claimed by the Canucks from the roster of the Toronto Maple Leafs in the 1970 NHL expansion draft.

A fan favourite who had played for the Canucks of the old minor-pro Western League, Quinn was a member of that first Vancouver NHL squad, paired mostly with Gary Doak. During one practice in that first season, Quinn twice fought Vancouver captain Orland Kurtenbach.

"We were a ragtag bunch," Quinn once told the Vancouver *Sun* of that 1970-71 team. "We weren't even what you'd call adequate by the standards of the NHL at that time. But we were good workers and I think every one was good people."

Former Canucks play-by-play man Jim Robson remembers being impressed with Quinn's honesty during a 1971 between-periods interview he conducted in Chicago. At the time, Quinn was being benched by coach Hal Laycoe in favour of Dennis Kearns; Quinn opened up during the interview about his frustration.

"By the end of it, he was in tears," Robson recalls. "He was so emotional." Robson's impression was vivid: Quinn cared so deeply, he couldn't hide his feelings.

Quinn has since instilled the same sort of passion in the players he has coached and managed during a post-playing career that has included NHL stops in Philadelphia, Los Angeles, Vancouver and Toronto.

He was claimed from the Canucks by the Atlanta Flames

during the 1972 expansion draft, and he captained the Flames to conclude his 606-game playing career. His first NHL head-coaching job came in 1980, when he led the Philadelphia Flyers to a Stanley Cup finals appearance.

Fired by Philadelphia in 1982 after three and a half seasons, Quinn spent three seasons as coach of the Los Angeles Kings before being hired in 1987 as the Canucks' president, general manager and, ultimately, coach. He immediately began retooling the team and, after missing the playoffs in two of his first three years, Vancouver began a streak in which it made the playoffs in six straight springs.

The best years came when Quinn was coaching the club. After taking over behind the bench for Bob McCammon during the 1990-91 season, he coached the team to 42-, 46- and 41-win seasons, the three highest victory totals in the first three decades of the franchise.

Quinn was also busy as a general manager, assembling the team that he would coach to within two goals of a Stanley Cup during the spring of 1994. Included among his best draft picks were Trevor Linden (second overall in 1988) and Pavel Bure (113th overall in 1989), but he landed his finest talent by trade, including Greg Adams and Kirk McLean from the New Jersey Devils in 1987; Jyrki Lumme from the Montreal Canadiens in 1990; Geoff Courtnall, Sergio Momesso and Cliff Ronning from the St. Louis Blues in 1991; and Dana Murzyn from the Calgary Flames the same year.

Quinn's high point with the Canucks came in 1994, when Vancouver emerged from a disappointing 41-40-3 regular season to go on a playoff tear. After rebounding from a 3-1 series deficit to beat the Calgary Flames in Round 1, the Canucks defeated Dallas and Toronto before nearly upending the New York Rangers in one of the finest Stanley Cup series in NHL history.

"Pat treated everybody with respect," says Lumme, who also played for Quinn in Toronto near the end of his career. "He treated everybody as a man. But you know, when he had to put his fist down he sure did it and, when he did it, you knew. But he wasn't in your ear every day just yelling and screaming and making you do this and that. He treated everybody with respect. And you don't want to let a guy like that down. I've always loved to play for him."

"Pat was very honest with all the players," adds Murzyn. "He was very stern, but at the same time he kept the game very simple and he was part of the team. He didn't put himself above the team or away from the team. He worked with the guys. When someone did something wrong, he'd say they did something wrong, but he never singled anybody out. He had a real sense of team with all of us.

*Long before he was the team's coach or general manager, Pat Quinn was a popular, rugged defenceman for the first-year NHL Canucks.* (Graphic Artists/HHOF)

He let us do our jobs and kept us kind of on line, but he never persecuted anyone and everyone respected that."

"The biggest thing is that he didn't treat you as a hockey player or as an employee, he treated you as a person, with the appropriate respect on both sides of the street," says Gerald Diduck. "You weren't just a tool in his tool belt, so to speak. And because of that you ended up playing for the guy. I mean, he's one of the few coaches where you were actually disappointed if he was disappointed, whereas so much of the business gets to be everybody kind of protecting their own ass ... Pat would put his neck out on the line, play guys when they were having slumps, and people responded to that."

Nevertheless, the Quinn years began to take a downward turn following those 1994 playoffs. Quinn stepped away from the bench, turning over the team to assistant Rick Ley. Ley lasted less than two seasons before Quinn returned, but the club's on-ice slide worsened. Vancouver lasted two rounds in the 1995 playoffs and just one the following spring.

Prior to the 1996-97 season, Quinn hired former Canadian national team coach Tom Renney to run the bench. Renney, who seemed to struggle to command the respect of the players Quinn had assembled, missed the playoffs in 1997 with a 35-40-7 record.

*Pat Quinn fields questions from the media during a scrum in Vancouver.* (Chris Relke/HHOF)

With the team floundering and new ownership growing impatient, Quinn was fired by Orca Bay Sports and Entertainment in November 1997. He received the news during a road trip at the team's hotel in Washington, D.C. It came as a shock to the proud man who had devoted 10 years of his life to the organization.

But it also gave him time to have the hip replacement surgery he had been putting off. And by the following summer he was working in hockey again, as head coach of the Toronto Maple Leafs, the team he had idolized as a boy and with which he had begun his NHL career as a player in 1968. A two-time NHL coach of the year, Quinn has also excelled as an international coach, leading Canada to the gold medal at the 2002 Salt Lake City Olympics and the 2004 Canada Cup championship.

"Good people find jobs quickly and they're back on their feet and I think that just kind of says what Pat's done," says former Canucks captain and now director of player development Stan Smyl. "Pat is a very patient man, a good teacher with the game, listens to you, gives his opinion, is under control — a lot of things that I saw in Pat's coaching are some of the things that I wanted to take in my coaching. I learned a lot from Pat Quinn." Although Quinn later admitted he had been frustrated working under

Orca Bay ownership, he has always taken the high road when discussing his departure from the Canucks. In an interview with The Canadian Press shortly after joining the Leafs, he summed up his feelings: "I had a terrific time there and like most people I'm hanging onto the positive things, the good things that happened there."

Judging by the loyalty his former players show, there were plenty of good things. That's what made the end difficult for many. Gino Odjick describes Quinn's departure as being "like our dad was gone and there was a new guy in our house."

"Certainly, if you look at a lot of the guys who played there in the '90s under Pat, we all had our career years under him," Odjick says. "We were a close team and everything was built around us feeling like a family and doing things together. What I liked about Pat when he was in the organization was he made it clear that being part of the community was very important. So not only did he make us better hockey players, he ended up making us better human beings. And for that I'll always be grateful."

Quinn was fired by the Leafs on April 20, 2006, after Toronto failed to make the playoffs.

## Strange Comings and Goings

Pat Quinn's arrival in and departure from Vancouver both were rather out of the ordinary.

In 1987, when he was still coaching the Los Angeles Kings, he accepted a US$100,000 signing bonus from the Canucks to join the team for the 1987-88 season. That resulted in NHL president John Ziegler suspending him from coaching for three years. Ziegler also fined the Canucks US$310,000 — later reduced to US$10,000 after a legal challenge — in an episode that became known as "Quinn-gate."

In 1997, three days after he had been fired as president and general manager by the Canucks, Quinn was reportedly telephoned by owner John McCaw and offered the coaching job. A stunned Quinn declined.

*Most of those who played for Pat Quinn in the NHL describe him as a players' coach. (Vancouver Canucks)*

# CLIFF RONNING

As a 16-year-old, Cliff Ronning was one of the estimated 100,000 Canucks fans who lined the route of the team's post-Stanley Cup finals parade in Vancouver in May 1982.

Twelve years later that Burnaby boy was part of another Vancouver championship series route, but this time he was on skates.

Ronning, who at 5'8" and 170 pounds beat the bigger-is-better mantra of professional hockey to carve out a 20-year career, clearly appreciates having had the chance to participate in one of the Canucks' finest moments.

"You know, when I was a kid, that's who I watched," he says. "Like most kids, where you're from is where you want to play, and my dream was to play for the Vancouver Canucks. My parents used to take me to the games at the Pacific Coliseum, so I grew up watching those players — Orland Kurtenbach and guys like that."

Ronning developed into a junior hockey star in the Lower Mainland, spending a year in tier 2 before moving on to the Western Hockey League's New Westminster Bruins. He became a scoring phenom for the Bruins, piling up 89 goals and a staggering 197 points in his final season of junior.

But his size made doubters out of most in the pro hockey world. Despite his obvious passing and skating skills, he wasn't selected until the seventh round of the 1984 NHL draft, when he finally went to the St. Louis Blues, 134th overall.

"You know, people have doubted me, I would say, all my career," Ronning says. "Every time I stepped on the ice, there was always a doubt — 'Can he do it again?' — because of my size, definitely.

"But I was always a guy who, when it came to competing, that came easy to me, because the more I got hit, the more I got bounced around, the more I wanted to win ... If you really look over the history, I had to make every game count, sometimes just to stay in the lineup, or every shift count just to show them I could still play."

Rather than join St. Louis right away, he suited up with the Canadian national team for the 1985-86 season and for part of the following year. He posted 55 points in 64 games for the Blues in 1988-89, but then he opted to jump to Asiago of the Italian league for the entire 1989-90 season.

"It wasn't about money or any of that stuff," he reveals. "It was just the competitiveness of the game and enjoying it. And at that time I wasn't enjoying just getting out five or six shifts a game [with St. Louis]. The game was a little political and I just went over there to Italy and really enjoyed playing the game again. It was a great experience, knowing that sometimes there are things that are out of your control, and that's what the situation was in St. Louis at the time."

Ronning returned to the Blues the following season, putting up 32 points over 48 games. Then, on March 5, 1991, came the opportunity he had been waiting for: he was traded to Vancouver. He was going home to play for the team he had idolized as a youngster.

"You know, at first I was so excited," he recalls. "And then all of a sudden, it hit me that it was my hometown, and that every play I'm going to make is going to be all of a sudden picked apart and analyzed. But then I just thought: if I can play to the level I think I can, well, that's part of the pressure, right? By me just going for it, it helped me become a better player all around."

Traded to Vancouver with Geoff Courtnall, Sergio Momesso and Robert Dirk, Ronning enjoyed the finest years of his NHL career. During his first three seasons with the Canucks he had 71, 85 and 68 points, respectively, often playing with a mixture of linemates and usually on the second line. His 85-point campaign in 1992-93, during which he collected 56 assists, was his best statistical season in the NHL.

"I'll tell you what, for a little guy he sure didn't back down," says former teammate Doug Lidster. "He may not have been the instigator type that Theo Fleury was, but you know, he'd get bounced every once in a while [and] he'd bounce right back up. He's got unbelievable skills, great vision, great hands, and he's super competitive."

Coach Pat Quinn used Ronning's superb passing skills with a

range of players, including Trevor Linden, Pavel Bure and Alex Mogilny. When the Canucks went to the Stanley Cup final in 1994, the skilled centre played with Sergio Momesso and Martin Gelinas on a highly effective second line. During those playoffs Ronning had 15 points in 24 games.

"I always played with the guys who were struggling," he says of his time with Vancouver. "And once I got them going scoring again, then I never saw them."

Although he had at least 67 points in each of the four full seasons he played in Vancouver, Ronning was allowed to slip away as a free agent in the summer of 1996. The Canucks asked him to take a pay cut of US$200,000, from the US$900,000 he had been making; the Phoenix Coyotes dangled US$1.1 million.

Leaving his hometown "was difficult to do," Ronning says. "But when they offered me even less than what I was making, I obviously knew that they had no plans for me being a part of anything, so ... I think maybe they were betting that I wouldn't leave my hometown, but there comes a point that there has to be some logic on my part but also on their part. I just wanted a fair deal."

Ronning has since proved a valuable veteran presence with Phoenix, Nashville, Los Angeles, Minnesota and the New York Islanders. He announced his retirement from the NHL in February 2006. "I've tried to enjoy every place I've gone to, but by far playing for my hometown was what I always wanted to do," he says. "If I could have played all 18 or 19 years with Vancouver, I would have loved that. But it's not a perfect world, right? So I enjoyed every minute everywhere else I played."

## Role Models

*Growing up in Burnaby, Cliff Ronning watched the Vancouver Canucks and imagined he would one day play for them.*

*"I enjoyed different players, different styles," he says. "I liked the way Gary Lupul tried on every shift. I liked the way Thomas Gradin skated and was just effortless in his skating and passing. I think those two guys stood out quite a bit.*

*"I remember the leadership of someone like a Stan Smyl, who didn't have tons of talent but showed up every game to play.*

*"I kind of idolized each player for different attributes of what they carried to the team."*

*Despite terrific offensive production, the Canucks let Cliff Ronning slip away as a free agent in 1996.* [Chris Relke/HHOF]

# A NEW YORK MINUTE

*For Vancouver players and fans, 1994 Stanley Cup playoffs were quite a ride*

## by Iain MacIntyre

A NEW YORK STORY: a man in a hurry to leave Central Park decides to take a shortcut by climbing a wrought-iron fence. He summits the fence, loses a foothold and impales himself on an arrow-like tine. Quite alive, he holds himself in place until firemen arrive and begin cutting through the fence to unhook the punctured man. It is the morning rush and hardened New Yorkers pass by the bizarre scene with studied indifference. Most don't even break stride on their way to work or school. This is New York, after all, the centre of the universe. What, you think they haven't seen a human being shishkabobbed on a fence before?

It takes a lot to make New Yorkers look, let alone to stop them in their tracks. But on the hot afternoon of June 14, 1994, the Vancouver Canucks did just that — or rather, their bus and escort did.

To traverse 16 shimmering blocks through the canyons of midtown Manhattan, from the Grand Hyatt Hotel to Madison Square Garden, the Canucks had a police escort to Game 7 of the Stanley Cup final against the New York Rangers.

Motorcycle cops, trained to speed heads of state through streets choked with limousines, cabs and double-parked delivery trucks, rode in teams ahead of the Canucks' bus, blocking off side roads and intersections to allow Vancouver players a non-stop ride to the arena.

Perhaps New Yorkers thought it was the Iraqi head of state, because there were a thousand one-finger salutes as the Canucks were whisked along. Canuck captain Trevor Linden doesn't think so. "They knew who we were," he says, with a grin.

It was the only easy ride in the greatest spring the Canucks had ever had. This was a team that did everything the hard way.

The Canucks who went to the 1982 final, a few miles east on Long Island, were an assortment of journeymen and labourers who elevated themselves at playoff time and surged beyond everyone's expectations.

The 1994 Canucks, by contrast, were deep and talented, but bumbled exasperatingly though the regular season. Vancouver set franchise records with 96 points in 1991-92 and 101 in 1992-93 and could have gone to the final either season. Instead, the Canucks were upset in the playoffs' second round both times.

The nucleus — Linden, Pavel Bure, Geoff Courtnall, Greg Adams and Cliff Ronning up front, Jyrki Lumme and Dave Babych on defence and Kirk McLean in goal — remained intact for the 1993-94 season. Much was expected. Little was delivered through the winter.

After a 7-1 start, the Canucks were five games under .500 for the rest of the season and sputtered into the playoffs as the seventh seed in the Western Conference at 41-40-3. Pat Quinn probably wouldn't have survived as coach had he not also been general manager.

As if their results weren't discouraging enough, the Canucks rarely escaped the smog of a messy contract dispute with emerging star Petr Nedved, who refused to re-sign in Vancouver. When Nedved eventually signed with the St. Louis Blues in March, an arbitrator awarded the Canucks smooth centre Craig Janney as compensation.

Janney's reputation as a playmaker was exceeded only by his reputation as a loafer. Janney to the Canucks would have been like corn chips to a man dying of thirst. Fortunately, he refused to report. Quinn somehow persuaded the Blues to take back Janney and part instead with Jeff Brown, Bret Hedican and Nathan LaFayette. That trade on March 21 saved the Canucks' season.

Brown was the offensive defenceman the Canucks had lacked since Paul Reinhart had retired in 1990, and Hedican dramatically upgraded the defence's mobility. LaFayette, a checking forward, would become that sweltering June night in New York an infamous trivia answer.

The trade had little initial impact. The Canucks trailed the Calgary Flames 3-1 in their first-round playoff series and the bleak season seemed mercilessly near its end. Bure was invisible, McLean was outplayed by Calgary goalie Mike Vernon and things seemed as they had always been: the powerful Flames superior, the Canucks willing to go meekly into the night or to Hawaii.

Courtnall's overtime slapshot that won Game 5 in Calgary roused the Canucks from their stupor. The awakening resulted in

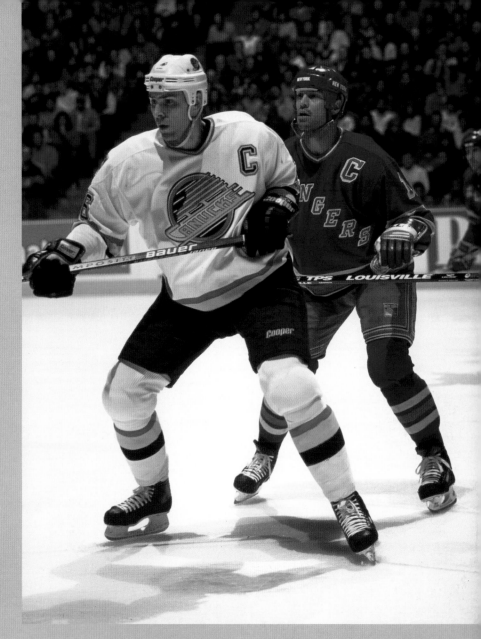

Linden's overtime winner in Game 6 and Bure's historic double-overtime goal in Game 7. Bure's breakaway deke, after a blue-line-to-blue-line pass by Brown, is regarded as the greatest goal in Canucks history. That game also featured the franchise's most famous save: McLean's overtime magic act on Robert Reichel during a three-on-one break.

But as cathartic and seminal as that victory seemed, wiping away nearly a quarter century of haplessness, the games that convinced Canuck players they could win the Stanley Cup were the next two.

Emotionally and physically spent and with only one day to recover, the team started the second round by marching into Dallas and sweeping two games from a rested Stars team that had, like the Flames, finished 12 points ahead of the Canucks. Vancouver brushed aside the Stars in five games, then dismissed the Toronto Maple Leafs equally quickly.

The Stanley Cup final against the Mike Keenan-coached Rangers is still considered the finest of the NHL's modern era. It was the crescendo for attacking, artful hockey, which died the next year when the neutral-zone-trapping New Jersey Devils won their first of three Stanley Cups and changed the way the game was played.

Cynical coaches' erosion of the game and NHL commissioner Gary Bettman's reckless expansion of the league have made fans more wistful by the year for another final like Canucks-Rangers.

As against the Flames, the Canucks rallied from a 3-1 deficit to force Game 7. Their 4-1 win in Game 6 is regarded as the greatest game ever played in Vancouver, but it was only the third-best of the series' final three games; in Game 5, with New York ready to explode with its first Stanley Cup in 54 years, Vancouver had recovered from blowing a 3-0 third-period lead and won 6-3.

Game 7 was a classic, a 3-2 Rangers victory that featured the best game of Linden's career. He scored twice. Vancouver nearly tied it with a minute remaining when Courtnall's centring pass found LaFayette in the slot. The clang of Lafayette's shot hitting the post resonates still. So does that spring run by the Canucks, who were a changed franchise.

Their stature around North America was elevated, and so was their payroll as the Canucks, under pressure from fans, rewarded and kept their best players. The dramatic inflation of salaries and the construction of a new arena caused Seattle billionaire John McCaw to be recruited as a new owner, which led eventually to Quinn's dismissal and Keenan's hiring in Vancouver.

Three days after game 7, fugitive retired American football star O. J. Simpson was driven by his friend Al Cowling down Interstate 5 in Los Angeles, trailed by dozens of police cars and nearly as many television news helicopters. North America was mesmerized by O. J. and his murdered wife, Nicole, and for most people June 1994 is best remembered for a white Ford Bronco and the famous suspect it contained.

To Canuck fans, it was merely the second greatest chase that spring.

*Iain MacIntyre has been a sports writer at the Vancouver* Sun *newspaper since 1981. He has reported on the Canucks and the NHL since 1991.*

# great expectations

The Vancouver Canucks have yet to make an appearance in the Stanley Cup final this decade. In fact, heading into the 2006-07 season, they had won only one playoff series so far in the new millennium.

That lack of postseason success has been a significant blemish on a predominantly handsome half decade. To many, playoff accomplishment is the only standard by which a NHL team should be measured.

Still, others could make a convincing argument that the early years of this decade have been among the brightest in the 35-season history of the Canucks.

Since the new millennium was rung in, the Canucks have compiled an excellent regular-season record.

They finished better than .500 for six straight winters and recorded more than 100 points in each of the 2002-03 and 2003-04 regular seasons.

*Facing page: Anson Carter and twins Henrik and Daniel Sedin enjoyed a terrific season together in 2005–06.* (Vancouver Canucks/Jeff Vinnick)

*Above: Trevor Linden has been part of the new-millennium Canucks, although in a reduced role from the 1990s.* (Vancouver Canucks/Jeff Vinnick)

Perhaps more important, the team has, until the 2005-06 season at least, consistently played an exciting, up-tempo brand of hockey. It has featured one of the NHL's most exciting lines in Markus Naslund, Brendan Morrison and Todd Bertuzzi and employed one of the best blue-line corps in the league, anchored by Ed Jovanovski and Mattias Ohlund.

That success has paid off in 124 straight sellouts of General Motors Place. It has also resulted in a much envied season-ticket base capped at 17,000 fans with a waiting list in the thousands.

The Canucks have gone from one of the most hapless NHL franchises during the late 1990s to one of the most successful, at least in the regular season. They have gone from money-bleeders to money-makers with a combined profit reported at US$50 million over the 2002-03 and 2003-04 seasons, compared with losses of more than US$100 million during the mid- to late 1990s.

In 2001-02, for the first time in its franchise history Vancouver led the NHL in goals scored. The next season the Canucks recorded 104 points, their best total in 35 seasons. They backed that up with 101 points in 2003-04, when the team also clinched its first Northwest Division championship and its first division title of any kind in 11 years. Only an inexplicable collapse down the stretch run of the 2005-06 regular season prevented the Canucks from making the playoffs for a fifth straight year in this decade, although the team still finished 10 games over .500.

Regular season results have, for the most part, been there for the new millennium Canucks. But playoff success has remained elusive. And don't think they aren't painfully aware of it.

"We've proven that we can be a great regular-season team with winning the division and having 100-point seasons ..." says goaltender Dan Cloutier, whose season-ending knee injury in 2005-06 was a factor in the team missing the postseason. "Everybody knows how good we [can be] in the regular season. Now we definitely have to prove it in the playoffs, and that includes myself."

That will be the remaining test for these Canucks. That is the hurdle on which general manager Dave Nonis will ultimately be judged. It is a difficult standard and he knows it.

Virtually the only thing left unaccomplished by Nonis' friend, mentor and predecessor, Brian Burke, was a significant playoff run. Vancouver fans have been craving a Stanley Cup since 1915, when the city's Millionaires captured the silverware in the days before the NHL laid sole claim to it. But even a berth in the Western Conference final would be a refreshing tonic for the frustration of recent springs.

Playoff experience is something most franchises seem to have to earn over time. The Tampa Bay Lightning might have come out of nowhere to win the Stanley Cup in 2004, but most squads have to pay their dues and suffer their share of postseason disappointments before winning the big prize.

Even the 1994 Canucks, the last Vancouver team to make the Stanley Cup final, experienced playoff despair after promising regular seasons in the years leading up to that magic spring.

"Playoff experience is something that you have to gain," Nonis said before the 2005-06 season. "You can't just snap your fingers and have it. Not that you want to compare yourself to some of the other great teams, but if you look at the history of a lot of the teams that have done well in the playoffs, they've gone through a lot of the same things that we've gone through. The Detroit Red Wings went through a stretch where they were out in the first round four out of five years."

The Canucks have had their share of disappointments so far in the new millennium. After missing the playoffs completely in the spring of 2000, they rebounded with a 36-28-11-7 record to make the postseason in 2000-01, the first post-Mark Messier campaign. But they bowed out quickly by falling in four straight games to the Colorado Avalanche, who went on to win the Stanley Cup.

That was generally accepted as a learning experience and the young Canucks emerged stronger for it, posting a 42-30-7-3 regular season in 2001-02 and nudging postseason expectations higher that spring.

Those hopes were elevated further when the Canucks won the first two games of their opening-round series on the road against the powerful Detroit Red Wings in April 2002. But four straight losses once again ended the team's postseason in abrupt fashion. This time, it was the Wings who went on to sip out of the Stanley Cup.

More determined than ever, the Canucks had the finest regular season in their history the following winter. They won 45 times in 82 starts and posted a franchise-best 104 points to place second in the Northwest Division. Two of their players, Markus Naslund and Todd Bertuzzi, emerged into bona fide superstars, respectively finishing second and fifth among league scorers. Vancouver became a team that everybody enjoyed watching, a franchise held up as an example to emulate. This time, fans had clear playoff expectations for the Canucks.

So when Vancouver lost 6-0 to the St. Louis Blues in the opening game of the first round and then fell behind 3-1 in the series, the pressure was on. The Canucks bounced back dramatically, clawing their way out of that deficit and triumphing over the stunned Blues in GM Place in Game 7. Vancouver supporters began to feel that 2003 was the year.

*The towels are waving in a jam-packed General Motors Place during the 2004 playoffs against the Calgary Flames.* (Vancouver Canucks/Jeff Vinnick)

Facing the third-year Minnesota Wild and with powerhouses Detroit and Colorado already out of the playoff picture, the path to the Stanley Cup final suddenly seemed clearer than ever for Vancouver.

But days after they had rambled back to beat the Blues on home ice, the Canucks themselves became the victims of a Cinderella team. Up 3-1 in the second-round series, Vancouver dropped three straight to the Jacques Lemaire-coached Wild and were outscored 16-5 over the final three games by a team that normally had trouble mounting any sustained offence.

To make matters worse, the Canucks blew a 2-0 lead in Game 7 in front of their home crowd to fall 4-2 and once again bow out of the playoffs. To a man, they realized they had let a brilliant opportunity slip away.

Dan Cloutier, the goaltender who had been outstanding in the comeback against St. Louis, surrendered 15 goals on just 60 shots over the final three games against the Wild, resurrecting all the questions about whether he was a money goaltender that had seemingly been answered days before. In the final game, Minnesota scored on Cloutier on four of its last seven shots.

Just as fateful, Canuck snipers were held in check by the tenacious Wild defence. Naslund failed to score after Game 1 of the series, and Bertuzzi was held to just a single marker.

"We're not at the level that we need [to be] to win a championship," coach Marc Crawford told the Vancouver *Sun*. "We didn't do enough ... We are learning lessons along the way ... difficult lessons."

Those lessons continued the following season, with similar results. After a 101-point regular campaign in which they overcame injuries to Jovanovski and Naslund and a controversial season-ending suspension to Bertuzzi to win their final six games and clinch their first Northwest Division title, the Canucks again suffered a heartbreaking playoff exit.

This time the villains were the physical, upstart Calgary Flames,

*The combination of Todd Bertuzzi and Markus Naslund was highly productive while it lasted in Vancouver. (Vancouver Canucks/Jeff Vinnick)*

a group that had finished seven points behind Vancouver in the regular season. Led by captain Jarome Iginla, the Flames would use a dramatic seven-game series victory over Vancouver as a springboard into the Stanley Cup final.

The Canucks played the series without Bertuzzi, whose physical presence might well have made the difference against a pounding Calgary lineup. Bertuzzi was serving an indefinite suspension for a controversial late-season attack on Colorado's Steve Moore.

The Canucks were also missing Cloutier after the first period of Game 3, during which he broke his ankle. With backup Johan Hedberg quickly losing coach Crawford's confidence, the Canucks' fortunes were left with rookie goaltender Alex Auld, who acquitted

himself well in a difficult situation but wasn't ready to steal a win on his own.

The Canucks battled the Flames to the end, keeping it highly entertaining if ultimately unsatisfying for their fans. After building a 4-0 lead in Game 6 at Calgary, the Canucks squandered that advantage, only to win 5-4 through an overtime effort by Brendan Morrison that forced Game 7.

In that Game 7 showdown at GM Place, the Canucks again provided prime-time theatrics. They appeared to be going down to defeat late in the third period until Matt Cooke scored with 5.7 seconds remaining, to send the game into overtime. But once again Canuck fans were deflated as former Vancouver favourite Martin

Gelinas scored the series winner for Calgary on a power-play rebound 1:25 into the overtime session. It was the third first-round exit in four years for the Canucks.

The defeat left Vancouver fans wanting more. But they would have to wait, enduring the NHL lockout of 2004-05 before their team would have a chance at redemption.

The lockout killed an entire season but the Canucks returned intact — save for the firing of GM Brian Burke — hopeful that 2005-06 would be their year. They jumped out to an impressive 8-3-1 start in October, too, and won 13 of their first 14 home games. But that early season promise gave way to an astonishing late-season fade.

Season-ending knee surgery to Dan Cloutier on December 15 and abdominal surgery to Ed Jovanovski that caused the defence-man to miss 38 games didn't help. But what really killed the Canucks was a lack of defensive discipline, a continuous rash of untimely penalities and a lack of urgency when they needed it most. They managed just one win during a crucial seven-game stretch at the end of the regular season, sealing their fate.

Needing a strong performance in a home-and-home series against the San Jose Sharks in mid-April, the Canucks blew a 2-0 lead at GM Place to lose 5-4 in overtime. The next night in San Jose, they squandered three leads to fall 5-3 and were eliminated from the tight playoff race.

Despite a 42-32-8 record, Vancouver missed the post-season by three points. Less than two weeks later, head coach Marc Crawford was fired, signaling the start of major changes in the Canucks' dressing room.

"This team was good enough to get in and didn't," general manager Dave Nonis told reporters after the season ended. "What went wrong? That's something we have and will take some time to analyze, but I don't think it was because we didn't have the horses to get in."

"I would say the lack of urgency down the stretch was the biggest disappointment," Nonis added. "We had lots of opportunities. We were two points out of first place with eight games to go ... The lack of urgency was disappointing from everyone's standpoint."

### BEST OF THE DECADE

The 2002-03 regular season shines so far. A franchise-high 45 wins and 104 points, 264 goals, two players among the NHL's top five scorers and an exciting brand of hockey. What's not to like?

### WORST OF THE DECADE

There are multiple options to date in this category — the second-round playoff loss to Minnesota after taking a 3-1 lead in 2003; the Todd Bertuzzi-Steve Moore incident and resulting suspension in 2004; the firing of successful president and general manager Brian Burke later that year; and the NHL lockout that scuttled the entire 2004-05 season each come to mind.

But the biggest disappointment of the decade to date has to be the 2005-06 Canucks missing the playoffs. Sitting two points out of first place in the Northwest Division with eight games to play, the team won just two of its last eight games and found itself sitting out the postseason.

### TOP CANUCKS OF THE DECADE

**Goal:** Dan Cloutier
**Defence:** Ed Jovanovski, Mattias Ohlund
**Right wing:** Todd Bertuzzi
**Left wing:** Markus Naslund
**Centre:** Brendan Morrison

# FRANCESCO AQUILINI

HE HAS FOLLOWED the fortunes of the Canucks since he was a 10-year-old East Vancouver "rink rat" living just blocks from the Pacific Coliseum. That kid never played high-level hockey, but 35 years later he owns half of the NHL team.

Francesco Aquilini grew up to become a successful Vancouver businessman and head of a widespread family enterprise. The Aquilini Investment Group, of which he is managing director, purchased 50 percent of the Canucks and General Motors Place from sole owner John McCaw in November 2004. Although terms of the sale were not made public, the half share was believed to have cost US$125 million.

The transaction gave the Canucks significant local ownership for the first time since 1995, when American McCaw took sole possession of the team from the Griffiths family. The new deal also was seen by many as a strong sign that the Canucks were not in danger of being relocated.

"Local ownership adds value, it puts deeper roots in the community," Aquilini told reporters during a press conference at GM Place to announce the sale. "I think it's a good thing. People have been wanting that for a long time."

The U.S. based McCaw remained the NHL governor for the franchise after the deal; Aquilini became alternate governor and also served as interim chief executive officer. Aquilini indicated that he was happy with the direction the club had taken in recent years and said he did not plan to be a meddling part owner. Although he lives in Vancouver and has a profile in the business community, he hinted that he was unlikely to become the public face of the franchise.

"We're committed to be investors and not managers," he told reporters. "We told John and the management team that we like the direction the team is going and it's our intention to leave the day-to-day running of the team ... to the people who do it best. They're only likely to see us at home games."

Aquilini had been attending Canuck home games for more than 15 years as a season-ticket holder. Ironically, the fall that his company bought into the club he was not able to watch the Canucks play, as the NHL labour dispute killed the season.

The 46-year-old Aquilini is a graduate of Simon Fraser University in Burnaby, where he earned a bachelor's degree in business administration, and the University of California at Los Angeles, where he obtained his master's.

The family business began in 1955 when his father, Luigi Aquilini, purchased a single East Vancouver house. Today, Aquilini Investments is active in property development and real estate as well as in cranberry and blueberry farming.

The family has given back to its community. Francesco was a key player in transforming part of Hastings Park into an Italian-style garden, a project to which the family contributed Can$125,000. They also donated Can$700,000 to save a wetlands area near Pitt Meadows, British Columbia.

Their purchase of a share of the Canucks was not without controversy, however. In January 2005, Vancouver businessmen Tom Gaglardi and Ryan Beedie filed a lawsuit in B.C. Supreme Court alleging that McCaw and Aquilini had ignored existing legal agreements and acted in bad faith when they cut their deal, thereby preventing Gaglardi and Beedie from exercising their negotiated option to purchase the team.

Nevertheless, the NHL's board of governors approved the 50-percent sale to Aquilini Investment Group on March 10, 2005.

"Today is a very exciting and proud day for my family," Francesco Aquilini said as the deal received formal league approval. "The Vancouver Canucks have been an integral part of British Columbia for almost 35 years and the team's fans have demonstrated unwavering loyalty since the franchise's first game in 1970. I grew up cheering for the Canucks, and I look forward to my responsibility to contribute and help grow this great franchise both on the ice and in the community. I am very proud to be a local owner."

# TODD BERTUZZI

ONE NASTY incident will probably forever define Todd Bertuzzi in the minds of many who follow professional hockey casually, or even not at all.

Infamy struck on March 8, 2004, at Vancouver's General Motors Place, in the dying moments of a 9-2 Canucks loss to the Colorado Avalanche. Aggressively pursuing Colorado centre Steve Moore, Bertuzzi chased down the Avalanche rookie from behind, levelled him with a hard punch and then proceeded to land on top of him. The result for Moore was three broken vertebrae in his neck and an end to his hockey career.

Bertuzzi's life also changed forever. The 6'3", 245-pound right winger instantly became the scourge of the hockey world, the poster boy for on-ice violence gone too far. Bertuzzi was suspended indefinitely by the NHL, stripped of more than a half-million dollars in salary and brought up on a criminal charge in British Columbia's courts.

A year earlier, Bertuzzi had broken through as the NHL's prototypical power forward. Just five months earlier, he had signed a four-year, US$27.9-million contract with the Canucks. While Steve Moore's world came crashing down as a result of the ugly incident, so did Bertuzzi's.

"I think all around it was a really unfortunate incident," says Brendan Morrison, Bertuzzi's former teammate and often linemate. "I know Todd, and did he intend to engage Moore? Yeah, I think he intended to confront him. But did he ever intend for the outcome to be the way it was? No. Not at all."

While the NHL lockout dominated hockey news in 2004-05, the Bertuzzi saga provided a secondary sideshow. The Canuck forward was charged in June 2004 with assault causing bodily harm. In December he pleaded guilty under an agreement with prosecutors that allowed a judge to give him a conditional discharge, which will leave him without a criminal record. He was fined $500 and ordered to do community service.

Many observers felt the punishment was too little for leaving Moore with fractured vertebrae and a severe concussion. Others felt the police shouldn't have become involved in what to some

was typical hockey justice — Bertuzzi chasing down Moore because the Colorado rookie had injured his linemate, Vancouver captain Markus Naslund, with a questionable hit a few weeks earlier. Nobody wanted the incident to end the way it did, however, with Moore seriously injured, his future thrown into doubt.

Two days after it occurred, Bertuzzi held a press conference at GM Place in which he tearfully expressed regret to Moore and his family.

"Steve, I just want to apologize for what happened out there," he said. "I had no intention of hurting you. I feel awful for what transpired.

"To the fans of hockey and the fans of Vancouver, for the kids that watch this game, I'm truly sorry. I don't play the game that way. I'm not a mean-spirited person. I'm sorry for what happened."

Bertuzzi was left off the Canadian team for the 2004 World Cup and his suspension also prevented him from playing in Europe during the NHL lockout. But he was reinstated by NHL commissioner Gary Bettman prior to the 2005-06 regular season and was included on the Canadian team for the 2006 Olympics in Turin.

The fall-out from the Moore incident seemed to affect the hulking winger's production on the ice, however. Bertuzzi seldom found the powerful stride and aggressive style that made him one of the NHL's most feared offensive threats in 2002-03. In the 2005-06 season, he posted 25 goals and 46 assists in 82 games. But that was 26 fewer points than his career high and he finished the season a miserable minus-17.

Compounding Bertuzzi's on-ice problems was a CAN$19.5-million civil lawsuit launched by the Moore family against him, the Canucks and Orca Bay Sports and Entertainment. Bertuzzi was also sued for fraud in June 2006 for allegedly transferring ownership of a home to his wife, Julie, in order to render himself judgement-proof.

As the 2005-06 season ended, Bertuzzi said he was looking forward to a "clean slate" in 2006-07.

That fresh start will come in Miami, not Vancouver, however. On June 23, 2006 Canucks general manager Dave Nonis ended

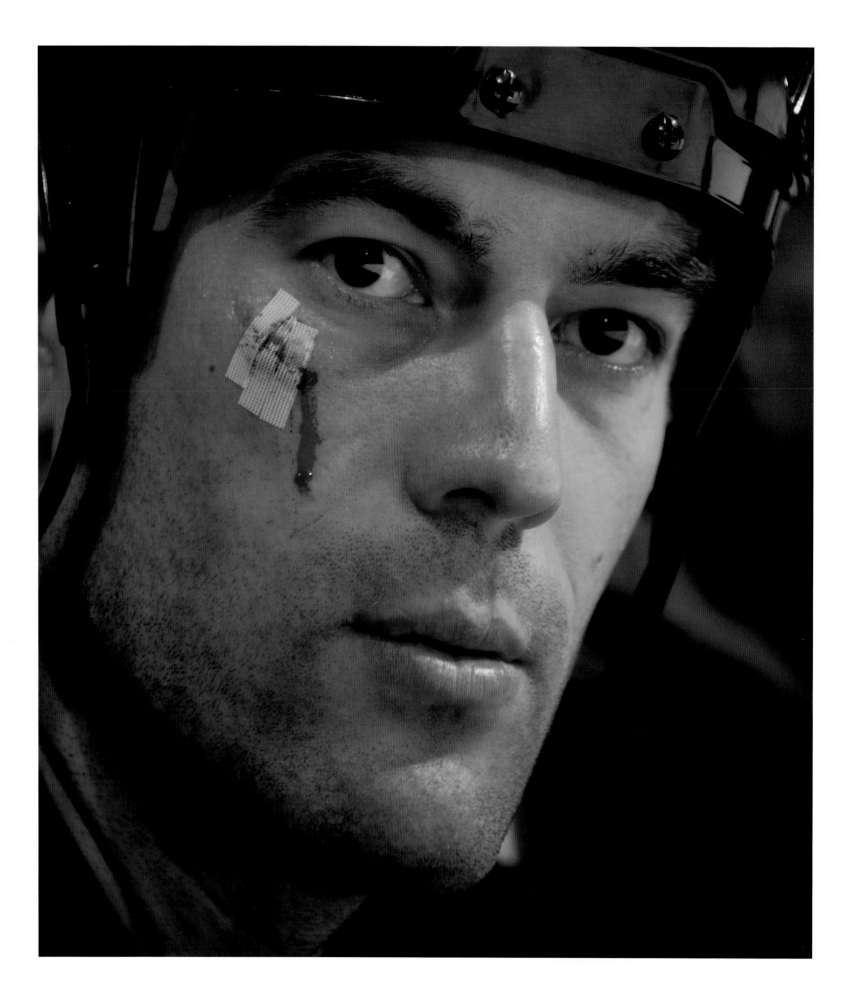

Facing page: *When at the top of his game, Todd Bertuzzi is among the finest bruising power forwards the NHL has ever seen.* (Vancouver Canucks/Jeff Vinnick)

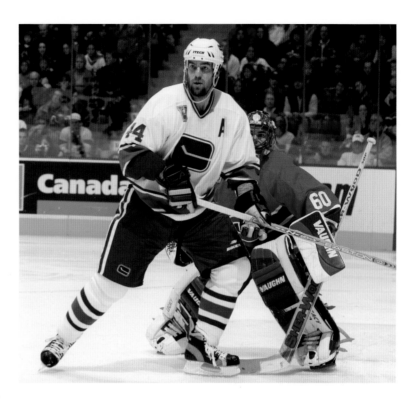

*The 6'3", 245-pound Todd Bertuzzi crowds goaltender Jose Theodore of the Montreal Canadiens.* (Vancouver Canucks/Jeff Vinnick)

Bertuzzi's often rocky tenure in Vancouver by trading the big winger to the Florida Panthers along with defenceman Bryan Allen and goalie Alex Auld in a blockbuster deal. Coming the Canucks' way were star netminder Roberto Luongo, defenceman Lukas Krajicek and a sixth-round pick in the following day's NHL draft.

Bertuzzi's professional career has had its share of ups and downs. He was selected 23rd overall by the New York Islanders in the 1993 NHL draft from the Ontario Hockey League's Guelph Storm, with whom the youngster from Sudbury, Ontario, had shown a penchant for both scoring and the rough going.

He posted an impressive 119-point effort in his final season of junior hockey in 1994-95, but Bertuzzi struggled to make an impact in the Islanders' lineup. He finished with a respectable 18 goals and 21 assists in his rookie season but things spiralled downward from there. His toughness and heart called into question by Islander management, he was traded 52 games into his third NHL season, going to Vancouver as part of the deal that sent longtime Canuck captain Trevor Linden to the Islanders.

Bertuzzi didn't make an immediate impact in Vancouver, either. His first full season with the Canucks was limited to 32 games due to a serious knee injury. But in his second year on the West Coast he began to show promise, scoring 25 goals and adding as many assists, easily his best NHL season to date.

Paired with Markus Naslund, Bertuzzi was moved up to the Canucks' number 1 line, where his promise as a bruising power forward with deft puckhandling skills began to be fulfilled. In 2000-01 he improved again, posting 25 goals and 30 assists. His career really took flight a year later, when Bertuzzi, Naslund and Morrison began skating together full-time. Bertuzzi scored a career-high 36 goals, added 49 assists and had 110 penalty minutes for his finest NHL season.

That upward curve continued in 2002-03, when Bertuzzi again posted career numbers and reached superstar status. Playing a full 82 games, he had 46 goals and 51 assists, finished fifth in league scoring and amassed 146 minutes in penalties. Not only was Bertuzzi posting eye-popping statistics, so was Naslund, who benefited from the open ice created by his bigger linemate.

"There aren't many guys in the league who have the combination of [Bertuzzi's] size and power and the finesse," says Morrison, who also benefited from playing with Bertuzzi.

"A lot of big guys create room, but initially they'll move the puck right away and then go to the net. Todd's a guy who can create room, but he can also beat a guy by putting the puck through his legs, you know? So he's a very special talent."

Special or not, Bertuzzi certainly has his detractors in Vancouver. His name was the one most mentioned in rumours leading up to the NHL's 2005-06 trade deadline. And as the post-mortem was conducted into the Canucks' absence from the 2006 post-season, rumours swirled around whether he would return. Some cited a strained relationship between Bertuzzi and head coach Marc Crawford as a major problem in the dressing room. When asked about their relationship, Bertuzzi simply told reporters: "He's the coach, I'm the player and that's it."

Vancouver fans reacted positively to the trade that sent Bertuzzi to the Panthers and so did the player himself. For whatever reasons, things never seemed the same for Bertuzzi in the city after the Moore incident. "Florida is a perfect fit for me," he told the Vancouver *Sun* in the aftermath of the trade. "Let's face the facts, it's beautiful out there, it's sunny year-round, and it's a place where you can kind of hide out. It's not hockey 24 hours like it is in a Canadian market."

*Todd Bertuzzi celebrates a goal during one of his happier moments as a Vancouver Canuck. (Vancouver Canucks/Jeff Vinnick)*

# ANSON CARTER

AT FIRST IT seemed like an odd match — two quiet, red-headed young Swedes paired alongside an outgoing, dreadlocked Canadian veteran with an active stake in the movie and music business.

But it turned out to be a perfect fit, both for the previously underachieving Sedin twins and their new Vancouver Canuck linemate, speedy right-winger Anson Carter.

Carter joined the Canucks as a free agent in August of 2005, signing a one-year deal for US$1 million. He would prove to be a bargain for Vancouver general manager Dave Nonis. Forming an effective line with Daniel and Henrik Sedin, Carter led Vancouver in scoring with 33 goals and his seven game-winning goals was also tops among Canucks. His 55 points were the second-best total in the 32-year-old's NHL career.

It was a nice rebound for Carter, who had plenty of doubters after posting just 15 goals and 28 points over 68 games for the Rangers, Capitals and Kings in the season prior to the NHL lockout. But maybe more importantly for Vancouver fans, his presence on the Sedins' line brought out the best in the twins — Carter was able to capitalize on their passing skills while at the same time helping them become more consistent scorers themselves.

"He's a guy that can make plays," Henrik Sedin said late in the 2005-06 season. "Daniel and I haven't had to do as much work in the corner this year. We just have to stay open and he's good at getting the puck to us. He prepares a lot for the game — talks a lot with us and goes over tape, etc. It's been real helpful."

The chance to play alongside the Sedins was one of the reasons Carter chose to sign with Vancouver in the summer of 2005. But as the summer of 2006 wore on, the free-agent had not re-signed with the Canucks amid heavy speculation that he was headed elsewhere.

Carter scored the winning goal for Canada in the gold-medal game of the 2003 world championships, beating Sweden in the process. Obviously, the Sedins didn't hold a grudge over that as the three have clicked marvelously, on and off the ice.

"The main thing about scoring goals in this league is puck protection and making smart, heads-up plays," Carter says. "It isn't always so much about dumping and chasing, although we dump and chase a fair bit for a skilled line but the key is we put the puck in the right area. With us we take into consideration, what's the other guy going to have once he gets the puck? We're not just giving each other the other guys' problems. Having said that, I knew [the Sedins] cycled the puck well, I knew they protected the puck, I knew they had really good hands — it was just a matter of creating more openings for them and giving them time and space to do what they do best."

Vancouver represented a fresh start for the 6'1" 209-pound Carter, a native of Toronto and a veteran of nine NHL seasons with seven different organizations. The Michigan State product, who was drafted 220th overall by Quebec in 1992, rose to prominence in 2001-02 and 2002-03 when he posted back-to-back 60-point seasons, including 28 goals, for the Edmonton Oilers in the first of those two years.

That production didn't stop the Oilers from trading Carter to the New York Rangers in March of 2003, however. During the next season, he juggled injury problems and teams as he moved to the Capitals and the Kings and dealt with the aftermath of late-season hernia surgery.

"It's good to bounce back. I mean, it's not like I'm 40 years old," says Carter who worked out under renowned Los Angeles trainer T.R. Goodman prior to the 2005-06 season. "You put in the hard work and you put in the training and you try to build your body back and every time you have major surgery ... there's always the fear you're never going to be as good as you were before ... But if you put in that time and that work into the rehab and the training; it's amazing what the human body can do."

Carter owns and runs a production company based in Los Angeles called Big Up Entertainment, which includes a record label and has also begun producing films. The label's first hip-hop artists were Virginia-based Main and Merc while the company's first motion picture was *Bald The Movie*.

# DAN CLOUTIER

DAN CLOUTIER has been a goaltender for long enough to know how it works: no matter what a netminder does in the regular season, no matter how steady he is or how many victories he posts, the most important thing is what he does in the playoffs.

"I think respect comes from winning in the post-season," Cloutier said in an interview while he was still a member of the Vancouver Canucks. "I think it's the same for every-body. Obviously, the goalies are always the guys that get the fingers pointed at them ..." That certainly happened enough to Cloutier in Vancouver, despite solid performances during the regular season. And ultimately it led to the Canucks trading him in the summer of 2006.

When Vancouver acquired Roberto Luongo from the Florida Panthers, the writing was clearly on the wall for Cloutier. On July 4, he was dealt to the Los Angeles Kings in exchange for future draft picks.

Cloutier has certainly gained his share of regular-season respect. Prior to being sidelined for most of the 2005-06 season with a knee injury, the 6'1", 185-pounder had posted at least 31 wins in three straight campaigns, including 33 victories in both 2002-03 and 2003-04.

Cloutier also lowered his regular-season goals-against average since joining the Canucks in 2001, dropping it from 2.43 to a career-best 2.27, and raising his save percentage from .894 to .914.

And he has proved he can handle a big workload, playing at least 57 games in each of his three full seasons after joining the Canucks in a trade that sent defenceman Adrian Aucoin and a draft pick to the Tampa Bay Lightning on February 7, 2001.

But with success in the playoffs still missing, with the Canucks winning just one series during Cloutier's three most successful seasons and his average inflating by more than a goal a game in the postseason, the goalie was criticized by many. After the 2003 playoffs, when the team was beaten in seven games by Minnesota though Vancouver had led the second-round series 3-1, a picture of Cloutier with an airbrushed beach ball going through his legs circulated on the Internet.

It was a biting reference to the fact that Cloutier had allowed 15 goals on 60 shots over the final three games against the Wild, but he seems to take such criticism in stride.

"I think it obviously goes with the position," he says. "It's just like being the quarterback, I guess, or a starting pitcher — you're the one that's going to have to face the media after the game and explain to them. It's not going to be the guy who hit the post or something like that, it's going to be the guy who lets the goal in, and it always has come down to that in this position, even if you're a peewee or bantam or midget. If you win you get the tap on the back, and if you lose they kind of stick it to you. But I think it only makes you stronger and hungrier for the year to come."

Cloutier felt he was poised for his postseason breakthrough in the spring of 2004, as the Canucks squared off against the Flames in the first round of the playoffs. But an ankle injury sidelined him early in Game 3 and the Flames went on to take the series in seven.

"I really felt that it was my year and I felt like I had a good record against Calgary, and so it was definitely very disappointing," he says.

Cloutier is from Mont-Laurier, Quebec, and he grew up less than a two-hour drive north of Montreal. He idolized the Canadiens' great goaltender Patrick Roy, but he was also a fan of towering Philadelphia netminder Ron Hextall and the latter's feisty style has rubbed off on Cloutier, who during his career has fought more than most NHL goalies.

"I just liked the way Roy approached every game, and I also liked the way Hextall competed," he says. "You know, it didn't matter if they were down five or up five, Hextall played the same. He always had that aggressiveness to him. I really liked that in him."

Cloutier was a junior star for the Sault Ste. Marie Greyhounds and the Guelph Storm of the Ontario Hockey League before being selected 26th overall by the New York Rangers in 1994. He split time between the minors and the NHL during his first two pro seasons and was looking forward to taking over from veteran Mike Richter in the New York crease, but Cloutier was traded to the Tampa Bay Lightning on draft day 1999.

*Goaltender Dan Cloutier was traded to the Los Angeles Kings after the Canucks obtained Roberto Luongo in July 2006.* (Vancouver Canucks/Jeff Vinnick)

The Lightning gave him plenty of playing time over the next two years, but the struggling team posted only 12 wins in his 76 starts. "I was getting a lot of work every night and I think it was a big part of improving," he recounts. "Even though the wins weren't coming, at least I knew myself that I was getting better."

Via a cellphone call from Brian Burke while out for dinner with Lightning teammates Vincent Lecavalier and Brad Richards, Cloutier discovered he'd been traded to the Canucks.

"Vancouver had 80-some points at the time and we were in last place and so I was happy for that," Cloutier recalls. "I was happy, too, to go to a Canadian team, to be able to play on *Hockey Night in Canada,* which people maybe don't think is a big deal, but when you're playing in the NHL, and you're playing in Tampa, you don't get too many [nationally televised games]. Suddenly I was playing in Vancouver and every Saturday night was one. It was a good move for my career, I think."

He feels he improved every year with the Canucks, his progress aided by well-respected Vancouver goaltending coach Ian Clark.

But Cloutier missed 94 regular-season games to injury over four seasons as a Canuck and some now question his durability as well as his stock as a playoff goaltender.

# MATT COOKE

EVERY SUCCESSFUL hockey team needs a player like Matt Cooke. In fact, most coaches would like more than one. And most fans wish all National Hockey Leaguers arrived at the rink with the same attitude as the feisty forward.

Cooke is an "energy guy," a player who never takes a shift off, never lays up when he can staple an opponent to the boards with a crunching hit, never stops moving his feet. In a professional sports world that has turned even the run-of-the-mill athlete into a millionaire, he still goes to work every night with a lunch-bucket mentality.

His statistics won't wow you. Neither will his 5'11", 205-pound frame. But his work ethic certainly will.

"I find it fun to go out there and be physical," says Cooke, who broke in with the Canucks as an NHL regular in 2000. "To me, setting the tempo or the tone of the game by getting a big hit early is just as effective as scoring a goal. It does the same mentally and energy-wise for your team."

But in the seasons where he has managed to avoid serious injury, Cooke has also become more than a player who runs around hitting opponents and creating havoc. He has developed into a valuable penalty killer and he can score when given the opportunity to play with offensive linemates. In 2002-03 he had 15 goals and 42 points, playing mainly on the third line and never on the power play. In that season he led the Canucks with a plus-21 rating.

The following year, despite being limited to 53 games due to injuries, he was elevated to the Canucks' first line late in the season after teammate Todd Bertuzzi received an indefinite suspension for his attack on Colorado's Steve Moore.

"Initially, when I started playing with them [Markus Naslund and Brendan Morrison], I was nervous being out there just because there's a lot of pressure and I wasn't totally used to that," Cooke admits. "I hadn't been strapped with that offensive performance pressure yet. Not that I minded it, but learning how to handle it was obviously a big step."

He has handled a lot of big steps during a hockey career in which he has had to continually prove skeptics wrong. As a high-scoring minor-hockey star from Stirling, a town of about 1,800 near Belleville, Ontario, he waited in agony as he was bypassed until the 10th round of the major junior Ontario Hockey League draft in 1995.

Snubbed or not, he went to camp with the Windsor Spitfires and earned a spot with his hard-nosed play. As a rookie he posted eight goals, 19 points and 102 penalty minutes over 61 major junior games in 1995-96. Determined to carve a career in the pro game, he then declared himself eligible for the 1996 NHL draft as a 17-year-old.

He went undrafted, but he swallowed his disappointment and attended the Toronto Maple Leafs' camp as a free agent. Once again he made a solid first impression on the ice and he earned a contract. But the Leafs failed to properly register the paperwork on time and Cooke's three-year deal was declared invalid by the NHL Players' Association. "That was a huge disappointment at the time," he says now.

Spitfires coach Paul Gillis persuaded Cooke to look it as another opportunity to enter the NHL draft. The young forward took that advice and posted a 45-goal, 95-point, 146-penalty minute season in his second year of major junior. That was enough to prompt the Canucks to select him in the sixth round, 144th overall, when the 1997 NHL draft rolled around.

After another year of junior, which he split between the Spitfires and the Kingston Frontenacs, Cooke turned professional. He used his flat-out style to impress then Vancouver coach Mike Keenan enough to surprisingly place the youngster on the Canucks' opening-night NHL roster for the 1998-99 regular season.

The energetic but unfocused rookie lasted nine games before being sent to the Syracuse Crunch of the American Hockey League. It's a move he now says was the best thing for him: "I think it was essential that I went down there, because I was allowed to go out and play 30 minutes a game against grown men, which was the big difference between [pro] and junior hockey."

*Feisty forward Matt Cooke enjoys setting the tempo with a big hit as much as he relishes scoring a goal.* (Vancouver Canucks/Jeff Vinnick)

After splitting time for two seasons between Syracuse and Vancouver, Cooke moved up full-time to the Canucks in 2000-01. Since then, he has become one of the team's most popular and dependable players. Once described by former general manager Brian Burke as a "wolverine" on the ice, Cooke has developed some big-league skills and focus to go along with his energized, agitating style.

Cooke believes he is capable of contributing more offensively and even earning some power-play minutes. He knows that he needs to capitalize more often when he does get chances.

"An area where I can improve is shooting the puck," he says.

"Not necessarily being selfish, but when given the opportunity to shoot the puck I should shoot the puck and not look for a better opportunity, no matter who I'm playing with ... And if I can optimize my chances by hitting the net every time, that's something I can work on."

Cooke also hopes he can avoid the injury bug which severely hampered him during the 2005-06 season when a combination of jaw, ankle and concussion problems limited him to just 45 games, 18 points and a disappointing minus-eight rating.

# MARC CRAWFORD

As a fringe forward skating for the Canucks of the 1980s, Marc Crawford's nickname was "747." The energetic left-winger was tagged thus because he always seemed to be the player shuttled back and forth between Vancouver and its farm team across the country in Fredericton, New Brunswick.

Crawford has, of course, soared much higher as a coach in the NHL than he ever did as a jet-setting athlete. During six seasons spent mostly between the Canucks and the Fredericton Express, Crawford the player managed just 19 NHL goals and 50 points.

As a player, he skated in the 1982 Stanley Cup finals with the Canucks. But as a coach, he has won a Cup, guiding the Colorado Avalanche to that honour in 1996. He also steered the Canucks to six straight winning seasons before being fired on April 25, 2006.

"I'd like to be able to say I was gifted as a player," Crawford says with a laugh. "But I was a good skater and I guess probably the best [description] was reliable, hard-working. I was probably a cross between Jarkko Ruutu and maybe a guy like Tyler Bouck — that type of player.

"You always kind of look back and say: 'I could have been better.' But at the same time, knowing the league as I know it now, I'm starting to realize that, boy, it's a huge accomplishment just to even make the NHL. You don't realize when you're in it just how great you have to be to even get there. That gives me a little bit more perspective now — being in the game and seeing how many great players don't really even ever get a sniff."

Although he was never an NHL star, Crawford was always a student of the game. Some of that, no doubt, came from his father, Floyd, a former minor-professional player who coached senior and major junior hockey in Ontario and played for a Belleville senior team that won the world championship in 1959. Hockey was never far from the dinner-table discussion, as most of Marc's six brothers and two sisters were heavily involved in the game.

When Canuck bosses Pat Quinn and Brian Burke offered Crawford a chance to become a playing assistant coach with Fredericton in 1987, he accepted. He followed that up with a similar stint for the Milwaukee Admirals of the International Hockey League the next season.

"Pat and Brian were the first ones to recommend [coaching] and I took them up on it," Crawford says. "And once I started in that profession, then I really found out that I enjoyed it, and I was having the best of both worlds there for the two years that I was a player-assistant coach at the minor-league level. It was a great way for me to segue into the coaching career and I've never looked back."

He became head coach of the Cornwall Royals, the same major junior team with which he had won two Memorial Cups as a player. After two years at the junior level, he became head coach of the St. John's Maple Leafs of the American Hockey League in 1991, spending three seasons there.

In 1994 Crawford was named an NHL head coach at age 33, taking over the Quebec Nordiques. A year later the franchise moved to Colorado and he steered the Avalanche to a Stanley Cup championship in 1996, the team's first season in Denver. In doing so, he became the third-youngest coach in NHL history to win a Cup.

Until that time his coaching star had been on a rapid rise. But the talented Avalanche were unable to get back to the finals over the next two years, and Crawford surprisingly resigned his position after losing in the first round of the 1998 playoffs. That winter he coached the Canadian Olympic team, which returned from the Nagano Winter Games without a medal.

"They had offered to keep me on [in Colorado] and I felt that it wasn't the right situation," he says. "At that time I made the decision to move on, and I have taken my lumps because of the decision. But you know, you can't look back in life ..."

Crawford became the Canucks' 15th head coach on January 24, 1999, relieving Mike Keenan, who had been fired by Brian Burke. For his first two years behind the bench, the rebuilding Canucks finished out of the playoffs. During the next three, they were one of the NHL's best clubs over the regular season.

In 2002-03 the Canucks recorded the highest point total in

*Former Canucks' head coach Marc Crawford couldn't stop his team's inexplicable slide out of the playoffs in 2006.* (Vancouver Canucks/Jeff Vinnick)

franchise history, with 104. The next season the club again surpassed the 100-point mark under Crawford.

But in nearly seven seasons as Vancouver's head coach, the Canucks managed to win only one playoff series. And after the team stalled down the stretch and failed to even qualify for the post-season in 2005-06, Crawford was quickly fired by general manager Dave Nonis.

"We felt that our team needs a kickstart, that we haven't played with the fire that we have been known to have," Nonis told reporters during a press conference to announce Crawford's dismissal. "And I felt that a change behind the bench was the first place to start."

Crawford, who in late 2003 had signed a three-year contract extension with the Canucks, was fired with more than US$1.3 million left on that deal. But that became moot when he was quickly hired as head coach of the Los Angeles Kings.

"It's not about Marc being a bad coach," Nonis said, explaining the Canucks' decision. "If I'm in another market today and I'm looking for a head coach, his phone is already ringing. That's what I think of him, but it doesn't mean we didn't need to make a change. We did."

Crawford's 246 wins were the most of any coach in Canucks' history. But two days after his firing, in a 40-minute farewell press conference at GM Place, he admitted they weren't enough.

"I'm sitting here because we're involved in a very, very difficult business," he told reporters. "There were a lot of distractions with this club and some you could control and some you couldn't. I'm not going to make excuses. The job in professional sports is to be as good as you possibly can as often as you possibly can. We didn't do that enough this year and that's largely the reason I'm sitting here today."

# ED JOVANOVSKI

FOR CANUCKS FANS, an NHL trade that involved seven players and a draft pick ultimately boiled down to just two young men: Pavel Bure for Ed Jovanovski.

On January 17, 1999, Jovanovski was traded to Vancouver by the Florida Panthers in a blockbuster deal. He was the player Canuck fans accepted in return for the Russian Rocket, the latter one of the most exciting skaters to ever grace NHL ice.

The sizable shoulders on Jovo's 6'2", 210-pound frame came in handy as the defenceman carried the weight of all those expectations while developing his game under a media microscope. He emerged as a star in his own right, one of the NHL's premier blueliners, a gold-medal-winning Olympian and a leader for the Canucks.

But that star will now shine in Phoenix for the foreseeable future. In a move that was as much about the new NHL economics as anything else, the Canucks simply didn't have the salary cap space to compete with a five-year US$32.5-million offer from the Coyotes. Jovanovski left Vancouver on July 1, 2006 to sign as a free-agent with Phoenix, ending his stint as a Canuck.

For more than six seasons, however, Jovanovski was a breath of fresh air for Canucks fans, considering that the superstar he had replaced didn't even want to be in Vancouver. And as his time as a Canuck concluded, Jovanovski had become one of the finest defencemen in franchise history.

Former Canucks general manager Burke once referred to Jovanovski as "a rare combination of skill and toughness," a hulking physical presence with surprising skills who in recent years has mastered the intricacies of defence in the NHL.

"Eddie is a hard-rock defenceman," Burke said back in 2003. "He brings a lot to the table every night. This is a guy who can take your head off with a bodycheck, can go end to end with a puck, has a great shot. He's a multi-dimensional player, and he adds an ingredient that's an important part of the way we want to play."

The son of Macedonian immigrants to Windsor, Ontario, Jovanovski didn't begin playing the game until he was 11 years old,

far later than most players who make it to the NHL. But by the time he was 17 he had already emerged into a blue-chip defensive prospect, posting 50 points and racking up 221 penalty minutes in 62 Ontario Hockey League games for his hometown major junior Windsor Spitfires.

That was enough for the Panthers to take the strapping Jovanovski first overall in the 1994 NHL draft. And after one more stellar year with the Spitfires, in which he had 65 points and 198 penalty minutes and helped Canada to the world junior gold, the 19-year-old jumped directly to the unforgiving world of the NHL blue line.

Few players can make that leap, but Jovanovski did. Although his play was at times erratic, he managed 10 goals, 21 points and 137 penalty minutes in his first season to make the NHL all-rookie team.

In the ensuing playoffs he contributed nine points and 52 penalty minutes as the upstart, third-year Panthers stunned the NHL by advancing to the Stanley Cup finals. Just eight years after he played his first organized hockey game, he was at the pinnacle of his sport.

Unfortunately for Jovanovski and the Panthers, that spring would also be the peak of his time in Florida. Over the next three years he played reasonably well, but not well enough for a struggling franchise looking to justify the number 1 pick used to select him. Jovanovski often sacrificed the smart play in order to go for the eye-opening hit, and his lack of judgment earned him the derisive nickname "Special Ed" in some NHL circles. So when the Canucks dangled Bure in front of the Panthers, Jovanovski was put on the trading block.

It was a deal that Jovanovski says was key. "When I got traded here, it turned my career around," he said in 2003. "And each year as a player I feel I've been developing with the coaching staff here."

Few would disagree with his self-assessment. In each of the three seasons in which he played the majority of games without injury to 2004, he surpassed the 45-point mark as he became an increasingly dependable defender. He is capable of hurting

*Ed Jovanovski, one of the finest defencemen in Canucks history, signed as a free agent with the Phoenix Coyotes in the summer of 2006. (Vancouver Canucks/Jeff Vinnick)*

*Defenceman Ed Jovanovski's stellar play with the Canucks made him a selection to Canada's Olympic team in both 2002 and 2006.* (Vancouver Canucks/Jeff Vinnick)

opponents with a huge hit, a timely pass, a surprisingly quick rush or a booming shot.

During the best stretch of his career to date, he made the NHL All-Star Game in 2001, 2002 and 2003. He was selected to Canada's Olympic team for the 2002 Salt Lake City Games and assisted on the gold-medal-winning goal by Joe Sakic.

Jovanovski's most impressive season statistically probably came in 2002-03, when he rebounded from an early-season broken foot to collect six goals and 46 points in 67 games. In 2003-04, a shoulder injury limited him to 56 games and 23 points and in 2005-06, abdominal surgery caused him to miss 38 games. Jovanovski, who still finished the year with 33 points in 44 games, returned to the Canucks' lineup with five games left in the season but his late comeback wasn't enough as the team missed the playoffs.

Canucks general manager Dave Nonis says Jovanovski matured nicely after arriving in Vancouver.

"His all-around game has improved," Nonis says. "He's always had the ability to change the game with one part of his game, whether it's scoring a goal or a big check ... But I think sometimes that can also cause problems and get you out of position, running around, and I think that was part of the learning curve for Ed. He's learned to control his game and he's much safer; he's a much better all-around defenceman than he was when he first came to Vancouver. He's more mature and understanding that, even though he has those abilities to change the game, to pick his time, to pick the right spot.

"You don't have to go out and do it every shift, because that can work against you. It can lead to pucks in your own net. I think there's been a big improvement in that area for him."

*Defenceman Ed Jovanovski was the key player obtained in Vancouver's trade of Pavel Bure to the Florida Panthers in 1999. (Vancouver Canucks/Jeff Vinnick)*

# RYAN KESLER

THE WORD MOST often used to describe Ryan Kesler during his early tenure with the Vancouver Canucks has been "mature." The kid is cool beyond his years, according to club management, coaches and fellow players.

Kesler himself remembers feeling anything but calm in November 2003 when he first received word that he was headed to the NHL. The call came from Stan Smyl, then his head coach with the Manitoba Moose, Vancouver's American Hockey League farm team. Kesler was being summoned to "the show" by the Canucks as a 19-year-old.

"I didn't believe him at first. It was kind of surreal, almost," Kesler recalls. "My dream had finally come true. I was really nervous before my first game, but once I got on the ice I was fine."

Indeed, he was. The steady teenage centre made his NHL debut against the Maple Leafs in Toronto less than three months after his 19th birthday. The next night, in Montreal, he earned his first assist against the Canadiens.

For a young man who thought he would be taking his second year of classes at Ohio State, things moved pretty fast for Kesler in 2003-04. After being drafted by the Canucks 23rd overall in June, he was persuaded to turn pro right away. Expected to spend at least a full winter seasoning in the American Hockey League, he ended up playing 28 games for the Canucks, chipping in two goals and three assists.

"I had no idea I was not going back to school," he says. "I was all set. I got an apartment in Ohio and got all my classes set and then, toward the end of the summer, my agent called me and basically told me that [the Canucks] wanted to sign me. I've always wanted to play in the NHL, so I didn't want to turn it down."

He went to his first training camp in Vernon that fall oozing confidence and even telling reporters that he believed he was ready to play at the NHL level. What they didn't realize was that he was right.

But even he admits to being surprised at how much time he spent in the NHL as a teenager. "I had big expectations going in but, I mean, I never really thought I'd play almost half the year in the NHL."

The league labour lockout came at an unfortunate time for Kesler, who many believed would have been a full-time regular with the Canucks in 2004-05 if there had been a season.

Instead, he spent the entire season with the Moose, working on his strength and his offensive game. At 6'2" he managed to gain about 20 pounds, bulking up to 210 through working out and taking protein supplements. Kesler played in all situations for the Moose and was named most valuable player of the AHL team, posting 30 goals, 57 points and 105 penalty minutes over 78 games.

Kesler jumped to the big club full-time in 2005-06, playing all 82 games for the Canucks. In Vancouver, he has thus far filled a checking and energy role, mostly centering the team's third line. In his first full season with Vancouver, Kesler had 10 goals, 23 points and 79 penalty minutes while finishing with a plus-one rating.

The Canucks have been impressed with Kesler's skating and defensive maturity, and he is seen as a key part of the NHL team's future. Although he has been described by many as a checking centre, he sees himself as a more offensive player. Many expect his offensive role with the Canucks to increase in coming seasons.

"I see myself in the future as a first- or second-line guy," he says. "I really don't want to be a checking centreman. That's what I've basically focused on, is to just be more offensive and improve my game a lot."

Growing up as the son of a Junior B coach in Livonia, Michigan, a Detroit suburb, Kesler admired the play of fellow Livonian Mike Modano and Colorado centre Joe Sakic. He is pleased with those who compare his game to that of a young Trevor Linden, who also broke into the NHL as a teenager.

Kesler learned the game following his older brother and father and playing in the competitive AAA midget leagues of Detroit. "When I was young, I just basically wanted to do anything my brother was doing."

# ROBERTO LUONGO

It DIDN'T TAKE long for Canucks fans to forget about the disappointing 2005–06 NHL regular season and to start looking forward to training camp even more than they usually do. The reason? Two words: Roberto Luongo.

You'd have to go back to the arrival of free agent Mark Messier in 1997 to find another acquisition that has created as big a stir as the Canucks obtaining the 27-year-old Luongo in a June 23 trade with the Florida Panthers.

It wasn't simply that the trade was a blockbuster, or that it divested the Canucks of the now-travelling Todd Bertuzzi soap opera. It was mainly because Luongo is widely considered to be one of the best — if not the best — netminder in the world.

"There's no doubt in my mind that as soon as I get there we're going to make a run for the Stanley Cup," the confident native of St. Leonard, Quebec, told reporters after signing a four-year contract with the Canucks less than a week following one of the biggest trades in Canuck history.

Luongo will need that confidence to live up to massive expectations in Vancouver, which has been searching for a crease saviour ever since the glory days of Kirk McLean. The fact that the Canucks gave up two solid, young contributors — defenceman Bryan Allen and goaltender Alex Auld — as well as the brooding Bertuzzi in exchange for Luongo, defenceman Lukas Krajicek and a late draft pick, puts the onus on Luongo to prove that he was worth it.

So does his US $27-million contract, which at US $6.75 million a season makes him the highest paid Canuck, ahead of even captain Markus Naslund. All this for a goaltender who has never played in a single NHL playoff game.

But Luongo, whose combination of size — he's 6'3" and 205 pounds — solid technique and lightning reflexes has led to a career save percentage of .919, is universally regarded as a goaltender capable of stealing games. In Florida, he played on poor Panther teams and was often forced to stand on his head just to keep them in the game. In Vancouver, the talent level is higher and the Canucks are banking that he is the star stopper capable of taking them to a Cup.

Luongo has always been a highly regarded prospect, since well before he was drafted fourth overall by the New York Islanders in 1997 out of the Quebec Major Junior League, at the time making him the highest goaltender ever selected. But in recent years, he has transformed from prospect into one of the two or three best netminders in the NHL.

Some have likened his ability to keep his team in games to that of former Edmonton Oilers' standout Grant Fuhr. It's an analogy that Luongo enjoys, since it was Fuhr whom he emulated as a youngster growing up in the Montreal suburbs. Luongo admired Fuhr's quick reflexes and his habit of making dramatic glove saves.

"Patrick Roy was the guy we saw on TV obviously, every night in Montreal and I really have a lot of admiration for Patrick," Luongo said in a 2003 interview. "But Grant Fuhr and his glove saves are really what attracted me to being a goaltender. Grant Fuhr was my idol growing up."

After an outstanding junior career in Quebec and a silver-medal performance with Canada at the world junior championships, Luongo played just 24 NHL games for the Islanders before being sent to Florida on June 24, 2000 along with centre Olli Jokinen in a trade for wingers Oleg Kvasha and Mark Parrish.

He spent the next five seasons for the playoff-less Panthers, facing a heavy barrage of rubber on most nights. Over six NHL seasons, Luongo has posted a respectable 2.72 goals-against average despite playing on weak clubs.

In 2003–04, Luongo was recognized for his efforts by being selected a finalist for both the Vezina Trophy, awarded to the NHL's top goaltender, and the Lester B. Pearson Award, given to the player voted by NHL colleagues to be most valuable to his team. During that campaign, Luongo set the NHL record for saves in a season with 2,303.

Luongo looks forward to playing in Vancouver, where hockey is king and expectations are high. "It's up to me to deliver," he says.

# BRENDAN MORRISON

BRENDAN MORRISON was having lunch with his fiancée and future family members when he heard the news that would change his hockey career.

It was March 14, 2000, and Morrison was a 24-year-old centre with the New Jersey Devils. On a day off, he was having a casual meal across the river in New York when his brother-in-law-to-be, former NHL goaltender Daryl Reaugh, received a call on his cellphone.

A hockey broadcast analyst, Reaugh was being interviewed by a Toronto radio station about the NHL's trade-deadline day. When Reaugh asked if the Toronto reporters had heard of any trades, he received some surprising news.

"Daryl hung up the phone and said, 'Hey, you might be going home,'" Morrison recalls. "I'm like, 'What are you talking about?'"

The buzz was that Morrison and Denis Pederson had been traded by the Devils to the Vancouver Canucks in exchange for Russian right-winger Alex Mogilny. By the time Morrison returned to his New Jersey apartment, the phone was ringing with official confirmation of the deal. The native of the Vancouver bedroom community of Pitt Meadows was, indeed, headed home.

"It was kind of funny how it happened," he says now. "But when I finally [confirmed] it was Vancouver, I was ecstatic about it. As a young guy, I went down to quite a few Canucks games at the old Pacific Coliseum, and to get the chance to come back and play in your hometown was a huge thrill."

Morrison has made the most of a rare opportunity, not only to play as an NHLer in the area where he grew up but also to play on what has in recent seasons been one of the most potent lines in professional hockey.

After skating mostly with Peter Schaefer and Matt Cooke during his first season with Vancouver, he was thrown together with various linemates and even asked to take some shifts on the wing. But just after Christmas of 2001 he was placed between star wingers Markus Naslund and Todd Bertuzzi. For the next three years, that line was one of the NHL's best.

At 5'11" and 185 pounds, Morrison is blessed with superb skating and playmaking skills. Although he garnered far less attention than Naslund or Bertuzzi, he was seen by some as the glue that held that line together.

"I think my speed on that line maybe pushes the defence back a little bit and at times maybe gives them [Naslund and Bertuzzi] a little more time with the puck," Morrison said in a 2004 interview. "A lot of times, when I'm with those guys, I just want to make sure they get the puck and they can do their thing.

"You have to be patient at times when you're with those guys, because they both like to handle the puck. And on a lot of lines you don't get that, where every guy is comfortable with the puck; a lot of times you'll have one or two guys who like to have it. But on our line, all three of us don't mind having it. So at times you have to be patient and pick your spots when you do have the puck. But overall it's been a good fit."

The West Coast Express, as the line eventually became dubbed, wasn't such a good fit in 2005-06, however, and was often broken up as the Canucks tried in vain to squeak into the playoffs. With the trade of Bertuzzi to the Florida Panthers in June 2006, the line is now NHL history.

In 2005-06, Morrison managed close to the offensive numbers he had posted in previous seasons, finishing with 19 goals, 56 points and a minus-one rating despite spending a considerable amount of time in coach Marc Crawford's doghouse.

Morrison scored the overtime winner against Colorado in the final game of the regular schedule. But despite solid statistics as a Canuck and hometown status, his name was prominent in off-season talk about which Vancouver players could be traded.

Prior to the NHL lockout, the speedy Morrison had enjoyed three straight seasons with at least 60 points. That included a career-high 71 in 2002-03, when he also posted his best scoring year as an NHLer, with 25 goals. Naslund and Bertuzzi, meanwhile, had become two of the league's most feared snipers.

*Pitt Meadows, B.C. native Brendan Morrison was ecstatic about coming home to play for the Canucks in 2000. (Vancouver Canucks/Jeff Vinnick)*

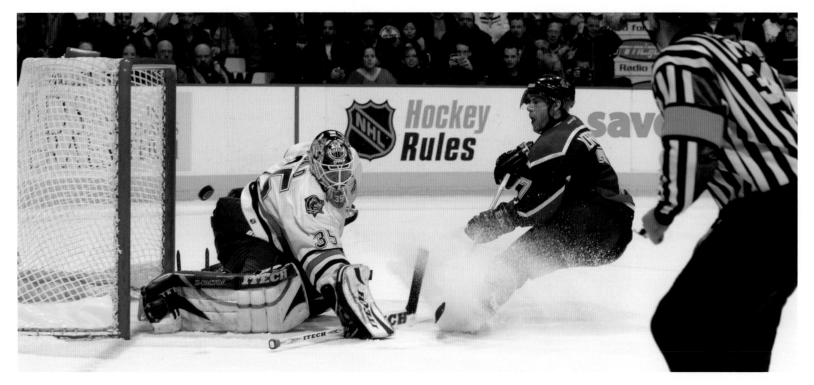

Centre Brendan Morrison compiled a career-high 71 points for the Canucks in 2002–03. (Vancouver Canucks/Jeff Vinnick)

Morrison believes the line as a whole picked up confidence with each year prior to the lockout.

"Any athlete — or, anybody, really, in all aspects of life — will tell you [that] when you're confident, you try more things," he says. "You're not afraid to do things out there. Whereas, when you're not fully confident, you might be a little bit hesitant at times."

Playing in Vancouver has been a terrific experience for Morrison and his wife, who have two young children. But the move from New Jersey hasn't allowed his parents to watch him play on a regular basis: several years ago they moved from Pitt Meadows to Hungary, where Ron Morrison works for a major modular building company.

"Ever since I've been back in Vancouver, they've been in Budapest," Morrison laughs.

Morrison himself left home when he was barely 17 to play in the B.C. Hockey League with the Penticton Panthers. After piling up 94 points in 56 games during his only season of junior hockey, he was selected 39th overall by the Devils in the 1993 NHL draft.

But he opted to accept a full scholarship to the University of Michigan, where he earned his economics degree and enjoyed a stellar four-year National Collegiate Athletic Association career under former NHLer Gordon "Red" Berenson. Morrison was a three-time all-American with the Wolverines, winning the NCAA tournament most-valuable-player award in 1996 and scoring the winning goal as Michigan captured the national championship. After piling up 31 goals and 57 assists in only 43 games as a senior in 1997, he won the Hobey Baker Award given to NCAA hockey's outstanding player.

But breaking in with the Devils wasn't easy. He played just 11 NHL games in his first professional season, spending most of the year with the Albany River Rats of the American Hockey League.

"Initially, it was a little frustrating, because a lot of players that I'd played against in college were getting opportunities to play in the NHL right away," he recalls. "And I knew I was as good a player as these guys, if not maybe a better player, but I just knew in New Jersey's system they're very patient, they want to make sure guys kind of learn the system and learn the ropes a little bit."

He had 13 goals and 46 points in his first full NHL season with New Jersey. After a holdout in his third pro season, during which he played in the Czech Republic, Morrison posted 26 points in 44 games with the Devils before being traded to Vancouver.

"System-wise, Vancouver was definitely a bit of a change from Jersey, and I think also confidence-wise," he says. "In the East it's a little more grind-it-out, with a lot of battles in the corner and things like that, whereas when I came out here it seemed to be a little more free-flowing game, a little more skating, and I think that suited me better."

*Prior to becoming an NHLer, Brendan Morrison won the Hobey Baker Award as U.S. college hockey's top player.* (Vancouver Canucks/Jeff Vinnick)

# MARKUS NASLUND

FEW, IF ANY, athletes are as closely scrutinized by British Columbians as Canucks captain Markus Naslund. While Vancouver hockey fans endured the frustrating NHL labour lockout of 2004-05, the question that seemed to loom as large as the future of professional hockey itself was whether the smooth Swede would ever be back in a Canuck uniform. And when he did return for a 2005-06 season that was plagued by injury, the question on the mind of most Canuck fans was why Naslund wasn't producing at his usual prodigious clip.

But just seven years ago, Naslund's injury status or even his future in a Canuck uniform wouldn't have mattered a whit to most Vancouver fans. The transition since then has been remarkable: from underachieving, enigmatic Swedish import to the face of an entire franchise and one of the finest players in Canucks history.

In the fall of 1998, Naslund wasn't getting even so much as a regular shift from head coach Mike Keenan as the Canucks lurched toward laughingstock status in the NHL. Naslund was benched during the preseason and found himself limited to just a couple of shifts a night or even a lonely seat in the press box early in the regular season. At the time he felt he had never played for a coach who disliked him so much.

Somehow, Naslund remained positive while in the coach's doghouse. And when he was finally given another chance by the unpredictable "Iron Mike," he responded in surprising fashion and finished that season with a career-best 36 goals and 30 assists.

"Once I got back in there, I thought: 'I'm just going to go out and dangle — have fun,'" Naslund would later reflect.

He has been "dangling" ever since, much to the delight of Canucks fans and a growing number of followers around the NHL. In the process he has fulfilled the great expectations that seemed to weigh him down when he arrived in the NHL as a slender 16th-overall draft pick of the Pittsburgh Penguins, a prospect dubbed by some as more promising than countryman Peter Forsberg.

That 1998-99 breakthrough was just a taste for Canuck fans, though. Growing more confident by the year, Naslund emerged into the NHL's most consistent scorer over the four seasons to 2003-04,

a stint in which he averaged 41 goals and 88 points a year. He has also grown into a team leader, and was made Vancouver captain when Mark Messier departed in 2000.

Naslund "has improved dramatically ... as a player, as a leader, as a professional," says Vancouver general manager Dave Nonis. "I think in all those areas you could say that Markus has grown significantly."

As with many European players, it took Naslund a lengthy adjustment period to find his legs in the NHL. It took so long, in fact, that his initial team, the Penguins, gave up. Although he had collected 52 points over 66 games in his third NHL season while skating with the great Mario Lemieux, Naslund was considered enough of a bust that Pittsburgh sent him west on March 20, 1996, for Canucks' draft pick Alex Stojanov, in what will go down as one of the most one-sided deals in league history.

Naslund didn't excel immediately as a Canuck, either. He had a promising 21 goals and 41 points during his first full season in 1996-97 but slipped backward the next year, falling to 34 points.

Back home in Sweden over the summer of 1998, he didn't feel much like returning to Vancouver for another NHL season under the demanding Keenan. Later, he would recall during that period feeling "like a fragile human being ... I was just sick of everything."

Though it began horribly, the subsequent NHL season would be the turning point for Naslund. Showing off the powerful wrist shot, silky moves and nose for the net that made him an NHL first-rounder, Naslund earned 66 points and served notice that he could be a force in the North American game.

In 1999-2000 Naslund posted 27 goals and 38 assists before taking a huge leap the following season. In 2000-01 the talented leftwinger broke the 40-goal barrier for the first time, totalling 41 goals and 75 points. He followed that up with a 40-goal, 90-point effort in 2001-02, as linemates Todd Bertuzzi and Brendan Morrison began to blossom alongside him.

Naslund turned in his best season in 2002-03, finishing second to Forsberg in the NHL scoring race with 48 goals and 104 points, by far the finest numbers of his career. That season he won the Lester B.

*Slick forward Markus Naslund took over as the Canucks' captain in 2000.* (Vancouver Canucks/Jeff Vinnick)

*Popular Markus Naslund was second in the NHL scoring race to fellow countryman Peter Forsberg in 2002–03. (Vancouver Canucks/Jeff Vinnick)*

instincts without having a tremendous vision of the ice," says former Canucks coach Marc Crawford. "A goal scorer gets himself to the position quite readily, and Markus has a great gift for that. On top of that he's blessed with a terrific shot and a quick release and some deception and that change of pace that allows him to elude people, so I think those combinations are quite good."

"He has a nose for the net," Nonis adds. "People talk about hockey sense, and it's something you can't really describe. Some players have the ability to know where to go and what to do and when to shoot, and Markus has that. He has something — an innate ability to know where to go. That's an area of the game where he just excels."

Naslund's numbers fell considerably in 2003-04, as he battled through a groin injury and then missed three games due to a concussion when he was hit by Colorado's Steve Moore in February. He suffered an elbow injury on the same hit, something that hampered his wrist shot down the stretch and required surgery to remove bone chips during the off-season.

His own injuries and the suspension of linemate Todd Bertuzzi seemed to weigh heavily on Naslund during the 2004 playoffs, when he was less effective than usual.

"I think I was just drained at times this year," he told reporters after the Canucks' season ended with a disappointing first-round loss to Calgary. "Everything just took its toll on me."

After doubt lingered during the NHL lockout about whether Naslund would ever return to the Canucks, the team's most popular player signed a three-year US$18-million contract in August 2005. Vancouver fans who had missed an entire hockey season rejoiced over having their Swedish sniper locked in as the NHL resumed play.

But injuries again took their toll on Naslund in 2005-06. Although he led the team in scoring for the seventh straight season, his 79-point output was his worst since 2000-01 and his minus-19 rating, one of the poorest of his career. An early-season groin injury never fully healed and although he played all but one game, he couldn't show the skating or strength on the puck that fans have come to expect. The injury was bad enough that Naslund passed on a chance to be part of the gold-medallist Swedish team for the 2006 Olympic tournament in Turin. But even the rest resulting from that sacrifice wasn't enough to bring the old Naslund back to the lineup.

The famed West Coast Express line of Naslund, Bertuzzi and Morrison just didn't click as it had in previous seasons, and was often split up by coach Marc Crawford. And as the Canucks faded down the stretch, with Naslund scoring just four times in the final 20 games, questions were raised for the first time about his leadership.

Naslund refused to use the lingering groin injury that troubled him all season as an excuse and said he remained proud to

Pearson Award, voted by his peers the NHL's outstanding player. He made the NHL All-Star Game for the third straight season and fourth time in five years.

"We've had some skilled players here in Vancouver over the last 35 years," Nonis says, "but if you look at some of the best players we've had and the most offensively gifted players — guys like Pavel Bure — I would say that Markus is much more consistent, in that he may not have a great night every night, but there are very few nights that he's not giving you 100 percent. And I think that's what makes him such a good player ... he's going to give you what he has every night."

"This is the best league in the world, and for you to notice one guy that much more than everybody else, it just shows how good he is," adds goaltender Dan Cloutier. "Not just on breakaways but on every aspect of the game — his shots from the wing, his patience, all the little things that other players can't do. And it's pretty spectacular to be able to witness that every day."

Nonis says there isn't one single quality that makes Naslund a standout. The friendly Swede is a strong skater, with a deadly shot, but he's also highly committed off the ice and keeps himself in top shape.

"He's got great scoring instincts, and you don't have scoring

*Swedish star Markus Naslund is under contract with the Canucks until 2008.* (Vancouver Canucks/Jeff Vinnick)

be captain of the Canucks. However, true to his nature, he said he would respect management's opinion if they wanted to make a change in leadership on the team.

"When a team is not performing as well as everyone hoped, you have to look at all the ingredients," he told reporters late in the season. "Being the captain, I have a big responsibility. It hasn't been a year I was hoping for and I think I speak for Brendan Morrison and Todd Bertuzzi, too. It's frustrating. We just haven't been able to click.

"I think everyone is going to be questioned and you're going to look at everything if the team is not doing as well as everyone is expecting it to. If someone has a suggestion or thinks that something can be done to upgrade this team, I'm all for it. That being said, I haven't changed anything in my leadership from when the team was winning to now. I think it's just that when things are slipping, people are trying to look for reasons."

Though Naslund says it is an honour to be team captain, there are parts of the job he doesn't like and he thinks too much is made of the captain's role in the success of the team both in good and bad times.

"A captain should be the one that's looked upon to lead the team but the drive has to come from within the team and the whole group," Naslund says. "If you don't have the whole group pulling the same way, then you're not going to be successful. It's not an individual sport, it's a team sport and you've got to have your team working."

Former Canucks coach Marc Crawford wasn't about to the lay the blame for the Canucks' slide out of the postseason at the feet of his captain.

"If he's guilty of anything it's caring a little too much," Crawford said late in the regular season. "He's a guy who cares passionately about the club. We all know he wears his heart on his sleeve."

# DAVE NONIS

AS A HOCKEY-CRAZY KID growing up in the Burnaby area of Greater Vancouver, Dave Nonis dreamed about playing for the Vancouver Canucks like his idols Andre Boudrias, Stan Smyl, Thomas Gradin and Curt Fraser.

That dream didn't come true, but another just as grand has materialized: instead of skating for the Canucks, he runs them.

On May 6, 2004, Nonis at age 37 became the youngest general manager in the history of the NHL franchise when he was named to replace his former boss, mentor and longtime friend, Brian Burke.

"When I do sit back and look at it, it's almost a little surreal," Nonis admits. "It's something I would never have expected to have happen."

It didn't surprise others, though. Nearly everybody in pro hockey circles had been predicting for several years that the capable, articulate Nonis would become an NHL general manager. As vice-president to Burke he had proved to be a shrewd contract negotiator, and he oversaw the team's minor league and scouting operations.

A finalist for general managerships in Calgary and San Jose, it seemed only a matter of time until Nonis ran his own NHL club. But he didn't see it coming in Vancouver, and he admits it was awkward being asked to replace his good friend Burke. During the press conference to announce his appointment, Nonis fought back tears as he thanked his former boss.

"It was difficult," Nonis says. "I'd worked for Brian for a long time and pretty much everything I've learned about running a team I've learned from him. And you know, we were very close. We remain best friends to this day. So it wasn't the way I envisioned getting my first GM job, that's for sure. And without [Burke] really telling me that it was the right thing to do to take the job, I would have had a difficult time doing it."

With Burke's blessing, Nonis assumed control of the team. But he was immediately hit with the uncertainty of the NHL labour lockout. That was followed by a 2005-06 season in which the Canucks were hit hard by injuries and faded miserably over the second half of the schedule to miss the playoffs for the first time in five years.

Just days after the regular season ended, Nonis made the most significant decision of his tenure thus far when he fired Marc Crawford, the winningest coach in Canucks history. The GM pledged to make more changes in order to "kick-start" the franchise.

He wasn't kidding. Nonis made several key moves in the 2006 off-season, the biggest trading Todd Bertuzzi to the Florida Panthers and landing franchise goalie Roberto Luongo in return. He also managed to extend the contracts of twins Daniel and Henrik Sedin and sign free-agent defenceman Willie Mitchell.

Nonis grew up not far from the Pacific Coliseum, the East Vancouver rink where the Canucks played before moving to General Motors Place. His father shared season tickets with business partners, so young Dave attended his share of games. As a teenager he was a die-hard fan, and he embraced the team's 1982 run into the Stanley Cup finals.

He himself played the game at a high level, first in the B.C. Hockey League and later on a four-year scholarship as a defenceman at the University of Maine. For his final two seasons of National Collegiate Athletic Association hockey he captained the Black Bear squad.

He played for a season in Denmark before returning to Maine to get his master's degree in business administration and serve as an assistant coach with the Black Bears. At 24, he was faced with the choice of heading to Sweden to play professionally or taking a front-office job with the Canucks, offered to him by Brian Burke and Pat Quinn.

"You know, when you get a chance to work for the team that you followed and continued to follow up until that time as your hometown club, that was something I really felt that I had to do," Nonis says now. "It was an opportunity I didn't know would ever come around again ... So I decided to quit playing and start working."

Canucks general manager Dave Nonis wasted little time putting his mark on the team with a flurry of moves in the 2006 off-season. (Vancouver Canucks/Jeff Vinnick)

The decision was a good one. He has developed into one of the NHL's top young administrators, somebody the team was afraid of losing to another franchise. His first stint with the Canucks lasted until 1994, when he left to join Burke at NHL headquarters in New York. He rejoined the Canucks as senior vice-president in 1998, with Burke hired as general manager and president.

Now the onetime fan finds himself in charge, the first GM in team history to have grown up in the Vancouver area.

"I didn't set my goals [initially] as being the general manager," Nonis says of his rise through the ranks. "I wanted to be part of a team that played in the National Hockey League. I wanted to be a part of a team that had a chance to win the Stanley Cup. And that's what I think everyone's ultimate goal is, and if we can't do it as players, then this is what we strive to do."

The average fan probably won't be able to distinguish between the Canucks as run by Burke or by himself, Nonis says. "There might be some differences in how I present myself — I mean, I am who I am. I'm not going to try to pretend to be Brian or act like him.

"[But] I can also tell you that most of the things that he taught me and that I learned from him, we've gone through a lot of those things together, and I don't see any reason to change the way the team is run."

# MATTIAS OHLUND

SOME QUESTIONED the wisdom of Canucks general manager Pat Quinn in the summer of 1997, when he committed nearly US$10 million over five years to sign a rangy 21-year-old Swedish defenceman named Mattias Ohlund.

The Canucks had selected Ohlund with the 13th overall pick in the 1994 NHL draft but hadn't been able to come to terms with the prospect, who was playing for Lulea in the Swedish Elite League. So when the Toronto Maple Leafs signed Ohlund to a generous offer sheet, some were surprised that Quinn matched it.

It turned out to be a shrewd decision. Ohlund has overcome a serious eye injury to become the Canucks' back-end rock that Quinn thought he could be, a true blue-chipper in even-strength, power-play and penalty-kill situations.

While former teammate Ed Jovanovski might get more attention, Ohlund has been a more consistent defensive force over his career and in many eyes is the Canucks' best blueliner, using his combination of strength, size, skating ability and hockey sense to provide one of the NHL's most complete defensive packages.

"I think he has turned out to be exactly what we looked at [when the team drafted him]," says Canucks European scout and former star Thomas Gradin. "We thought that this is the way he'd be able to play in the National Hockey League, and he has proven he can."

Ohlund has become a workhorse on the Vancouver blue line, consistently averaging well over 25 minutes a game. He has typically been asked to take on the opposition's top forwards but also to contribute significantly on the offensive end. In fact, he has surpassed the 30-point mark in each of the five seasons in which he was not sidelined for significant chunks of time.

The 6'2", 220-pounder considers himself fortunate to have managed a lengthy NHL career at all. It very nearly ended prematurely during the 1999 exhibition season, when a stray puck struck his right eye during a game against the Ottawa Senators.

That injury kept him out of 40 games during the 1999-2000 season and resulted in permanent partial loss of vision in the eye.

Since then, he has undergone a number of surgeries to relieve pressure and correct the problem. While some wondered if it would hamper his effectiveness as a professional hockey player, it hasn't.

"I was scared when I returned to the ice," Ohlund told NHL.com in a 2004 interview. "It took me a while to regain my confidence. But the mental part of one-on-one competition took still longer. Think about it: it was so fast. One second and it could have all been over.

"For years, doctors told me I might never have more than 70 percent of my sight. I'm lucky to still be playing. It's scary when it's your eyes. But going through that ordeal has helped me appreciate the game and what I have in my life even more."

Ohlund grew up in Pitea, on the northeast coast of Sweden, admiring the play of Leafs defenceman Borje Salming. Ohlund represented Sweden in three consecutive world junior tournaments and emerged as a standout with Lulea, leading the club to its first Swedish Elite League title in 1996.

The strapping defenceman didn't miss a beat after jumping to the NHL, posting seven goals and 30 points in his rookie season and finishing runner-up to Boston's Sergei Samsonov in Calder Trophy balloting in 1997-98. Despite his tender age Ohlund served as a Canucks assistant captain, finished with a plus-3 rating on a struggling team and went on to represent his country at the 1998 Nagano Olympics.

The next season, he upped that production to 35 points and logged more than 26 minutes a game for the Canucks. His efforts didn't go unnoticed around the league: he was named to the World Team for the 1999 NHL All-Star Game in Tampa Bay.

That fall, when a puck deflected off a stick and struck his right eye during the preseason, Ohlund's career was in jeopardy. But he bounced back from surgery to record 20 points and play a career-high 27:41 minutes per game for the Canucks during the last half of that season.

In 2001-02 he posted a career-best 36 points and 10 goals while playing in all but one regular-season game for Vancouver.

*Swedish defenceman Mattias Ohlund has become a rock on the blueline for the Canucks since 1997.* (Vancouver Canucks/Jeff Vinnick)

He also made the Swedish lineup for the 2002 Winter Olympics in Salt Lake City.

Although a knee injury limited him to 59 games the following season, Ohlund still managed 29 points. In 2003-04 he played in all 82 games for the Canucks, scoring a career-high 14 times and finishing with 34 points. He was second among all NHLers playing an average of more than 35 shifts per game. Following the season, he signed a new US$14-million four-year deal with Vancouver. This time, nobody questioned the amount he was making.

In 2005-06, Ohlund posted 13 goals, including eight on the power play, and finished with 33 points while averaging more than 25 minutes a game, a team high. He was voted by fans as the team's top defenceman for the fourth time in his career, although

his minus-six rating was his first negative plus-minus in four seasons, reflecting the problems the Canucks as a team had in keeping the puck out of their net

"Mattias is extremely competitive and that often goes unnoticed, because he's such a mild-mannered guy," says former Canucks coach Marc Crawford. "Because his strength and his size are so overwhelming in a lot of cases, he's a dominant defenceman."

Although disappointed in not making the playoffs with the Canucks in 2006, Ohlund did win an Olympic gold medal as a member of the Swedish team, recording two assists in six games. He endured a cracked rib and a shoulder injury during the Olympic tournament but missed only four NHL games as a result.

# JARKKO RUUTU

IN THE SPRING of 2003, Jarkko Ruutu had begun to think that his NHL career was over. In his fourth season with the Canucks, the left-winger had too often been the odd man out, spending much of his time in the press box as a healthy scratch.

But then came the 2003 playoffs. During that postseason Canucks head coach Marc Crawford seemed to discover that Ruutu was capable of playing hard-nosed, responsible, two-way hockey, and the Finn emerged as an NHL regular.

"I had thought my career was basically over in the NHL that season," Ruutu says. "I had played in not even half of the regular-season games. But after the first playoff game, he [Crawford] just threw me in. I had nothing to lose. And then he started playing me a lot. In some games I played over 17 minutes, at the most important time of the year.

"I think that kind of made him understand, too — I kind of gave him a picture that I can play at this level."

What Ruutu showed was that he was capable of being an effective agitator — the kind of player able to throw opponents off their game — without taking too many of the ill-advised penalties for which he had become known earlier in his career.

The 6'2", 195-pound native of Helsinki played in 13 playoff games that spring, winning a regular job in the process. The following season Crawford played him in 71 regular-season games. In 2005-06, he skated in all 82 contests for the first time in his NHL career and posted highs of 10 goals, 17 points and 142 penalty minutes.

While he still takes some penalties that hurt his team, Ruutu has generally picked his spots better, regularly drawing opponents into retaliating and proving to be an effective penalty killer.

"When you know that your coach trusts you, you play a lot better," Ruutu says. "When you're in and out of the lineup, you can't show a lot of things because you're so nervous and you're trying to avoid mistakes."

His feisty style and penchant for jawing at opponents seems to foster frustration and distraction in them. After one game in Denver

during the 2003-04 season, then Avalanche star Peter Forsberg told reporters: "Ruutu causes trouble every time he's out there."

Many assume that Ruutu patterned his style after Esa Tikkanen, a Finnish forerunner in the NHL. But Ruutu says he plays his own style, and that he actually idolized Wayne Gretzky while growing up.

"My problem [early in his NHL career] had been taking stupid penalties," Ruutu says. "But I've tried to cut them down ... I've always thought of myself as a playoff player. I've played fairly simple and it's nothing fancy, I don't do the great moves. But I try to play very simple and effective, and I think that kind of makes it more important and effective in the playoffs."

Ruutu believes he has more offensive potential than he has shown so far in the NHL — something he displayed during the 1999-2000 season with the American Hockey League's Syracuse Crunch, when he had 26 goals and 32 assists in 65 games.

"I know that I can be better offensively," he says. "I don't think I'll be the guy that scores 30 goals. I think I can get close to 20."

For a European, Ruutu took a slightly unusual route to the NHL. After playing junior for HIFK Helsinki, he accepted a hockey scholarship to Michigan Tech University as a 20-year-old in 1995. He played just one season for the National Collegiate Athletic Association school, scoring 12 times and adding 10 assists and 96 penalty minutes in 38 games. He then returned to Finland and played three seasons with HIFK in that country's premier league.

Ruutu had felt he would develop more as a hockey player by returning home. The move paid off as he was drafted by the Canucks in the third round, 68th overall, in 1998. After one more season with HIFK, he returned to North America in 1999 and began a four-year process to crack the Canucks' regular lineup.

In the summer of 2006, Ruutu opted to continue his NHL career elsewhere, however. In July, he signed as a free-agent with the Pittsburgh Penguins, accepting a two-year deal that will pay him an average of US$1.15 million a season.

# SAMI SALO

MOST PLAYERS can tell you exactly where they were and what they were doing when news came that they had been drafted into the NHL. Sami Salo can't. In fact, the Finnish defence-man can't even remember being told that he had been drafted.

The news came during a major holiday festival in his home country. Salo's former agent, then the player personnel director for the Ottawa Senators, telephoned to inform him that the Senators had selected him 239th overall in the 1996 draft.

But the news didn't sink in until three or four days later, when Salo finally read about it in the newspaper.

"It's kind of a funny story," Salo says. "If you're a Finnish guy, you would know about the midsummer festival. It's a special thing where you get together with all the families and you have fun for 24 hours or so, because it's a time of the year where it's pretty much light for 24 hours ... I was in the middle of the party and had a little too many drinks also, I think. So I didn't remember that he had called me ... I wasn't expecting to be drafted."

Salo was 21 at the time and the NHL seemed far away. The 6'3" defenceman wasn't ready to test the waters in North America and spent one more season with his Finnish club, TPS Turku, followed by a subsequent season with Jokerit Helsinki.

By then, he was ready to take the NHL plunge. When new Senators general manager Rick Dudley made a pitch, Salo decided to go to Ottawa in time for the 1998-99 season.

"It wasn't a great offer, but I just felt it was time for me to try, so I wouldn't be disappointed later on that I didn't even try to make it to the NHL," Salo says. "We just felt, with my family and the agents, that it was time to give it a go and see what happens."

What happened was a little surprising for a player who hadn't been drafted until the ninth round. At the time, Ottawa was short-handed on the blue line due to holdouts and injuries and Salo slotted in immediately as a regular, playing 61 games and recording 19 points as a rookie.

But even as he saw immediate ice time, Salo was still adjusting to the more intense pace and travel of the NHL and feeling unsure of his future. When he suffered a groin injury not far into his first season, he was sent down for some season-ing with the Detroit Vipers of the International Hockey League. He thought that was the beginning of the end.

"Obviously, I was disappointed, and I thought that okay, that was it — that maybe I wouldn't be back," he says. "But I think it was five games that I played, and then I came back and they kept me for the end of that year and then three more years."

There was no doubt he could contribute at the NHL level, but shoulder and wrist injuries would severely hamper his effective-ness with the Senators, limiting him to 37 and 31 games during his second and third seasons, respectively.

In his fourth campaign he rebounded by playing 66 games and recording 18 points. Nevertheless, the Senators decided to move him, shipping him to Vancouver in exchange for holdout forward Peter Schaefer on September 21, 2002.

"At first I was disappointed," Salo says now of the trade, which came just before the 2002-03 regular season. "Starting in Ottawa, you get used to all the players and the people around the team and it was a good organization.

"But over the last couple of years with Ottawa I seemed to have kind of an injury problem. Every year something happened. I think it was the right time to move on and start from zero again and I couldn't have asked for a better place to be than in Vancouver."

Salo, a native of Turku, Finland, didn't know much about his new city prior to the trade. Eastern Conference teams travel west only once a year at most, so Salo hadn't seen a lot more than his hotel, the airport and GM Place.

"But after the first couple of weeks I started feeling really good about myself with the city, and the fans in Vancouver were great," he says. "I think they are probably one of the best fan [groups] in the NHL."

Salo has given Vancouver fans plenty to cheer about and probably more than they had expected. He has become one of the Canucks'

*With the departure of Ed Jovanovski, Finnish defenceman Sami Salo has become even more important to the Canucks.* [Vancouver Canucks/Jeff Vinnick]

premier defencemen, with more than 20 minutes a game of ice time as well as regular penalty-killing and power-play duties. In 2002-03 he led Canucks defencemen with a career-high nine goals, and he had career bests of 21 assists and 30 points while finishing plus-9 over 79 games.

But physical problems struck him in the playoffs that year. A serious foot infection kept him out of Games 6 and 7 against the Minnesota Wild; the infection put him in hospital for eight days and even threw his career into doubt.

But he bounced back the following season to record 26 points and a plus-8 rating in 74 games, cementing his place as one of the Canucks' most trusted defencemen.

Salo played for Frolunda of the Swedish Elite League during the NHL lockout, allowing him to be closer to family and friends for a winter. He also skated for Finland in the 2004 World Cup of Hockey, helping the team to a silver medal.

In 2005-06, Salo again posted NHL career bests of 10 goals and 33 points, including nine power-play goals, despite missing 23 games due to a shoulder strain suffered while playing for the Finnish team which captured silver at the Turin Olympics. He was also an impressive plus-nine for the season.

"He's a great defenceman," former teammate, Ed Jovanovski told the Vancouver *Sun* during the 2003-04 season. "He moves the puck well, he skates well and he has a boomer of a shot. He's a solid, all-around player and I'm sure he's going to get a lot of opportunity here."

# DANIEL AND HENRIK SEDIN

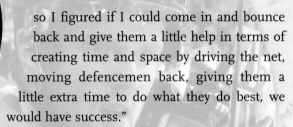

THEY WERE ONCE billed as "twin Forsbergs" and hailed by others as the hottest Swedish combo since ABBA topped the music charts, so Daniel and Henrik Sedin have only just begun to match the hype that emerged with them out of the 1999 NHL draft.

On June 26 of that year, then Vancouver general manager Brian Burke pulled off the blockbuster deal of draft day, securing the number 2 and 3 overall picks and convincing the Sedin family that their quiet red-headed twins should play professionally together on the west coast of Canada.

The fancy footwork was seen at the time as a bold move by Burke to solidify the long-term future of the Canucks. But it wasn't until the 2005-06 season, when paired with veteran winger Anson Carter, that the twins finally blossomed into a true NHL offensive force.

Meshing with Carter better than any of their previous linemates, the Sedins enjoyed breakout NHL seasons and also helped Sweden to a gold medal in the 2006 Turin Olympics.

Henrik finished second in Canuck team scoring only four points behind Markus Naslund, posting 18 goals and 57 assists while Daniel wasn't far behind with 22 goals and 49 helpers. All totals were easily career highs for the twins. In fact Henrik, a centre, eclipsed his previous best for points by 33 and Daniel, a left-winger, by 17.

Their performance represented a changing of the guard on the Vancouver franchise with the Sedins line becoming, in many eyes, the team's top combination. Not only did they produce points, but the twins also managed to retain their sound defensive and positional play, each posting positive plus-minus ratings.

Perhaps no forwards in the NHL are as skilled at "cycling" the puck in the opponents' zone and their style clicked well with Carter, whose 55-point showing was also among his finest NHL campaigns.

"I knew they were really good hockey players," Carter says. "I don't want to say it's been better than expected because when you're drafted second and third overall, you have to have some talent. I knew the potential was there. I saw their points, their stats and the minutes they played. I saw they were pretty effective, so I figured if I could come in and bounce back and give them a little help in terms of creating time and space by driving the net, moving defencemen back, giving them a little extra time to do what they do best, we would have success."

They have certainly enjoyed success, the sort that was envisioned when Burke scrambled to draft the twins in 1999. And the twins were rewarded in June 2006 when general manager Dave Nonis signed them each to three-year US $10.75-million contracts which will almost certainly be accompanied by an increase in ice time.

Daniel, the younger twin by six minutes, believes the Sedins' seemingly overnight success has come from a mixture of improving strength and confidence as well as the play of Carter. But the twins have always insisted that the amount of ice time they receive is a huge factor in their offensive production.

It's difficult to put up superstar numbers playing on the second line and getting second power-play minutes. The twins are looking to move into the 20-minute-per-game range as they enter what figures to be the prime of their careers.

"It all depends on how much ice time you get and how much coaches play you," Daniel says. "I mean, you can't score 80 points if you only play like 13, 14 minutes a game. So it's pretty much up to the ice [time]."

Daniel admits there was pressure on the twins when they arrived in Vancouver. They played an extra season in Sweden after the draft in order to finish their high school and mature as players, which heightened fans' anticipation of their arrival. And when they were drafted, the Canucks were a bad team in desperate need of a saviour, or two.

"I don't think we ever felt pressure from outside," Daniel says in hindsight. "I think we had all the pressure from ourselves. And I think that's a good thing — that we didn't care what the media said and all that. We knew it was going to be tough, so we just had to put that aside and just play our game."

*The Sedin twins, Daniel (left) and Henrik, had a breakthrough season for the Canucks in 2005–06. (Vancouver Canucks/Jeff Vinnick)*

# STEVE TAMBELLINI

THERE HAS BEEN one constant in the front office of the Vancouver Canucks for the last 15 years. His name is Steve Tambellini.

Now vice-president and assistant general manager of the team, Tambellini has worked through three management eras. He was hired by Pat Quinn in 1991, kept on by Brian Burke in 1997 and continued with Dave Nonis in 2004.

During that time he has done everything, from community and media relations to player personnel to marketing and ticket sales. And he considers himself lucky to have had the chance to get all that experience with one team.

"I don't hear those stories any more, where one guy gets to go through an organization and really learn it," Tambellini says. "Sometimes you'd have to move five or six times throughout a career to get that experience. So I have been extremely fortunate with this organization."

He joined the Canucks for the first time as a player, in 1985. Vancouver was the final NHL stop in a 10-season pro career for the forward from Trail, British Columbia.

After retiring from the NHL in 1988 following three seasons with the Canucks he went to Austria, where he played professionally while working toward a business degree in the off-seasons back home. Going into a management career in hockey wasn't his priority until Quinn, who had managed him during his final NHL season, came up with an offer that was difficult to refuse.

"Pro sport at that time was maybe third on my list as far as my agenda to go ahead," Tambellini recalls. "I was more interested in heading toward [non-hockey] business. But when I met with Pat and Brian, what they had planned and the opportunities were too much to pass up, so obviously it was a very good choice for me.

"Pat was magnificent as far as trying to accommodate a young guy's goals in the business. I told him what my goal was, that at the right time I wanted to take over my own club. And he was great. He was so open about it. He said: 'Look, we're going to put you in a lot of different positions that are going to require no ego. But you've got the hockey side, and you're going to learn the busi-

ness side from the ground up' ... I got to learn the business side of the sport."

Tambellini was raised on the game in the interior of British Columbia, where his father, Addie, was a slick centre for the world championship Trail Smoke Eaters senior team. Seeing his father playing with such a group was an experience that shaped young Steve's life.

"I grew up in a community that housed basically — from a small town of 15,000 people — a team that won a world championship. So growing up, in that dressing room with this group of men that were probably Canada's most famous amateur team, to go to that room with Dad, as a young kid, was like walking into the Montreal Canadiens' dressing room for me."

Steve Tambellini became a junior star with the Lethbridge Broncos of the Western Hockey League. After putting up 75 goals and 80 assists in his final junior season, he was selected 15th overall in the 1978 NHL draft by the New York Islanders and after one season in the Central League with Fort Worth he cracked the Islanders' lineup. In his rookie year, he was part of the Islanders' first Stanley Cup team in what would eventually become a four-year championship dynasty.

But the next season Tambellini was traded to the dismal Colorado Rockies, a move he now describes as going "from the penthouse to the outhouse." It was in Colorado that he had his best offensive season in the NHL, however, with 29 goals and 30 assists in 1981-82.

Over his 553-game NHL career, which included stops in New Jersey, Calgary and Vancouver, Tambellini posted 160 goals and 310 points with just 105 penalty minutes.

He followed in his father's footsteps when it came to international play. In 1978 Steve was a teammate of Wayne Gretzky on Canada's world championship junior bronze-medal squad; he also skated for Canada in the world championship and Izvestia tournaments and on the fourth-place host squad at the 1988 Calgary Winter Olympics.

That connection with the maple leaf has continued. Tambellini

*Before becoming a constant in the Canucks' front office, Steve Tambellini played 10 seasons as a pro.* (David Klutho/HHOF)

was director of player personnel for the Canadian teams that won gold at the 2002 Salt Lake City Olympics and the 2004 World Cup. He was also general manager of Canada's gold-medal-winning team at the 2003 world championships before serving as director of player personnel for the Canadian team, which fell in the quarter-final round of the 2006 Turin Olympics.

The international playing legacy has continued with Steve's son, Jeff Tambellini, a first-round pick of the Los Angeles Kings in 2003 who has represented Canada at the world under-18 and junior tournaments. It is the first time three generations of one family have played for Canada at the world level.

"That part of hockey — the international part — has always been a very significant, special part in our family," he says.

Tambellini was in the running for the general manager's job in Vancouver after Burke was fired in 2004. Ownership chose Nonis, but Tambellini remained loyal to the club that has given him a terrific post-playing career.

"I've been so fortunate," he says. "With the right situation I would like to run my own [NHL] club, but I've also got a wonderful job here with Dave and myself in Vancouver. There's a lot invested in this organization — and I still would like to be a part of this organization when it does win."

# ALAIN VIGNEAULT

ALAIN VIGNEAULT is well aware that hockey is a year-round obsession in Vancouver. But far from being a negative for the 16th head coach in Canucks' history, it is actually one of the reasons he wanted the job.

The 45-year-old Vigneault was hired on June 20, 2006 to replace Marc Crawford, who was fired after the Canucks failed to live up to huge expectations during the 2005–06 season and, in fact, failed to even make the playoffs.

Vigneault is no stranger to coaching in a puck-passionate environment. He spent three-plus seasons as head coach of the Canadiens in Montreal, where hockey isn't really a religion; it's far more important than that.

During the press conference to announce his hiring by the Canucks, Vigneault related a story about precisely when he knew he wanted to be a head coach in Vancouver. Vigneault, who coached the Canucks' American Hockey League affiliate in Winnipeg in 2005–06, and the rest of the Vancouver organization's coaching and management contingent went out for dinner to a Whistler, B.C. restaurant during Canucks training camp in September 2005.

"By the time we got to our table people realized who had walked in and all of a sudden throughout the restaurant people started chanting 'Go, Canucks, Go'," Vigneault recalled for reporters.

"Right then and there, not wishing any bad things to happen to anybody, but I said to myself internally, 'I'd love to coach here. I'd love to coach in a place where hockey means something.' I'm getting that opportunity."

Vigneault got that chance after the Canucks won just twice during the final eight games of the 2005–06 regular season and failed to make the playoffs for the first time in five years. That mysterious fade cost Crawford his job and ultimately elevated Vigneault, who led the Manitoba Moose to a 44-24-7-5 record in the same season.

Although general manager Dave Nonis interviewed other candidates for the job, he eventually went with the man from inside the Canucks' organization whom he had hired one year earlier. "All of those things that we were looking for [in a head coach] we had in our organization," Nonis said as he introduced Vigneault as Crawford's successor.

Vigneault, who played 42 NHL games as a defenceman for the St. Louis Blues from 1981–83, has coached for 19 years in the Quebec junior, minor pro and NHL circuits. He won a Memorial Cup and Canadian junior coach-of-the-year award behind the bench of the Hull Olympiques in 1987 and 1988 and his experience includes four seasons as an assistant coach with the Ottawa Senators as well as two seasons as a scout for the Blues.

In his only previous stint as an NHL head coach, which came at just 36 years of age, the native of Quebec City posted a 109-113-39-5 record over more than three seasons in Montreal. The bilingual Vigneault was a nominee for the Jack Adams Award as NHL coach of the year in 1999–2000 but was eventually fired by the Habs after they failed to make the playoffs for two straight seasons and then got off to a slow start in 2000–01.

Vigneault has the reputation of being a tough coach and he describes himself as "blunt and direct" in his dealings with players.

"Some guys say I'm a disciplinarian, some other guys say I'm a players' coach," Vigneault said the day he was named Canucks' bench boss. "I frankly believe that I'm just a business-type coach. There's a job that needs to be done and when you're in charge of the business you have to make sure that it is done and you have to create the right environment for your personnel to do it. Sometimes, it's making sure that the reins are a little bit tighter and sometimes it's loosening things up so guys can go out there and play. It's a matter of reading your team, reading your players and getting a feel for when they perform their best."

Vigneault says he noticed certain Vancouver players during post-game television interviews in 2005-06 saying that they believed the team hadn't worked hard enough or had been outworked by its opponent. "I'm pretty confident we can fix that with the proper direction."

"I know this group might not have met expectations, but there's a solid base here," he said. "I'm going to coach the group that is given to me and I'm going to make sure that they're well-prepared, they work hard, they play with commitment and passion."

# CANUCKS NATION

## by Kevin Woodley

TREVOR LINDEN spent almost two full seasons in a Montreal Canadiens uniform so he was familiar with the concept of being cheered on the road.

He'd certainly been on the wrong end of it enough times during his first 10-year go around with the Canucks, most often when those same Canadiens or their fellow "Original Six" squad from Toronto visited Vancouver.

Nothing, however, could have prepared him for hearing it while he was wearing a Canucks uniform. So he'll never forget the puzzled expression as he looked down the bench at captain Markus Naslund's face as the cheers rang out in Calgary after a Canucks' goal during the 2003-04 campaign.

It was a look of shock and surprise that Linden, then in the second full season of his second stint in Vancouver, is pretty sure mirrored his own.

"We were both like, 'What the heck is going on here? Where are all these cheers coming from?' It was really loud, and we were like, 'Wow, this is kind of cool!'"

For the Canucks, life on the road in the new millennium had become, in Linden's words, "almost like when Toronto comes to Vancouver."

"I had a reporter in Detroit come up to me and say, 'God, it's great to see you guys in town,' and I kind of looked at him, like, 'What do you mean?'" offers Linden. "And he told me how people can't wait for us and the Wings to play each other because the games are always good, and we both play the game the right way, and it's just always great hockey. That's the type of reaction I've gotten."

That reaction changed on March 8, 2004. Cheers for the Canucks were replaced with league-wide boos for Todd Bertuzzi, a constant reminder of the on-ice assault that left Colorado's Steve Moore with broken bones in his neck, a severe concussion, and questions about whether he would ever play again.

Two years and one lockout later, the boos infiltrated GM Place as the Canucks, true to the roller coaster form that dominated franchise history, ended a season that started with Stanley Cup expectations by missing the playoffs entirely. It was a tragically appropriate

bookend for a five-year stint that will be looked back on by long-suffering fans as the most successful in the team's first 35 years.

The Canucks, a franchise that had finished at or under .500 in 24 of its first 30 years, were above the break-even mark in each of the five years before the lockout cancelled the 2004-05 season. They set a team record with 104 points in 2002-03, then followed it up with their first division title in 11 years.

That success was mirrored in the stands: 124 straight sell outs to end 2005-06. Season tickets were capped at 17,000, a dramatic increase from a base that slipped under 8,000 as the 1990s wound down with a string of missed playoffs.

The turnaround can be largely credited to since-fired president and general manager Brian Burke, who re-established a connection with fans and a business community alienated by absentee ownership. He put together a younger, faster, hungrier team through trades that shed salary and the Canucks' fat-cat image.

Perhaps most important, Burke hired Marc Crawford to coach what he insisted be an up-tempo, entertaining style of hockey. "We've had a fun team to watch," says Linden.

Unfortunately, the Canucks have also at times been fun to play against. After trying to outscore their mistakes for years, the defensive deficiencies that often led to early playoff exits left them without a playoff spot in 2005-06 and cost Crawford his job.

Ironically, the things that made Crawford's Canucks entertaining also made them beatable at crunch time. But at least it was enjoyable to watch for five years.

A fast-growing new generation of fans agreed, but it's the ones who have been there since the beginning who reaped the biggest reward. Those are the fans who showed up for three mostly miserable decades knowing the best they dared hope for was a good effort and a close game, who went Mardi Gras crazy when, every 12 years, the Canucks went on an unlikely run to the Stanley Cup final.

"For us, the last five years aren't so much a reason for staying as a reward for being there," Darcy Puri, who was 11 when his dad bought season tickets in 1971, said during the NHL lockout. The family has renewed them ever since.

*These female citizens of the "Canucks Nation" celebrate during a game in General Motors Place.* (Vancouver Canucks/Jeff Vinnick)

Looking back on three decades of ticket stubs, Puri wasn't ready to label the first five years of the new millennium the best. He looks back on Orland Kurtenbach and Stan Smyl eras as the Canucks "good old days," laments the sometimes-stale corporate atmosphere at GM Place, and the fact he knows parents who have to save all year just to take their kids to one game.

There are too many nights, said Puri, when the ticket price stays the same but the quality of play is dragged down by less-skilled teams playing trapping, defensive hockey. The NHL agreed, and emerged from its one-year shutdown with an attempt to legislate such styles out of a game they had smothered.

The run-and-gun Canucks were supposed to benefit from the changes, but a strange thing happened while planning the Stanley Cup parade route. Teams that had tried for so long to stymie Vancouver's attack found it easier to generate one of their own, and the Canucks, who always struggled in retreat, found playing in their own end even more difficult under the new rules.

Add in some early season indifference and a rash of injuries to top players and it ended with earlier-than-expected tee times, leaving Canucks fans with an all-too-familiar feeling. They did not, however, leave the building or their television sets.

The unprecedented numbers watching before the lockout continued throughout an up-and-down 2005-06, which also ended with more than 4,000 on the season ticket wait list. Thousands watched pay-per-view broadcasts in movie theatres, bars and restaurants across British Columbia. Regional broadcasts sometimes outdrew even the Maple Leafs in a much larger Ontario market, and Vancouver radio shows fielded calls from overseas fans listening on the Internet.

That such support continued through the lockout and a season of disappointment wouldn't surprise University of British Columbia graduate student Clayton Munro, who argued in his master's thesis in sports management that Canucks fans had formed a "brand community": one defined not by geography, but by the unique social relationships that develop between enthusiasts.

Usually used to define the way social groups form around products such as Apple computers or Harley-Davidson motorcycles, Munro believes he's the first to apply this sociological concept of shared consciousness, rituals and traditions, and a sense of moral responsibility to a sports team. He didn't set out to define fans as individuals or a group, but now believes being a part of the Canucks community, whether at a game or in a chat room, is a big part of the attraction.

Different fans, he says, are drawn to the Canucks for different reasons — from the style they play, to the way jerseys look, to the kind of person Linden is — but the biggest reason they return is to remain a part of the larger group. "People think fans buy a ticket to see a game. It's so much more than that," Munro says. "You buy a ticket to be a part of the community, to feel that connection to the team and everyone else who is there to cheer for them with you." The best five years in history extended that Canucks community. Whether it remains intact and continues to grow could depend on just how long another team turnaround takes.

*Freelance journalist Kevin Woodley reports on the Vancouver Canucks for the Associated Press news agency.*

# conclusion

A t times during the 35-season history of the Vancouver Canucks, it has seemed as though the gods themselves were conspiring against the hockey fans of British Columbia.

How else do you explain acquiring Dale Tallon instead of Gilbert Perreault? The team's first owner going to jail? A dozen years without winning a single playoff series? Thirty-five seasons without a No. 1 overall draft pick? A reluctant Russian superstar who wants out of town but won't say why? A suspension to a brooding power forward that not only spoils a promising playoff picture but also sours the star's very relationship with the city?

The Canucks have had 16 head coaches, nine general managers and 11 captains; they have worn four distinctively different uniforms; and they have posted more than 1,000 National Hockey League victories over the years. But they have never once sipped from the Stanley Cup. And the only two times they made it to the league finals also represent the only two times in 35 seasons that they have advanced past the second round of the playoffs.

*Facing page: Faces on the Canucks' bench during the 2005–06 season included Daniel Sedin, Richard Park, Brendan Morrison, Jarkko Ruutu and Sami Salo.* (Vancouver Canucks/Jeff Vinnick)

*Above: Alexandre Burrows had 12 points and 61 penalty minutes in 43 games for the 2005–06 Canucks.* (Vancouver Canucks/Jeff Vinnick)

Right: *Defenceman Kevin Bieksa appeared in 39 games for the shorthanded Canucks in the 2005–06 season.* (Vancouver Canucks/Jeff Vinnick)

In short, there is no great history of success here. But there is a tremendous bond between the people of the province and the Canucks, judging by the faithful who support the team, year after year, playoffs or no playoffs.

That is the real strength of the Vancouver Canucks. The team's fans have been there, through thick and mostly thin. At times, their support has wavered but they have hung around, waiting for something, someone to cheer. They are as much a part of the history of this franchise as the players themselves. And as the Canucks move into their next 35 years in the NHL, they remain the backbone of the club's future.

Never has that support been more evident than following the NHL labour lockout of 2004-05. Despite the Canucks not playing a single game for an entire winter, Vancouver recorded 41 straight sellouts the following season, making it 124 capacity crowds in a row at General Motors Place.

And despite a disappointing end to the 2005-06 regular season, when the team folded down the stretch and missed the playoffs entirely – for the 15th time in franchise history, no less – there was still a lineup for season tickets. If the franchise doesn't have a win-loss record to envy, its support is certainly the thing of most NHL general managers' dreams.

With that kind of backing, it is difficult for this franchise to be labeled a failure, despite its well-documented lack of success in the playoffs. And there are now several signs that point to a bright future for the Canucks both on the ice and in the financial ledgers.

The labour settlement that emerged out of the NHL lockout will benefit the Canucks, its yearly cap on total team salaries meaning that Vancouver, in theory at least, should be able to ice as competitive a team as any major US market. As well, a strong Canadian dollar will help the Canucks, who like other franchises in this country pay most of their expenses in US currency.

The Canucks, thanks in large part to the foresight of Arthur Griffiths, also have the advantage of playing in a fan-friendly, modern, downtown building in GM Place. And thanks to the presence of Francesco Aquilini, the team once again has the local ownership that ties it to the city more securely than when American John McCaw was sole owner.

Though questions remain about some of the Canucks' older core players and pending free-agents, there is plenty of reason for optimism among the young.

Swedish twins Henrik and Daniel Sedin emerged into two of the top forwards in the NHL during the 2005-06 season and their production figures to increase as they are granted more ice time and power-play minutes. The Canucks' defence is capably anchored by Mattias Ohlund, Sami Salo and free-agent acquisition Willie Mitchell. And Roberto Luongo now gives Vancouver the kind of game-stealing goalie it has rarely boasted in 35 years.

Centre Ryan Kesler, with a solid frame, aggressive attitude and great wheels, figures to be a core building block, while winger Alexandre Burrows and defenceman Kevin Bieksa acquitted themselves well for the short-handed Canucks during the 2005-06 season.

Waiting in the wings is more young talent. Defenceman Luc Bourdon, a standout with Val d'Or of the Quebec Major Junior League and for Canada in the 2006 world junior championships, was taken 10th overall by the Canucks in the 2005 draft and nearly made the NHL roster as an 18-year-old. And the Canucks added a player they think will be able to score at the NHL level when they selected Austrian Michael Grabner — a 6' 1", 182-pound forward who has played in North America with the Spokane Chiefs — in the 2006 draft held at GM Place.

The Canucks also have a bright young talent in the general manager's chair in Dave Nonis, who is now putting his stamp on the team he took over from good friend and mentor Brian Burke in 2004.

So far, Nonis seems to be responding strongly to the disappointment of missing the playoffs in 2005-06, a key to the immediate future of the Canucks.

"I think we will have to make some changes, but when you look at some of the positive things we have on our roster and some of the positive people we have here, I don't see any reason

*Quebec native Alexandre Burrows was a junior star with Shawinigan before turning professional.* (Vancouver Canucks/Jeff Vinnick)

why our team can't look at [missing the playoffs] as a hiccup and have a very competitive club going forward," Nonis said after the 2005-06 season concluded.

"I'm not going to rule anything out. This isn't a team that needs to be torn apart completely. [But] we will be open to change more than we have been for five or six years. I don't believe everyone should be back for another kick at the can."

What that change will bring for Vancouver hockey fans remains to be seen. Perhaps it will be the Stanley Cup championship that

has eluded the city since 1915 and craved by Canucks fans ever since the team entered the NHL in 1970. If and when that day comes, expect the city and the province to explode with a celebration like never before.

Until then, the journey will continue to be interesting, the characters colourful, the fans mostly patient and always passionate, and the wet West Coast winters focused squarely on Vancouver Canucks hockey.

*Left-winger Josh Green, a native of Camrose, Alberta, appeared in 33 games for the Canucks in 2005–06.* (Vancouver Canucks/Jeff Vinnick)

# Acknowledgements

THE AUTHOR WOULD like to thank the following current and former Canucks players, coaches and management staff for providing their personal insights on the team: Greg Adams, Bryan Allen, Alex Auld, Dave Babych, Rick Blight, Ivan Boldirev, Andre Boudrias, Garth Butcher, Anson Carter, Dan Cloutier, Matt Cooke, Geoff Courtnall, Russ Courtnall, Marc Crawford, Gerald Diduck, Robert Dirk, Thomas Gradin, Arthur Griffiths, Gary Doak, Doug Halward, Glen Hanlon, Charlie Hodge, Dennis Kearns, Ryan Kesler, Orland Kurtenbach, Rick Lanz, Don Lever, Doug Lidster, Trevor Linden, Lars Lindgren, Jyrki Lumme, Gary Lupul, Phil Maloney, Kevin McCarthy, Jack McIlhargey, Kirk McLean, Alex Mogilny, Sergio Momesso, Brendan Morrison, Dana Murzyn, Markus Naslund, Harry Neale, Dave Nonis, Gino Odjick, Rosaire Paiement, Barry Pederson, Paul Reinhart, Cliff Ronning, Darcy Rota, Jarkko Ruutu, Sami Salo, Jim Sandlak, Tom Scallen, Bobby Schmautz, Daniel Sedin, Henrik Sedin, Stan Smyl, Harold Snepsts, Patrik Sundstrom, Dale Tallon, Steve Tambellini, Tony Tanti and Tiger Williams.

Thanks to former Canucks broadcaster Jim Robson for his generosity in sharing many memories and anecdotes instrumental in putting this book together.

Thanks to Kevin Woodley for conducting several supplementary interviews with current Canucks players and for his valuable contributions to the writing of this book.

Thank you to the following people and organizations for their expertise in this project: Michelle Benjamin (publisher), Chris Brumwell, Teresa Bubela (designer), Derek Fairbridge (editor), Tony Gallagher, Norm Jewison, Iain MacIntyre, Archie McDonald, David Poile, The Vancouver Canucks, The Nashville Predators, The St. Louis Blues.

Thanks also to Craig Campbell at the Hockey Hall of Fame, Kristina Edmondson at Orca Bay and Jason Beck at the BC Sports Hall of Fame for their enthusiasm and for all of their help collecting the wonderful images in this book.

The following publications were consulted in researching this book: *Hockey Chronicles: An Insider History of National Hockey League Teams, Island of Champions, The NHL Official Guide & Record Book,* and *Vancouver Canucks: The First Twenty Years.*

The following newspapers, magazines, news services and websites were consulted in researching this book: The Associated Press, *The Calgary Herald,* The Canadian Press, Canucks.com, *The Ottawa Citizen, The Detroit Free Press, Forbes Magazine, The Globe & Mail,* Hockeydb.com, Legendsofhockey.net, *The National Post,* NHL.com, NHLPA.com, *The Portage Daily Graphic, The Prague Post, The Syracuse New Times, Toronto Maple Leafs Game Day Magazine, The Vancouver Sun, The Vancouver Province, The Victoria Times Colonist, The Winnipeg Free Press, The Winnipeg Sun.*

Thanks to the following for use of photos in this book: The Hockey Hall of Fame (HHOF), The Vancouver Canucks, The B.C. Sports Hall of Fame (BCSHF), Pacific Newspaper Group Library and Jim Robson. See individual captions for credits. Otherwise, photo credits are as follows:

O-Pee-Chee/HHOF: 7, 27, 42 (background), 78 (background), 88, 89 (inset), 98 (background), 100 (background), 114 (background), 117, 243; Robert Shaver/HHOF: 22 (background), 23, 39 (background), 54, 56, 62, 72 (background), 80, 89 (background), 91, 93, 96, 98 (inset), 100 (inset), 106, 114, 122, 126, 132; London Life-Portnoy/HHOF: 22 (inset), 28, 30 (inset), 32, 39 (inset), 41, 58, 72 (inset); Graphic Artists/HHOF: 29, 42 (background), 46; DiMaggio-Kalish/HHOF: 30 (background); Paul Bereswill/HHOF: 74, 82, 108, 112, 116 (inset), 128, 165, 218; David Klutho/HHOF: 78, 95, 110, 116 (background); Doug MacLellan/HHOF: 144, 148 (background), 150, 162, 167, 170, 171, 176 (inset), 179, 187, 188 (inset), 198 (inset); Chris Relke/HHOF: 148 (inset), 151, 160, 163, 190, 198 (background); Ottawa Senators/HHOF: 166, 176 (background); Dave Sandford/HHOF: 183; Steve Babineau/HHOF: 185, 188; HHOF: 218, 243 (background); Vancouver Canucks: 37, 43 (inset), 102, 194, 225, 243 (inset), 245; Vancouver Canucks/Jeff Vinnick: 5, 208, 209, 213, 214, 216, 220, 224, 226, 230, 234, 236, 238, 239, 241; BCSHF: 36, 43 (background), 118; Dave Paterson/*The Province*: 45; Bill Cunningham/*The Province*: 48; Robson Private Archives: 50; Dan Scott/Vancouver *Sun*: 52; Wayne Leidenfrost/*The Province*: 178.